COLONIAL MENTALITY IN AFRICA

Nkuzi Nnam

Hamilton Books
A member of
The Rowman & Littlefield Publishing Group
Lanham · Boulder · New York · Toronto · Plymouth, UK

Hamilton Books
4501 Forbes Boulevard
Suite 200
Lanham, Maryland 20706
Hamilton Books Acquisitions Department (301) 459-3366

Estover Road
Plymouth PL6 7PY
United Kingdom

Printed in the United States of America
British Library Cataloging in Publication Information Available

Library of Congress Control Number: 2007922451
ISBN-13: 978-0-7618-3291-1 (paperback : alk. paper)
ISBN-10: 0-7618-3291-2 (paperback : alk. paper)

™ The paper used in this publication meets the minimum requirements of American National Standard for Information Sciences—Permanence of Paper for Printed Library Materials, ANSI Z39.48—1984

Dedicated to

My wife Nkeiruka

and children, Adora, Obiora, and Zikora

Contents

Preface

If Africans fail to tell their story, it will be told by foreigners. He who lets an outsider tell his story, according to a Tiv proverb, should not complain that it is biased. This book is an attempt to tell the African story, by an African, in the African style.

I have researched "the African problem" and I have discovered that "colonial mentality" is the primary cause of it. Colonial mentality is an unintentional attempt by Africans to continue to live and behave like we did during colonization, even several decades after our independence. It makes us appear to be ashamed of our culture, customs, and who we are. We pretend to be what we are not by trying to dress like foreigners, speak like foreigners, and even alienate our God in order to pray like foreigners. We become estranged in our motherland. We begin to see everything African as bad and inferior. African festivals, masquerades, folktales, proverbs, native names, attires and even languages begin to disappear because they are diabolic, evil, backward, primitive, and uncivil.

The worst of all is when we question our physical and mental appearance. We use expressions such as *oyibo kariri madu*. It begins to affect our psyche, our mentality, and our *modus cogitandum*. Then we bleach our skin and straighten our hair. We separate church and state, only because the foreigners do so. Consequently, we alienate God, and the fear of Him, from our lives. Then we begin to wonder why we are so corrupt.

This book is about colonial mentality in all of Africa, with particular reference to Nigeria and the Igbo ethnic group.

I am indebted to all of my students at Dominican University, especially those whose dexterous hands have make this work possible. They include: Erika Neumayer, Lea Marzolo, Teresamarie Cervone, Francesca Tinnirello, Ebony Benson, Stavros Georgikos, Omar Abdelgader, Sarah Cano, Erendira Lopez, Jason Swan, Sr. Cecilia Madu, OP, Sr. Perpetua

Chime, OP, RoJenia Judkins, and Latricia Varnado. I am also grateful to my colleagues in and out of Dominican University—without whose supple minds this work would not have been possible. They are: Dr. Lou Tenzis, Sr. Elwyn McHale, OP, Dr. Kelly Burns, Dr. Jeff Carlson, Sr. Melissa Water, OP, Dr. Chris Colmo, Dr. Monti, Dr. Donald Shaffer, Dr. Aly Drame, Dr. Roger Oden, Dr. Martin Okoro, Dr. Odeluga, Ms. Robbi Byrdsong-Wright, and Mr. Solomon Maduko. I am grateful to Dominican University for the Summer Grant, with which I was able to complete the final phase of this research.

Finally, I would like to make a special mention of those who edited this work. The credit will always belong to them, since the mistakes are certainly mine. They are: Ms. Angela Frazier, Sr. Jeanne Crapo, OP, Mr. Donald White, Sr. Angele Spehn, OP, and Mrs. Dorothy Albritton. May God bless each and every one of you on my behalf for your selfless and painstaking efforts.

Chapter 1

What Do You Know About Africa?

Misconceptions About Africa

Africa is the most misunderstood continent in the world. That is one of the reasons why it is considered a dark, uncivilized, underdeveloped continent and regarded as the most backward in recent memory. However, this stereotype is not true at all. Such misinformation stems either from ignorance or conspiracy. Personally, I think it is from both. Why would any organization, government, or individual in the Western world choose to spread wrong information about Africa? What benefit would it serve to them? Why is it that nine out of ten times when Africa is in the news in the United States it is about something bad? Why is it that when something good happens in Africa no one cares to report it? For instance, when the Junior Eagles from Nigeria won an Olympic championship in soccer, it hardly made the news in America. In contrast, whenever there is a *coup d'etat*, a disaster, a civil war, famine, or rioting of the minutest magnitude, it makes the news everywhere, even if it happens in the remotest village in Africa. Why is that?

Worse, it is not simply that the reporters and writers who catalogue African events are woefully pessimistic; it is that they bend the truth when they report or write about Africa. Such falsehoods are what I shall refer to as misconceptions about Africa in this passage. They include the following:

1. Africa is a Small Continent

The African map has, as a matter of habit, been deliberately represented as much smaller than it is in reality. This has gone on for several decades! What could one individual, an organization, or a state gain from such a misrepresentation? Besides such a calculated attempt to mislead the world regarding the actual size of Africa, the world, especially Americans, thinks seriously of Africa as extremely small. Some refer to it as a country. Others refer to it as an ethnic group. Upon learning that I come from Africa, an American would say, for instance, "One cousin of mine, John Adams, has lived in South Africa for ten years. Do you know him?"

The fact is that Africa is the second largest continent in the world, next only to Asia. Africa is bigger than the United States of America, China, all of Europe, India, Argentina and New Zealand put together, with room to spare. These countries combined encompass 11,668,035 square miles. Africa, by itself, encompasses 11,706,166 square miles.

2. Africa is Homogeneous

Quite the contrary, Africa is probably the most heterogeneous society in the world. Every tribe represents a unique language (not dialect), and hence a unique culture. Africa has about 53 countries today. Nigeria is only one of those countries, but it alone has more than two hundred uniquely different languages.

3. Animals Roam Wild Across the Continent

Many Americans want to visit Africa, neither to meet the people nor to study their graceful culture, but simply to see their wild animals. Most tourists to Africa are drawn towards the safari. Unfortunately, they fail to realize that the safari is only a big zoo in Africa. They go back to their various countries thinking that animals run wild everywhere.

Fr. Brigham visited my hometown in 1982 from Chicago with Fr. George Clements and two of their adopted children. They stayed with us for two weeks, and as we drove them to the airport, Fr. Brigham said, "I can't believe I have been in Africa for two weeks and not seen an animal." I was next to him in Chief Nneji's Mercedes car. I heard him and simply chuckled. Such an observation was remarkable.

I lived in Nigeria for almost twenty years before coming to America. Nevertheless, I saw an elephant for the first time in my life in the Lincoln Park Zoo. My mother saw both an elephant and a lion for the first time at a Ringling Brothers' Circus, performed at the United Center in Chicago in 1999.

Even African Americans have been misled to think of Africa similarly. Take for example Eddie Murphy, a talented African American movie actor, who had a movie called *Coming to America*. One feature of this movie that struck me as an African, was first, that an African would come to America, of all places, to look for a wife, and second, that a wild animal such as a giraffe could be seen frequently crossing the street, supposedly in Africa.

4. Africans Run Around Naked

Actually, more people run half-naked during the summertime in the Western world than they do in Africa, given the fact that many parts of Africa have summer weather almost all year round. Whereas there are numerous nude beaches and nude resorts in the Western world, they are non-existent in Africa.

In certain African locations, women are required to dress up very conservatively at all times so that only their eyes and their palms are visible. Males are expected to be appropriately clothed as well, though not as extremely as women.

5. Africans Swing from Tree to Tree

Such a misconception stems largely, if not totally, from the *Tarzan* movies on television. Americans often ask me how close to reality those shows are. I reply that they have no foundation in reality. As a matter of fact, the creator of *Tarzan*, Edgar Rice Burroughs, is said to have been raised in Oak Park, Illinois, and might have never been to Africa. Finally, I want to point out that no single episode of Tarzan was recorded in Africa.

6. Africans are Uneducated

The most educated immigrants to the United States are from the continent of Africa, and the Immigration and Naturalization Services (INS) of the United States knows that best. The average African is bilingual. Americans find it hard to believe that most Africans come to the United States to enroll in universities because the ones in their various homelands are so competitive that they are filled to capacity.

7. African Women are Subservient to Men

One of the most notorious misconceptions about Africa is that African women are loyal, humble, meek, subservient, and helpless in the hands of their male counterparts. The expression is that when men ask them to jump, their only response would be simply to ask, "How high?" Whoever harbors such a notion has never met an African woman. African women are very assertive, intelligent, demanding, and most of the time, unyielding.

Until the Europeans introduced their patriarchal system into Africa, many African communities were matriarchal. Any sign of mistreatment of women today in Africa is a direct result of Western imperialism and the colonization of Africa.

I often compare and contrast to show that African women are not only more assertive, but that they are also more liberated than American women. The reasons that demonstrate that are:

a. Whereas America has never had a female president or even a female vice-president, Africa has had queens who ruled and governed states, tribes, and empires before Christ was born.
b. Whereas women are not allowed to become part of the clergy in some denominations of Western Christianity simply because of their gender, African communities have never ever excluded women from such an important fabric of society. Women have always been priestesses in Africa. As a matter of fact, priestesses are revered and sought after more than male priests in Africa because they are believed to be more clairvoyant than their male counterparts.
c. Whereas American women were not allowed to vote until 1920 AD, African women have always voted, and they could always be voted for, since the origin of humankind.
d. Whereas American women are not allowed to take part in combat even in the 21st Century, African women, especially the Amazons, have always fought in wars. Queens such as Amina and Ngui Nanaramama were known to have led soldiers in wars. They were fierce warriors.
e. People tend to conclude that African women have no power from the fact that there is polygamy in Africa. What such people fail to realize is the exact meaning of that word "polygamy." They fail to realize that polygamy does not mean

polygyny. Polygamy is the presence of both polygyny and polyandry in the same society. Polygyny is the marriage of several wives by one man at the same time. Polyandry is the marriage of several men by one woman at the same time. What Africa's critics fail to realize is that polygamy applies to men just as it applies to women. Those critics mistake polygyny for polygamy. They emphasize polygyny without mentioning polyandry at all. The fact that polygyny is more frequent does not mean that polyandry is non-existent. Also the fact that polygyny is more frequent is not at all a result of male chauvinism in Africa; instead, it may be due to the fact that there are a lot more females than males in Africa. Having more females than males is a direct result of the transatlantic slave trade, which targeted more young African males than women. Another reason for such a shortage of males in Africa is war. Though women could go to wars in Africa, there were still far more males in combat; that is because women also had the additional role of being pregnant and/or taking care of children. The final reason why there are more females is that throughout the history of humanity males have been known to take more stupid risks than females.

f. Another reason to show that African women are more assertive than American women is that in many parts of Africa, such as in Igboland, women have the right to marry fellow women, not as lesbians. However, no man is allowed to marry a fellow man in Africa. The origin of this tradition is unclear.

g. A common Igbo name is "Nneka," which means that mother is "superior." No man would dare to call his child "Nnaka," meaning father is "superior."

h. An African proverb states that if all snakes were to unite, they would overtake any community they might choose. In the same way, if women were to unite, they would overrun men because they outnumber males on every continent. The problem with Western women, especially Americans, is that they have consistently failed to unite. If they would, then they might be able to vote one of their own into the office of the president of the United States, for example. Also, most donors and most ardent members of the Catholic Church in the United States are female. If they were to unite and go on strike against the Church, the Vatican will think twice about not allowing women to become clergy. American women do not try any of the above because they are disunited. African women, on the other hand, have united time after time to fight and overcome a common enemy. The greatest example is the Aba Women War of 1929 in southeastern Nigeria. The Europeans imposed taxation without representation on Igbo males who hated it but lacked the courage to do something about it. When their wives could not stand it anymore, they assembled themselves and took up arms against the entire British Army. Though the Igbo women lost that battle, they had won the war. They had gained everyone's respect and even fear. By the time the war ended, the Europeans had understood the message that they could never impose such taxes on women, and they never tried it again.

i. The circumcision of women in Africa makes outsiders think that African women are helpless. The fact is that it is imposed on women by women, just like the circumcision of males is imposed on the males by the males. In other words, circumcision is imposed on children by both of their parents. It is imposed on the society by the culture, and that version of the culture needs to be uprooted from the rest. Female circumcision is bad, awful, inhumane, and simply ignorant. It has nothing to do with male chauvinism or the superiority of men over women. It has everything to do with ignorance. The practice goes further than the simple tradition that both males and females are circumcised. Mothers insist that their daughters are circumcised because to them it is like a religious rite of passage. It has a spiritual meaning to mothers. It is to them what Baptism is to Christians. Remember, this is done when the children are babies. In Igboland, children are circumcised exactly on the eighth day after birth. Unfortunately, some people actually end up cutting off some parts of the human anatomy in the name of religion/tradition. It is egregiously wrong. It can be likened to the Christian baptism where the priest or the minister is supposed to pour a little amount of water on a child's forehead as a symbol of the Holy Spirit. Unfortunately, some churches end up almost drowning little babies in cold water during baptism. It is wrong, but it does not stem from male chauvinism. Everyone, both males and females, needs to be better educated about circumcision.

Africans believe in the natural law theory, and female circumcision is one of the direct results of it. Other ill-fated results of the natural law theory in Africa are the castigation of homosexuals, human sacrifice, and killing of twins. The practice of the last two—human sacrifice and twin killing—has been stopped completely, thanks to missionaries such as Mary Slessor who did not pass judgment on a person's culture. Instead, they showed human understanding, and that is why they were able to make a breakthrough. Female circumcision is in the same category as twin killing, human sacrifice, and stoning of homosexuals to death. All constitute a shameful aspect of the African culture that needs to be destroyed. To help end those practices, one needs to study why they are practiced, as a good anthropologist would or as Mary Slessor did in Calabar. Mary Slessor lived in Africa, and she knew that Africans had nothing against women. She understood that such practices took place because they did not know any better. Every culture has a bit of such ignorance. St. Augustine abhorred masturbation because he believed that semen was made up of little people and masturbation terminated their lives. He wrote that because he did not know any better. Some church doctrines emanated out of such false biology, yet we look at it today as simply out of date, not out of malice, tyranny or chauvinism. America has caused slavery, racism, and violence (like in Hiroshima and Nagasaki). Europe has experienced world wars, Nazism, the Mafioso, colonization, and imperialism. In other words, every culture has something of which it is not very proud; unfortunately, those Westerners who are preoccupied with circumcision in Africa have failed to remove the log in their own eyes before the speck in an African eye. They have failed to read their own Bible where it is written, "Only he who is without sin should cast the first stone." They have failed to reread their own Bible in which it is written, "that thou shall not judge." If they read it, then they would have known that it is with the judgment that they pass unto others that they in turn will be judged. African proverbs say it more succinctly as follows:

i. Ashes fall back on the face of him who throws them.
ii. When one points an accusing finger towards another, three fingers of the same hand point towards himself.

j. Another reason with which to show that African women are more assertive than American women is the concept of *uzii* in Africa. Some authors have incorrectly referred to *uzii* as a fattening period in the life of a newlywed bride. For one reason or another, African women, especially in Igboland, were able to get men to agree to keep them in the house for a period of three to twelve months right after marriage, during which they were nourished, catered to, and spoiled with love and affection from everyone within the community. No man is allowed to undergo this privilege. Women have a monopoly on it. Women from the extended family and from the entire community take turns in coming to beautify the new bride with *uli*, *ufie*, *odo,* and *agalo,* herbs that make the new wife's skin soft, smooth, and healthy. Further, the new bride is fed with the best food and delicacies that the family can afford. She is not to lift her arm or finger to work. She is taught about the facts of life, entertained with songs and music, fed constantly, beautified, allowed to sleep at will, or simply nurtured, pampered, and spoiled for an average of six months. At the conclusion of an *uzii* she is paraded and decorated with ornaments and shown off to the community in the public squares and in the market places. Little girls carry calabashes and follow her. People, who are pleased with her mother-in-law (who gets most of the credit), give the "fattened girl" presents. Gifts range from very expensive trinkets to money. Females will never get such a privilege and exclusive first-class treatment in a society in which the female species is not viewed as sacred.

k. Africa and ancient Mesopotamia historically have the oldest form of matriarchy in human history. The disappearance of such matriarchy today in Africa is traceable to the Western colonization of Africa during which the "imperial majesties" deposed and replaced African women rulers with males. However, the traces of matriarchy have not disappeared from Africa completely. Take, for example, *Nneka*, which is still a popular common name in Igboland. Also, Yorubaland still has *Lyalode,* otherwise known as female leaders, who oversee the affairs of the entire female group of the society. This is because male leaders are not allowed to rule over females in some African communities. These communities have to have female leaders who are not answerable to anyone (including the male leaders) except their subjects.

l. Prior to the colonization of Africa, a majority of the sub-Saharan African ethnic groups like the Asante of Ghana were completely matrilineal. That is, they traced their ancestry through their mother-line. They chose or determined their last names through their mother-line. Where can such matriliny be observed in the history of the Western world?

m. Western languages, such as English, have personal pronouns for male, female, and even neutral genders (he, she, it). Such an ugly distinction has been known to serve as a vehicle with which to carry out serious gender bias, gender prejudice, and gender discrimination. Most African languages such as Igbo have only one word for all the personal pronouns, hence they are unable to distinguish or discriminate between genders.

n. In Western languages such as English, one can distinguish a married from a single woman using the titles "Mrs." and "Miss" respectively. Males, on the other hand are represented with only the title "Mr." whether he is married or single. Such a double standard is not found in any of the African languages that I know. In the Igbo language, for example, "*Mazi*" is for both married and single males, the same way that "*Lolo*" is used to address both single and married females.

8. Africans are Pagans and Their Religion is Animism

Westerners tend to say that Africans believe in many gods and they worship their ancestors. They worship false gods, and they bow to images, objects, and idols.

The above information about African traditional religion is completely false. First, Africans are monotheists who believe in one supreme being that is ubiquitous, omnipotent, omniscient, *summum bonum,* and the creator of heaven and earth. They have no concept of heaven and hell, but they believe in life after death. They have no bible, or angels, and they do not believe in Jesus Christ or the saints. Instead, they have minor gods, goddesses, oracles and deities. They also revere and honor the ancestors in such a special way that it is often mistaken for ancestor worship. Directly beneath the ancestors in the hierarchy of their religion are priests and priestesses who are divinely inspired.

According to the African traditional religion, everyone has a goal in life, and that goal is to rest in peace. They equally believe in two worlds: the world of the living and the spirit world. Every African aspires to reach the spirit world. Such is attainable by three means. The first means is by living a virtuous life, the second is by getting a righteous burial, and the third is by getting a righteous funeral. This religion calls for a communal life since two out of three criteria for resting in peace depend on what the community does for the deceased after death.

Africans believe in reincarnation, and the number of times that one comes back to life differs from one ethnic group to another. The Igbo people maintain that everyone comes back to life seven times. In other words, according to the Igbos, one has seven chances or opportunities to ascend to the spirit world. Those who fail to enter the spirit world do not go to hell. Instead, their souls remain on earth as ghosts. That is why ghosts are always angry and haunting people.

9. Africans are Cannibals

One misconception is that Africans eat human flesh like cannibals do. This is one of the first misconceptions that I experienced in America. It was my first week of class in America. I sat in the front row of the classroom in order to observe the teacher's mouth since I was having a difficult time with American accents. It was a nighttime history class. It was during January and I was shivering with cold. I had a muffler around my neck and all of a sudden the teacher stopped his lecture. He stared at me, walked towards me, and asked, "Where do you come from?" I responded, "Africa." He then said, "You must be very cold. I know it's always very warm over there in Africa." I kept quiet. Then, he went on, "Are your people still cannibals?" I was shocked and embarrassed at the same time. "What?" I responded in disbelief. He said, "Do your people still eat human flesh?" I looked at him as though I were hungry and said, "Yes!" The class laughed.

At first, I thought that he was joking, but eventually, I realized that he was serious. I was not surprised that an American thought that Africans eat human flesh. I was mostly surprised that such a public, or classroom, display of ignorance was coming from a university professor.

10. Africans are Starving

All Africans do not starve. Most of them are farmers who grow what they eat even if they do not export the goods. I was raised in rural Nigeria where 80% of adults are farmers, 15% are traders, and the remaining 5% are teachers or something else. My parents were both farmers and traders, just like the majority of the population who grow more farm products than they need and sell the surplus.

Civil servants in the cities felt the sting of inflation almost immediately, but we never did because we grew our own foods. Food was never rationed or measured in my family. We had yams, cassava, palm oil, vegetables, cocoa yams, bananas, oranges, rice, and beans in abundance. We also grew palm trees from which we tapped the palm wine for social gatherings and to entertain guests. We also raised animals such as goats, cows, and chickens. With the above we never lacked meat for our daily consumption, sacrifice, or worship.

We did not have enough money to buy cars, have a refrigerator, or install telephones. We did not even have an account in the bank; most people from our village never did. However, one thing we had in abundance was food. No one starved in the entire village. There were no homeless people. No one was ever spotted begging for food since one who needed food would get it from his/her extended family.

Africa is still that way with the exception of urban areas that are built to look and function like the Western world. Once in a while, a natural disaster such as famine or war befalls a tribe, a country or a group of Africans and they would starve for a while. Such an example is what happened to the Igbos of Eastern Nigeria during their civil war, 1967-1970 (Rwanda and Burundi suffered similarly during their civil wars). It also happened to the people of the Chad Republic of West Africa in the1980s when they were hit by an unprecedented famine. The Ethiopians also went through that in the 1980s during their famine. Finally, southern African countries such as Zimbabwe suffered similarly during the apartheid regime and during various wars of independence. During such occasions, people ran away from their homes as refugees. The women and children especially were shown on television all over the world as starving Africans. Unfortunately, people fail to understand the causes of these problems. Instead, they see them as "starving Africans." Then, they conclude that all Africans starve. This is quite unlike the American perception of Europe as it would be reported as starvation taking place in Czechoslovakia at one time, then Italy at another period, and Greece in the next period. When it happens in any other part of the world, especially Europe, it is understood as a result of war or natural disaster. When it is Africa, then it is seen as a normal occurrence. Why? One of the reasons is that Africa is the least understood of the seven continents of the world. Another reason is that there is already a general negative view or biased view of Africa all over the world, even among Africans themselves. The third reason is that many Westerners are not aware that Africa has 53 countries; hence, if war or starvation is reported in Ethiopia and next time in Nigeria, the western media reports it as taking place in Africa. After a while, Americans have developed the understanding that all of Africa is the same.

11. Africa is Full of Jungles

To put it succinctly, according to the Field Museum in Chicago, Illinois, there is not a single jungle in all of Africa.

12. Africans Live in Huts

I am not from an affluent African family. My family is average and yet we do not live in a hut. I show students pictures of well-designed homes in my hometown and in the cities. Some of them were designed and built by my peers and former schoolmates. Africa, particularly Nigeria, is the only place that I know of where people spend more money and use more space building guests' homes before the main building.

I bought land in Africa and wanted to build myself a modest bungalow, the type that I am used to in America, but everyone I know cautioned me, telling me that it was a bad idea. They did not understand why I was insistent on being different. The bungalow that I had in mind, according to them, was not good enough to constitute even a guest's home. I drove around and discovered that they were correct. They guided me, and at the end of the construction, the guesthouse that I built before my main house became better than any house I have ever owned in America.

Unfortunately, most Americans do not know that, even the educated ones. One day, I went to a lounge with a group of graduate students to write an outline in preparation for our Ph.D. comprehensive examination. First, the six of us sat down chatting, as we waited for the rest to arrive. One of them said,

"Nkuzi, you are from Africa, aren't you?"

I said, "Yeah."

She said, "Is it true that over there people live in trees and in huts?"

Cynically, I said, "Yeah, my family lives in trees."

She said, "How do you get up there?"

I said, "We use the escalator."

She appeared confused and responded, "This does not make sense." The conversation continued. Of course, she understood later, but it amazed me.

Chapter 2

Life in Africa

I was born to a polygamist from Ogonogo Eji Ndiuno Akpugo, Nkanu Local Government Area in Enugu State. My father, Nnamigwe, was married to four wives at the same time. My biological mother was not only the youngest of the four wives but also the last to be married. Hierarchically, she was the lowest.

My parents could neither read nor write. My mother was economically independent and traded *Okpa,* bean pie. My father was a successful farmer, locally speaking. He took all of the titles allowed on the land. The first title is *ichi isi iyi*. The second is *isaku*. The third is *igo ji I*. The final is *igo ji II*.

I, like most Africans, was born and raised in a rural area. I was the second of six children from my biological mother. My date of birth is unknown because it was never documented. Birthdays were not celebrated. It was impossible to keep track of age, needless to say, it was not considered important. At first, children are described to be one year, two years, three years or even five years old. However, as they get older, no one cared to keep track of one's precise age. Days are calculated by night time. Four market days make a week—*Nkwor, Eke, Orie* and *Afor*. A month is calculated by the cycle of the moon, and a year is depicted by the two seasons—the rainy and the dry seasons. I was neither delivered in a hospital nor in a maternity home. There were simply none around. Instead, I was delivered in my parents' compound with the aid of a local midwife and some other women. Men (even the fathers) were not allowed in delivery rooms.

My parents wanted me to acquire a Western-type education just like most kids around. Consequently, I was taken to a Catholic primary school around the corner every now and then. Nothing was determined by age. Even school was determined by having children place their hands over and cross their heads in an attempt to reach one of the ears at the opposite side of the head. A child was only considered old and mature to start school if, and only if, he or she could touch one of the ears from the other side of the head. I was rejected many times.

I was not needed at home, so I went to school with one of my older siblings. Eventually, I was able to reach an ear and quickly got enrolled into the school. My father refused to enroll any of his daughters into school. He enrolled only the boys. It was either because our father was a male chauvinist or because he did not deem it wise to spend time and money educating women who would eventually marry and move out of the family.

I, unfortunately, was not very good at school. I simply could not comprehend any of the school materials. I was not good in arithmetic, English, the vernacular, nature studies and so on. As time went on, I developed a very low self-esteem. Additionally, I hated school and refused to go to school anymore. My father forced me to attend anyway. I left home in the mornings, walked around aimlessly, went back home, and pretended to have gone to school. My father punished me severely by whipping me after he had uncovered my little scheme.

Then, I went to school, and received poor marks from teachers. I changed the teachers' marks from incorrect to correct. My parents, particularly my mother, could not read; hence she could not distinguish my handwriting from the teachers'. One of my siblings revealed the trick to my mother and she whipped me. I never did it again. Then, I resorted to sitting close to the smartest kids in class and copying the right answers from them during tests. The smart kids were Eze Nnaji, Aboyi Be Okenwanta, and Moses Nnaji.

I was beaten quite a lot while growing up; after all, it was considered a necessary act of discipline, not abuse. My parents, uncles, nieces, neighbors, siblings and even distant cousins beat me. At a very tender age, perhaps eight, I was removed from school and sent to live with my grandmother in the neighboring town of Ihuokpara (a.k.a. Agabi). I was being trained in the art of farming since I was no longer in school. Suddenly, a cousin of mine who was a grade school teacher asked me to live with him. With his high school teachers' training education, he was the most educated person in his family. My parents sent one of my paternal uncles, Aneke Oko, to go and get me from Ihuokpara. In the coming week, we left for the northern region of Nigeria from the Southeast. It was quite a shock to me. They spoke a different language, had different tribal markings on their faces, lived and behaved differently, ate different foods, and got their drinking water from wells. Their school systems were different since they built dormitories even for primary schools. Most of the people were Christians; animists were nowhere in sight. They made fun of those from the Igbo tribe and called us *Wankpa Igbo,* which means Igbo Aborigines.

A few months later, conflict arose between my cousin and each of his house helpers, first with Godwin, then with Ahile, and finally with Francis. Before then, I had learned to cook, clean, and do the laundry in the stream of running water. I was glad to become the house helper. I continued with my primary education and kept the house at the same time. I fetched water from the streams, fetched firewood from the bush and the forest, and went to the markets once or twice a week for groceries. As a school teacher in a Roman Catholic Primary School System, my cousin was often transferred. First, we were transferred from Koriya to Ukan, and then to Alabasa—all in the Tiv tribal division of the Benue Province of Northern Nigeria.

I lived in Koriya for only four months before our next transfer. I lived in Ukan for about one year, which seemed to me like several. We lived in Alabasa for about one year, but it seemed as though we lived there forever as well.

Many things happened to me while I was in Tivland, which I will never forget. Some of them serve as good memories, and others are bitter reminders. I was forced by circumstances to learn to speak both English and Tiv. I learned to be a responsible housekeeper since I would be disciplined severely each time that I lacked or fell behind in my duties. There was a group of thugs known as *Atem Tio*, which means the be-headers, who roamed the nights singing and dancing. I was always scared at night when I heard them singing, especially when my cousin left me alone in the house to spend the weekend at Ihue or Gboko, the nearest metropolis. I still was not very good in school. In fact, I failed and consequently repeated classes. Mid-year and end of the year were dreadful time for me because of the examinations. It became much worse since my cousin was well educated and could read the school report cards much better than my parents.

One night, as I lay down on the mat in the living room (parlor) floor, a couple of burglars dug a hole from the outside of our house below the foundation to the inside of one of the bedrooms. They crawled into that bedroom, got to the parlor, walked across me as I lay on the floor, and entered the second bedroom. There they stole clothes, money, a radio, and my cousin's only means of transportation, his bicycle. They then went back into that parlor where I was lying asleep on the mat, with my fellow housekeeper, unlocked the entrance door and left undetected. It all happened while a teacher lay in each of the bedrooms and two boys lay in the parlor. No one woke up during the entire episode. It was not until the next morning that everyone discovered that our house had been burglarized. I imagined how the buglers walked across me, as I lay asleep, and became frantic and traumatized. The entire town lacked electricity, and it was always very dark and appeared scarier to me than ever before. A few months later, those individuals were caught, and both the radio and the bicycle were recovered. They were tried and sentenced to prison, but it never made me feel any better. In fact, that made the experience more real.

My parents were farmers, and I knew quite a bit regarding African farming techniques and methods. Thus, it did not take much time for me to be struck by how fertile their lands were. The Tiv did not have to irrigate their land for their yams to grow big, long, and fat. Unlike the Igbo, they did not have to dig their farms into big mounds of soil into which to plant their yams, cassava, soybeans, rice, and millets, yet they grew fruitfully and multiplied. I nearly collapsed with shock the first time I paid a single penny for a huge tuber of yam. That was about ten times less than what it took to buy one where I came from, in Igboland.

The first time that we were transferred from Koriya to Ukan, my cousin stayed behind and sent me along with another house helper, Ahile Yaji, to the new school. We went by public transportation to the road corner from where we would trek. It was about 30 miles from the junction to the school; however, the road was not paved with tar. Motor vehicles drove there only once a market week and those were Igbo traders who drove there for some food crops. It was about 8:00 p.m. when we got to the junction. We walked for about one hour, and it became extremely dark. Neither of us had ever previously been there.

Ahile might have been ten years old. He could speak Tiv, and he understood the culture better. He suggested that we walk into the next compound and spend the night there since it had become too dark to see. Almost one mile later, we saw some light. It was a home in a compound. I was terrified as we walked in the home. Ahile spoke to them in their native tongue or vernacular, telling them that he and I were stranded on the way to Ukan, twenty-five miles away. They screamed with sympathy and started to shower us with hospitality. They provided us with a spare room, water and soap for a bath, a sumptuous meal and detailed directions to our destination. It was too good to be true, I thought as I lay down, scared and sleepless all night long. At 6:00 a.m., one of the hosts woke us up and gave us breakfast before we left. We had to leave early in order to cover a reasonable distance before getting overtaken by the tropical sun's heat.

My cousin had a habit of spending most of his weekends in the big cities, getting out of the barren country lifestyle for a change. After all, he was a young man probably in his late twenties. I loved the lonely weekends at home because I saw it as a chance to be free, doing whatever I wanted and not getting beaten up for it. This particular weekend, one of my fellow housekeepers and I had a misunderstanding, and it was reported to Mr. Okeke. Mr. Okeke was another Igbo school teacher living in the next mud house among eight other houses in the teacher's quarters. He was a very heavyset, middle aged, single Igbo man. He lived there with two young boys of about my age—Emeka and Emmanuel. Mr. Okeke had just been transferred to Alabasa as a punishment for impregnating one of his teenage Tiv students in a Roman Catholic school. It was quite a notorious scandal in the entire parish. Mr. Okeke was embarrassed, humiliated, and quite bitter for getting caught, for being punished severely, and for committing fornication in the first place.

When Mr. Okeke heard that I was having a quarrel with Polycap, he quickly summoned Polycap, who told his side of the story. I stood by Mr. Okeke's side as he recounted what went on between Polycap and me. Then, all of a sudden Mr. Okeke bent down as though he was washing his hand in a bucket of water and then jumped up and slapped me, an eight-year-old boy with all his might. First, I felt a flash in the form of lightning, and then, I was flat on the ground. A couple of years later, I started to go blind in one of my eyes. We consulted optometrists and several ophthalmologists to no avail. It even started to spread to the second eye as time went by. Finally, I was sent home to my parents in the village who took me to a herbalist. He quickly ran to his backyard and reappeared twenty minutes later with some tree roots. He soaked them in water for about one hour and blew at one end, letting the juice come out of the other end into my eyes. This procedure was repeated several times each day. I regained complete sight in less than three months.

My cousin was transferred once again. This time, it was to a secondary school, which was more like a promotion for him. He was also being sent back to Igboland from Tivland. We were happy for his homecoming. Unfortunately, we were sent to Umuezeoka, a town considered by some to be the most backward, in terms of Western civilization, in all of Igboland. They lacked paved roads, electricity, clean water, and post offices. They had thatched homes, and many adults were half-naked most of the time. Though they were considered Igbos, they spoke quite a different language.

Motor vehicles came there only once in a long while, mostly during Afor Izo market days. Even then, transportation by motor vehicles was not guaranteed, especially during the rainy season, except for Long John, a huge lorry that was owned and operated by a tall man called John. The villagers drank from ponds called Okpuru, which were infested with water-borne diseases. Most adults and children had guinea worms hanging from inside their legs. I never drank out of such water sources because we lived on the high school premises where Father Collins, a missionary and school principal, had dug a well for the students. I might have drunk Okpuru only occasionally while swimming in the rivers with friends. This became evident years later when I observed traces of blood in my urine. Twenty years later, I underwent a successful surgery at Illinois Masonic Hospital to correct the problem. The surgeon and the urologist said that I had schistosomiasis, a disease commonly contracted from drinking bad water.

What has remained memorable to me about the transfer from Tiv to Igboland is that I did extremely well in school after that. Despite flunking all of my tests, my report card, which was written to enable me to transfer easily into my new school, read that I was excellent in all subjects, giving me the second highest score in my entire class. This was a totally contrary to my test results because I might have been the second student from the last. Though unethical, such falsification was done in good faith and out of expediency. It was simply to facilitate my transfer into St. Mary Catholic School, the nearest primary school from my cousin's school, St. Aidans Secondary School, Umuezeoka.

Such falsification was known only to whoever did it and to me. Even my cousin the school teacher did not know about the falsification because he kept praising me for "a job well done". We had gone to our hometown during those holidays before going to Umuezeoka. My cousin showed my report card around at home. People showered me with praise, and my cousin heard people call me smart for the first time. In the new school, I was quickly accepted into the right class, and both my class teacher, Mr. Nnabuenyi, and my headmaster (principal), Mr. Mgbahurike, announced that I was extremely intelligent. I started to believe that I was intelligent. I carried myself like John Omaka, one of the brightest students. I asked intelligent questions, made intelligent comments in class, and studied like an intelligent student. Further, after the first examination, I out-preformed John Omaka and became the brightest student in my class.

My life changed from that point on. This is concrete proof that a child will believe whatever he is told. I was transformed from the weakest student to the brightest scholar in my class simply because I was praised and called brilliant. I was aware of the fact that my result was falsified, yet I came to believe that I was brilliant. The only effect that this knowledge continued to have on me was occasional fear, self-doubt, self-deprecation, and lack of self-confidence. I graduated from the primary school with the highest score in the history of my school. I performed equally as well in high school.

About six months after we left northern Nigeria, the northerners started to kill and maim southerners in their land. News had it that Mr. Okeke, the one who slapped sight out of me, was one of the first Igbos to be killed. Some of the Igbos escaped. One of our closest Igbo neighbors, David, a carpenter by profession, had his Achilles tendons severed and was sent home to Igboland. It is unknown as to what would have happened to me and my cousin if we had not left the North just a few months earlier. Why were the northerners killing and maiming all of the southerners and Igbos?

Some young army officers from the south decided to conduct a coup d'etat in Nigeria. They sent officers to kill Prime Minister Sir Abubarkar Tafawa Belewa, a northerner. Others were sent to do the same thing to the Saduana of Sokoto, the western, mid-western and the eastern prime ministers. The officers were all supposed to perform their assigned duties at the same time. Everyone preformed his act of assassination except the Igbo officers who were sent to kill the Igbo Minister. For reasons best known to the Igbo army officers, Dr. Okpara's life was spared. The Hausa prime minister and the ministers from other regions were killed.

President Dr. Nnamdi Azikiwe was also Igbo, but no attempt was made on his life. In fact, no Igbo lost his life in this entire mutiny. Instead, Igbo musicians composed songs and made fun of Hausa leaders as they "cried like goats" during the assassinations. The most famous song about that was called "Enwu Nebe Akwa". The straw that broke the camel's back was the fact that an Igbo army officer, Aguiyi Ironsi, was made the head of the state. That was why and when the northerners took it upon themselves to show the Igbos that the Hausas were not the fools that the Igbos thought they were.

The Hausas fought back. They killed Ironsi and then they began to kill all Igbos in the North. Igbos seceded from the rest of Nigeria and independently declared them as the Federal Republic of Biafra. The rest of Nigeria united and declared a civil war against Biafra. Yakubu Gowon gained charge of the northern army, while Emeka Odumegwu Ojukwu remained in charge of Biafra. Britain, Russia, and the entire Arabic world came out in support of Nigeria. They supported Nigeria with money, ammunition, and manpower. The Biafrans got similar help from Israel and France. America was never directly involved with either because they did not want to go against Great Britain or simply because they were so deeply involved with the Vietnam War. Biafra surrendered in 1970, and the war was over.

The war lasted for three consecutive years during which I, like many other Igbo children, stopped going to school. I was also a refugee. However, I was not living in a refugee camp. Instead, my parents were always able to reside with friends and sometimes with close or distant relatives. Shelter was hard to find, but food was even harder to come by. People had no jobs. Biafran money was so devalued that it was almost worthless. The only people who were being paid with money and who were equally being fed at all were the soldiers.

As a result, most young people enrolled with the armed forces voluntarily. There was also an organization called the Boys Company reserved for those who were not old enough to join the army. It was a company of young boys who were specially trained to spy against the northern army. They also ran little errands for the soldiers who were not at the war front (battlefield). They were equally clothed, fed, and provided with shelter. Unfortunately, I was too young to join the Boys Company. Consequently, I starved.

Many children suffered from *kwashiokor*. The victims had swollen feet, swollen stomachs, swollen faces, anemia, and loss of hair. This illness was caused by acute malnutrition. Due to the economic blockade against Biafra, food items, especially salt, were nowhere to be found. Finally, my parents migrated to a section of Igboland that was getting clothes, salt, dried fish, dried milk, rice and beans from the Red Cross. For the first time since the war started, I received food.

Eventually, my town, Akpugo, surrendered and reconciled with the northern troops who had laid siege. Akpugo villagers became free once again to settle in their own homes. Most homes were already looted and burned so the resettlement process was not easy. Most of the restlessness was also due to the fact that the war was still going on, and Akpugo was being used as a battleground. Innocent civilians were often confused for soldiers in disguise and the consequences were often deadly.

Many wives ran after soldiers, giving them sexual and domestic services for money, which was sent to their husbands and kids for survival. Some people praised the women for their ingenuity. Others cursed them as unscrupulous deviants who were ready to prostitute themselves at the expense of both integrity and civility.

I could speak Tiv, Igbo and English. I was quickly recruited by one of the Nigerian soldiers first to translate Igbo to Tiv. Later, I was needed as a servant. I lived with a soldier, his girlfriend and two of her children in one tiny trench. At night time, I was asked to sleep above the trench in order to give the soldier some privacy with his girlfriend. However, I was allowed into the trench whenever it was raining and whenever an attack was expected from the Briafran soldiers.

My duties were to do the laundry for everyone, fetch firewood, clean, and run errands. However, the most difficult of all my duties was to fetch water from over a mile away for everybody to use. I would carry a six-gallon bucket on my head back and forth seven times each day. As a servant, I was not paid with money. Instead, I was fed, and I loved it. I was very happy, content and felt lucky to be chosen. My master, Dan Almagiri, was a kind soldier, but his girlfriend was not as kind. It was she who made me fetch water so many times each day because she had to bathe her children.

Clothes were purchased for his girlfriend and for all her children, even those who were not living with us, but clothing was never bought for me. As a matter of fact, up to this point, I had neither worn nor owned pants, a pair of shoes, sandals, canvas (gym shoes), or even slippers. One day, he gave her money to purchase articles of clothing for herself and "all the children including Michael." She traveled to Enugu for about one week, and upon return, she gave me a pair of slippers. It was my first pair ever. I was elated. I did not care as to whether she had purchased clothes and shoes for her own kids. When I wore my slippers, I was on top of the world.

Though he was kind, Dan Almagiri was quick with his temper. He often took action before he thought about it. One day, I did something that might have annoyed him which was so trivial that I cannot even remember it, and all I heard was "*Ka gaya maa Michael ya tefi gida nshi yenzu yenzu.*" He had said that to me a thousand times before so I knew what it meant, "Tell Michael to leave for his home now, now!" At first, I thought that he was not serious, but he repeated it over and over until I started to pack my bag that contained nothing but my new slippers. He reached into my bag and took them from me, and at that point, being so young and little, I felt as though my entire worth was just snatched from me. I looked up to his girlfriend to help me, but she did not care. I cried all the way home, empty-handed after so much dedication and service.

Then, I went to Abakpa Nike, where I started to serve another soldier, Corporal Ibrahim, who not only fed me but also paid me two British pounds each month. It was the first time that I had earned money for service, and I felt like being charitable.

As the Nigerian-Biafran war ensued in 1967, all hell broke loose. Propaganda spread all over Biafra, giving the impression that Nigerian soldiers were dying like flies daily and that the Biafrans had almost won the war. This made every young man and woman want to join the army. Many young men and women were rejected. Those who were turned down joined the civil defense. The younger ones joined the boys' company. The propaganda, spearheaded by Okoko Ndem, seemed truthful and useful until the following year when individual Biafran soldiers accepted money from the federal troops to betray us as well as reveal secret plans and decoded the secret codes of their own battalions. The Biafran soldiers headed towards Lagos, the federal Capital of Nigeria. They crossed the River Niger, then Agbo, up to Benin and passed Ore, not too far from Lagos. At this time, most people, at least in Biafra, thought that the war was coming to an end once Biafran troops reached Lagos, especially since they were quite determined and fearsome enough that nothing could stop their advance. Then, all of a sudden, one of the Biafran leaders accepted money from Nigerians and decided to betray his own army. He commanded his soldiers to keep withdrawing and retreating until they gave up all of the Federal land that they had gained and more.

The second shock was when suddenly the Nigerian army was known to have taken the stronghold of Enugu, the Biafran capital. It was later attributed to sabotage from another notorious Biafran army commander, Njoku. That was the final and strongest betrayal; greed, avarice, and bribe taking by Igbo soldiers who single handedly lost the war for all Igbos. No Hausa nor Nigerian solider was ever known to accept money from Biafrans in order to betray their fellow troops. They were all patriotic, loyal, tenacious, and honest as they fought for a single, unified, and common objective, which was like they put it, "to keep Nigeria One." They proclaimed that it was a task that must be done. Indeed, they got it done, not only because they out-numbered Biafrans by a ratio of about 5-1 but also because Nigeria had help from Great Britain, Russia, and a host of Arabic and Muslim countries. They also succeeded because Nigeria had more money, a better army and a backbreaking economic blockade against Biafra. Mostly, Nigeria completed the work mainly by staying true to its course and not betraying one another for their love of money, as the Biafrans did.

As the war continued into Eungu, my cousin, his wife and I left Umuezeoka to Akpugo. The travel was at night. It was in the company of Mr. Godwin Okenwa, the then owner of Republican Hotel, Enugu, who owned a Volkswagen beetle. He sat in front. The driver was a famous chauffeur called Peter Atu from Obuno Akpugo. My cousin, his wife and I sat at the back seat of the car. Between Umuezeoka and Akpugo is Enugu, a dangerous zone by virtue of its domination by the federal troops. Peter and Godwin decided to drive through Oruku, an outskirt of Egnugu. As we got close to Enugu, Peter and Godwin decided to turn off the headlight and he drove for several miles in the dark. We were out of any possible ambush from Nigerian soldiers; it was the greatest darkness I have ever seen. It soon disappeared due to a huge searchlight above us coming from the federal troops. The two experienced men in front cursed, ranted, and raved, as bewilderment descended upon us in the back. I prayed and prayed like never before. It was the longest 20 minutes of my life. Then as I anticipated, there was a cacophony of gunshots pouring incessantly. I was sure that they were directed towards us as I said my final prayers, but I was wrong. Those shots must have been directed towards somewhere else because we did not see or hear any bullets fly towards our direction. I still cannot get over how they could have missed us even with their state-of-the-art searchlight directly above us. We later heard that a Biafran jeep, full of Biafran soldiers was directly behind us. The Nigerian soldiers spotted both of us, but chose to shoot at the Biafran troops over pathetic civilians.

Shortly after we settled at Akpugo, the federal troops marched into Akpugo. My mother grabbed me, and the next morning we were refugees on our way to Ihuokpara, where I lived for about one and a half years. Those were the most memorable years of my life. I was very happy throughout those years because I knew that life could have been much worse for my family and me. My parents and my siblings moved back to their Akpugo farmland (Ndiagu) leaving me to stay with my maternal grandmother in Ihuokpara. Nigerian troops never came to Ihuokpara until the war ended, even as Akpugo became a battlefield only ten miles away. I felt lucky and fortunate. We grew our own crops and ate well. Everyone else lacked salt, but we never did because my grandmother traded for it. Salt was a rare commodity during the war.

In retrospect, I pity myself for thinking that I was having fun then. Meat was very scarce, so we ate snakes, wild birds, squirrels, chickens, dogs, cats, fishes, crickets, frogs, wild mushrooms, and rats. There was no indoor plumbing anywhere around. Instead, every family had shallow holes that they used for toilets. Vultures, mice, and chickens were often seen feeding from those shallow holes. I was worry-free in those days, but I feel quite sad today when I reflect on the fact that I was happily eating some mice and chickens that must have fed from those shallow holes of human waste. Though I was too young to make such conclusions, I might have done exactly the same thing in order to survive even if I were older. Ihuokpara had no perennial spring water that lasted beyond the rainy season into the dry season. As a matter of fact, they have no single source of water during the dry season. We traveled several miles to the nearest town, Amagunze, carrying clay pots of water on our heads to Ihuokpara. We fetched water twice a day - very early in the morning and late in the evening. We went to the farms in between. Schools were considered to be out of the question. All schools were closed indefinitely.

Sometimes, we went hunting for wild animals rather than going to the farm. We equally went into bushes and forests looking for wild mushrooms, wild African yams, cocoa yams, and carrots. We went hunting for frogs at night in the dark by waterfronts in the rainy season with a torch in one hand and a machete in the other. I was very fearful of snakes, and I remember stepping on one once and I never went back again. We would set forests on fire in order to kill wild animals that would run from the flames.

One day, my uncle Nnaji and I saw a burning bush and ran there to hunt down animals. At the scene, we saw a hole, the type that would be occupied by one of those edible wild mice. We started to dig the hole, looking for any sign of life. As we dug it with our machetes, we extended our hands into the hole to remove the debris. We were so relaxed, telling stories and cracking jokes, but all of a sudden, we saw *enwu agwo*, the most dangerous snake known to people in that part of the world. It is so poisonous that a single bite takes a human life in about ten minutes. First, the snake pulled out its ugly head as Nnaji and I fell backwards in shock and awe. We watched it slither toward the southern end of the field with speed until it disappeared there. We went home confused and not speaking to one another, especially as we realized that that wild snake could have killed either of us each time we extended our hands into that hole. It has become one of those indelible marks in my memory today. Several of my American friends, such as Tina Pucilowski, always wonder why I tend to be always happy and never fond of complaining about the vicissitudes of life. This near-death experience in wartime might explain it.

It was at this time of my life that I acquired a new respect for my parents and for my grandparents as well. They were all successful farmers, and I had found farming to be extremely difficult. Farming was not mechanized. All the labor was manual, under the sun and the rain. There were no fertilizers. We traveled very far by foot to grow crops such as cassava, maize, yams, cocoa yams, pumpkins, and garden eggs. I found digging up the soil in order to build hundreds of mounds to grow crops the most arduous and most energy-draining task. That is simply the reason why I vowed to acquire an education.

I dreaded working on the farm. I dreamed of an opportunity to indulge in an occupation that would not be performed while standing out in the rain or under the sun. I realized that going to school and acquiring degrees would enable me to work with my head for a living rather than with my hands. I worked very hard as a student because I knew that the only alternative was to become a farmer or one of those who pushes trucks or wheel barrows in the marketplaces to scrape a living daily.

When the Nigerian civil war ended, my immediate older brother who was in the Biafran boys' company brigade came home safely. For several weeks after the war, no one had seen my maternal uncle Pius Nnamani who joined the army very early in the wartime. No one saw my father's eldest son Nnamoko, "Mr. emotion-free guy". A lot of people returned from the war with amputated legs and hands. We just wanted to see my brother alive. One evening, we heard shouts of joy at my uncle's house. We ran out there, and behold, it was Nnamoko. I thought of my father's secret prayers, and I rejoiced. Nnamoko came home healthy with neither a missing limb nor a broken bone. A few days later, he told us that Pius, my maternal uncle, had died seventeen months before the war ended. He explained how he died in detail, how he helped to bury him, and how he wore a ribbon on his wrist for one year in his memory. It was sad. My mother wept bitterly.

I sacrificed a lot of my time serving Nnamoko, trying to help him get on his feet again and get on with life. He promised me that he would take me to Enugu City where I would live with him and go to school. I received that with elation and unsurpassable anticipation. Eventually, he went back to driving a cab at Enugu City as he did before the war. However, he failed to do as he promised: to take me with him. He avoided me like a plague, and the memory still haunts me today.

Eventually, I drifted to my brother-in-law Okorie, who had no choice but to accept me. He and his family gave me an unforgettable opportunity, a dream of a lifetime to live in an urban city the size of Enugu, a state capital. I was excited to be in Eungu city even though I was not in school and had to hawk in the street. Though the four of us, my brother-in-law, his younger brother, my sister, and I lived in one tiny, single room, it was still a thrill to reside at Enugu.

As time went on, I started to look at students as people with the greatest opportunity. I had no one to send me to school or pay for my education. I was beginning to settle for a life of abject poverty when my father visited Enugu to buy and sell seed yams. I bid him goodbye as he sat at the back of a lorry, happy that he did not have to walk or ride his bicycle home as usual. Then, an inward spirit moved me as I saw a boy hawking fresh meat right there. I quickly grabbed two heaps of the meat, paid the boy two shillings and gave it to my father as he sat in the truck waiting for Chinweze, the owner, to drive off. He accepted the meat with joy, and to my astonishment, he asked, "Why don't you come home and complete your primary education at Akpugo rather that waste your youth hawking bread here at Enugu?" It was the best and the sweetest question that I had ever been asked in my life. I responded, "Yes, I will be very happy to do that". I would rather go to school sitting in the shade than walk around under the sun shouting, "Buy Mazi Ejidike Bread," day in and day out. Within a month, my father arranged for my return to the village.

Earlier, I had not been very successful in school, perhaps due to the fact that I had always been forced to go to school, at first by my dad, and later by my cousin with whom I lived in Northern Nigeria. This time, however, I became so good in school that I was becoming afraid of myself. I knew this because Moses Nnaji was the smartest lad in our class at St. Thomas Catholic School a few years earlier. As a matter of fact, we sat alphabetically in class and since he was Nnaji and I was Nnam, we sat next to each other. I found myself copying from him during examinations, tests and exercises. This time I was lucky to meet him in the senior class at Sacred Heart Catholic School, a different institution. To my surprise, he was still as smart as ever, yet I was so far ahead of him in class it was unbelievable.

I started at primary five. At the mid-term examination, I was second to Benjamin Oko. At the final examination, the promotion examination, I beat Benjamin and came out at the top of my entire class for the first time in my life. This victory was also sweet because we had Sylvanus Eneh in class, another brilliant scholar who had unintentionally intimidated me some years earlier at St. Thomas Primary School Amede, Akpugo.

That year was the first time that all primary five students in all of Akpugo took examinations together. At the end, the headmaster, Mr. Joseph Obitulata, offered me an award from the Divisional Headquarters for scoring the highest mark among my entire class. In primary six, I continued to lead the class in every examination until we graduated. I was also the headmaster's monitor, the number one goalkeeper for the school's "first eleven" soccer team, a troop leader in the Boy Scouts, the founder of a "block rosary" society, the president of a Legion of Mary group, an altar boy and the teacher of our village girls' Igberi dancing group.

Nevertheless, I had two most unfortunate setbacks—my parents were so poor that they were unable to send me to any secondary school in the country after I finished elementary school, and I was having such a bad luck with external examinations that my First School Leaving Certificate Examination result came out with only a "credit." My headmaster, my class teachers and I rejected it, arguing that I should have received nothing less than a distinction. Upon further review, the examiners agreed that they had made a mistake. They sent me a different result with apologies. This time, it was worse than the "credit" that I had received earlier. This time they gave me an ordinary pass. Everyone, especially my teachers and classmates, knew that they were unfair to me.

The injustice continued when I sat for a Common Entrance Examination, and most of my classmates were placed in their schools of choice except for me. That was simply a sign of failure. My headmaster had a cousin, Mr. Ogbuke, who worked at the State School Management Board (SSMB), Enugu. The headmaster sent a letter to him that urged him to verify my grade and look up my school placement using my number. Mr. Ogbuke showed me my aggregate of 36, the highest possible score anyone could get. I saw it with my own two eyes. I still do not understand why he could not help me any further. I went back to my school with the note that he wrote to the headmaster, telling him that I had the highest possible aggregate and that I should have been placed at my first choice of schools, St. Teresa School in Nsukka. However, the Nigerian system was so corrupt that even the headmaster could not help me. I had no choice but to go to the junior seminary or to resort to my third choice, which was to enter the Benedictine Monastery at Awhum. I chose the junior seminary. I entered the Sacred Heart Junior Seminary at Nsude. I was quite determined to become a Catholic priest. I did not go in with the intention of gaining an education, which I could not afford in the secular institutions. I started to have some doubts regarding my vocation to the priesthood many years later.

My father gave me my first school fees. It was twelve pounds, which I handed my brother Nnamoko for safe keeping due to the fact that Father Mike Aluma, my parish priest, had paid my first tuition. Unfortunately, Nnamoko has not given that money back to me yet. Rev. Fr. Aluma ended up paying for my entire first year in the junior seminary. By the second year I had become a *Primus interparis*, the House Captain of Saint Godfrey's House; hence, Rector, Rev. Father Anih decided not to expel me when he expelled other debtor students.

By our third year, Father Anih was going to Rome to study. I was afraid of being expelled for my lack of tuition by the next Rector. Even if Father Anih had stayed, I would have still moved to Isienu Nsukka, at St. John Cross Junior Seminary where I was to continue with the third year. Fortunately, I had gotten the highest score at Nsude right before we moved to Nsukka. Our new Rector, from Amurri in my parish, Father Animba, had two scholarships from two German families. He quickly gave me one of them because I was the best in my class and awarded the second scholarship to Jude Anih, perhaps because he had a brother in the seminary and a sister in the convent. I used that scholarship for three years, until I obtained my high school diploma. We were neither allowed to write nor contact the foreign benefactors. I remember that a picture of each of us was taken and sent to them. I will be forever indebted to that unknown German family and to Fathers Anih, Animba, and Aluma for paying my tuition, thus enabling me to get an excellent Catholic education.

I was very lucky to be chosen by Father Egmehelu to spend vacations with him, especially when my own father disowned me for standing up to him when he tried to force my sister, Nwuka, into marrying a man who she did not like. My father liked him because he was very rich, but as I told my father, it was my sister, not he, that was getting married. My relationship with Father Emehelu helped me tremendously at St. John's due to the fact that our Rector, Father Aduaka, knew me as one of "Father Emehelu's boys."

I was equally lucky at Nsude since the Rector, Father Akubue, picked me from the crowd several times to ride with him to Enugu and to visit several families, such as one of my classmate's, Ferdinand Orji's. Being a house captain did not hurt either. During my first year, students were starving a lot, and some children even resorted to stealing food from the rich kids. Luckily for me, one of the teachers chose me to serve him his food. It was the greatest privilege. The teachers ate *semolina* while the rest of the student body fed on *garri*. They left me so much food at each meal that I had shared it with other friends, such as Innocent Nnajike, Emmanuel Ugwu, Felix Anah, and Sylvester Mbah.

Once the teachers were on strike, the Rector hired teachers from outside to administer the examinations. One teacher, whom I served, a history teacher, called me into his cubicle and told me in advance the questions for the exam. Not expecting this to be true, I walked into the examination hall to find the questions to be exactly what he had read to me word for word. I still do not understand why a teacher would do that; was it because he liked me that much, because he was trying to get back at the Rector, or simply because he lacked moral scruples?

Sacred Heart Nsude was new, and we uprooted trees in an area where they were developing a soccer field. I remember the dark and big scorpions that used to crawl out from underneath the trees. I remember planting the only coconut trees in my quadrangle as a house captain. Father Anih advised me to spread the coconut trees, and that meant planting them at Santa Maria's quadrangle, thereby helping Captain Basil Ogbozor, my rival. I did not like the idea, but I saw the reasoning behind it. Today, those coconut trees have grown to be huge and fruitful.

I remember introducing a marching band at the school and bringing an acrobatic dancing group from Akpugo called Odesha to teach my house how to dance and attract an audience. I remember sitting in the dormitory performing my administrative duties as other students went to the farm to perform manual labor. One day, Ferdinand Okonkwor was carried home by a group of boys. They said a dangerous snake bit him. Today, I ask, in retrospect, why they did not carry him to the hospital instead. I cried all night with Father Anih, the Rector consoling him. He almost died. That was the night that I realized why I am afraid of all snakes, even rubber snakes.

The night my name was announced as the new house captain of St. Godfrey's house, to replace Mr. Christopher Agalamayi, an older guy; I was so shocked that my sadness disappeared. We had just returned from a two-week break. I had seen people suffering from typhoid. Being a hypochondriac, I quickly started to suffer all of the symptoms. I came back to school as sick as a dog. I was even throwing up. I was getting ready to leave school in order to be treated in the hospital. I found out that it was psychosomatic illness when I forgot about my sickness for several weeks after I became a house captain, the greatest honor that could be given to a student in the junior seminary under Father Stan Anih. Finally, I remember making a lot of money through photography and winning the first spot as a mile runner in Nsukka Zone by beating the famous miler from St. Theresa's Nsukka.

By my fifth year, my classmates, such as Sylvester Mbah, Innocent Nnajike, Christopher Agalamayi, John Bosco Okafor and Master Ifeonu, were already transferring to the secondary schools in order to sit for the West African School Certificate (WASC) given by the West African Examination Council (WAEC). I could not transfer because my scholarship applied only as long as I was in the seminary. Luckily for me, the seminary got approved, and my set was the first at St. John Cross Seminary Nsukka to sit for the WASC in the history of Enugu Diocese.

Unfortunately, my bad luck with external examinations continued. Many of my classmates passed enough subjects to enter any of the Nigerian universities. I had grade two with an ordinary pass in English, my favorite subject. Once again, every one of my teachers and classmates agreed that a mistake had been made. I refused to protest. Instead, I went to the senior seminary, leaving my classmates behind.

In my first year in the senior seminary, Urbana University Rome approved it for BA honors after four years there. I was happy until Dr. Okere, the dean, announced that everyone had to have five credits including English in WASC or GCE in order to be awarded a bachelor's degree after four years. I became very sad. It caught up with me. I wanted to disappear from the face of the Earth. At this point, I was already one of the four top philosophy students out of over a hundred in the first year from the five dioceses in the eastern providence, or Onitsha ecclesiastical region. It would have been a shame for me not to sit for the BA examination at the end. I was the only top student in that situation.

I wrote Father Emmanuel Edeh Cssp, telling him that I was planning to leave the seminary because they would not let me take the BA examination after four years with my classmates. He wrote back to say, "Would you let me down if I bring you to the United States to complete your education?" I replied to his letter, reminding him how I listened to him when he advised me not to go to the secondary school to sit for my WASC even when half of my classmates had left. I also reminded him how I stayed with him, serving him from a week before his ordination until about a month later when I had to go back to school. I went on to remind him of how he had had a misunderstanding at one time or another with other seminarians simply because they refused to heed his instructions. Finally, I reminded him of how I had stuck with him all those years at Ihiala and Akpugo, along with Franka Anih and Ngozi Nnamchi until 1978 when he left Nigeria to the United States and eventually with Franka.

He replied to my letter and said that he had discussed it with Franka, and she agreed that he should bring me to the USA. He asked me to promise that I would remain obedient to him after I came to America and that I would continue to be steadfast to my vocation to the priesthood, especially after acquiring an education. I did. Then, he wrote back, sending me application forms to Kennedy King College and DePaul University in Chicago. I was more interested in Kennedy King College, because it appeared more familiar than DePaul. Eventually, he convinced me to pick DePaul over Kennedy, for which I will always be grateful.

Eventually, DePaul granted me admission. They sent me a letter of admission along with a form 1-20, both of which I needed to obtain an F-1 Visa from the American Consulate located at 2 Eleke Crescent, Victoria Island, Lagos. I discovered that I had to pay an entire year's tuition in order to be able to obtain the Visa. I wrote Father Emmanuel, begging him to pay the tuition on my behalf, but he wrote back urging me to use my "ingenuity" to get the money from "my rich uncles," Chief Samson Nneji and Chief Gabriel Nnaji.

I went straight to Chief Nneji and explained the entire situation to him. He and I were already quite familiar with each other only because then I was the president of the Akpugo students' union, and Chiefs Nneji, Nnaji, Nwobodo C. Nwobodo and Chukwuma Nwankwor were the Patrons. Chief Nneji was extremely sympathetic, kind, and understanding. He agreed to help but made it clear that he would not do it alone. He suggested that I should approach other Akpugo men, women, and social organizations to help me. We both agreed that the next person I had to approach was his cousin, Chief Gabriel Nnaji. Chief Nneji called him by telephone and told him that he and I would be coming to his house the next morning for a special discussion. The next day, Chief Nneji brought along with him a bottle of expensive English wine and asked me to offer it to Chief Nnaji when we got to his house. I did so when we got there, but he was not available and the meeting was rescheduled. It was agreed that Chief Nnaji would meet us at a different venue, Chief Nneji's office, the next evening. At 7 o'clock, Chief Nnaji arrived, and the discussion commenced. I told both of them the entire story and they asked me to step out for a moment to allow them to deliberate. I walked out humbly. Thirty minutes later, they asked me to come back and to listen to what they had to say in response to my request. When I came in, they told me that they have both agreed to help me with my first year tuition. They urged me to work hard and win a scholarship for subsequent years' tuition when I got there.

They went on to add that I had to do my best to give other Akpugo indigenes a chance to help me. Hence, we decided to organize a fundraiser on my behalf the next month. That gave me a chance to invite everyone I knew who was capable, in my opinion, of helping me. I even traveled statewide, asking many wealthy individuals to come to my aid. I was shocked by the way people failed to respond favorably to my appeal.

First, I went to Onitsha, where I visited Chief Ogbu, Unateze I of Nara. He was probably the richest man from the Nkanu local government. He was very sincere with me in his house. He told me that he had helped Father Emmanuel a year earlier to travel to the United States, and he never wrote him to tell him he got there safely, let alone thank him. He told me that he would not give me a penny as a result of such ingratitude. Then, I visited Mr. Onoh of Ngwo one evening in one of his offices at Coal Camp Enugu. He equally told me that he could not help me right then but maybe later. By the way, Chief Onoh was not only famous and influential; he was also probably the wealthiest politician in the entire state. My friends could not understand how I could have had the nerve to even come up with the idea of meeting such a larger than life fellow.

Nonetheless, there were many kind people who responded to me. Daniel Anike, Kenneth Nwatu, Sunday Oruruo, Christopher Asa, Stephen Nnamoko and quite a few other individuals pledged to give me some money, but none of them came to the actual fundraising. The only ones who showed up were Chief Nneji, who paid for all the drinks, Chief Nnaji, Mr. Michael Nwatu, my father, my three uncles, and myself. Then, my uncle Aaron addressed my two guests. Mr. Mike Nwatu was there only to serve as a secretary. Aaron told them to accept the little drink as a token of our appreciation of their presence. He went on to tell them that many were invited, and like in the Bible, only a few responded. He said that we would rather have a few people who were sincere show up than have millions show up who had come to laugh. Chief Nnaji stood up after him. He proceeded to say that they would pay for my first year's tuition, and if that was all they could afford, then they would inform me. Chief Nneji spoke only to agree with his cousin a hundred percent. We applauded them. Everyone went to them and shook their hands, thanking them. Aaron asked me to bow in gratitude to their magnanimity and benevolence. I did. At the end, we loaded their vehicles with the leftover drinks, and they drove off.

All said and done, I went to the American Consulate in Lagos for a visa interview. It was unsuccessful because they handed me a paper with a list of what I had to bring in order to obtain a student's visa. Mr. Nnejico and I were both disappointed because it was he who took me there by motorcycle from number 60 Aroloya Street, Lagos. He was only an apprentice then to Chief Nneji.

All of the requirements were provided overnight except for the recommendation letter from the Student Advisory Board, which became impossible because the man placed in charge of it made life miserable for anyone who was not ready and able to give him a bribe. I did not because I did not have it. Luckily, I had a friend, Ngozi Nnamchi, who was a classmate to his wife. She bought a live chicken, which she took to his house, and the next morning, he recognized that I existed for the first time even after I had been there daily for the past two weeks. He included me among his next batch of students to whom they gave lessons in preparations for study abroad, especially in the United States. We were taught how to tie ties, how to study, and how to behave while abroad without bringing shame to our country. In the end, I went back to Lagos and I was able to get a two-year visa. That was when I started to believe that I might actually be traveling abroad to study. I became giddy. The Akpugo Students' Union gave me a very big send off party, coupled with an expensive sweater, which they offered me as a gift. I started to visit my dearest friends and relatives to inform them that I would be traveling abroad.

I had only a few days left with many places yet to visit, and I became desperate. One day, I saw "Joseph-the-twin" at Sacred Heart, driving one of his uncle's vehicles. It was a Peugeot pick-up truck to be precise. I persuaded him to drive me to Umuzii village for an urgent message, and he agreed. After we passed Unuzii, he realized that we were only about four miles away from my grandmother's house at Ihuokpara, a neighboring town. He knew because my grandmother, Nwa Nnaji Nwa Nshi, was also his aunt. Therefore he stopped. I broke down and told him that I had just a few weeks to leave to the United States, and I had not visited most of my relatives, including my grandmother. I begged him to take me there as the last favor that he might ever get a chance to do for me for the rest of his life. He reversed his vehicle and went right back home without granting my wish. I thought of asking him to let me out on the way because I was too angry to ride home with him, but it was an isolated farmland where anything could have happened to me. Besides, it was getting dark. I remember asking him if he would treat his twin sister the same way or if it was because I was not related to him closely enough. He was probably a second or third cousin. By the way, I have forgiven him. After all, he was only a teenager.

Finally, I left Nigeria on December 29, 1979. That morning, members of the Akpugo Student Union started to march into our compound as early as 5 o'clock. By 7 o'clock, my compound was already full of people coming to escort me to the airport. There were between fifty and a hundred people. Patrick Onovo, my successor, and the new president of the Akpugo Student Union went and hired a third vehicle that morning because more people came than expected. At 8 o'clock, we left Akpugo for Emene Airport, which was only about a 30-minute drive from my home.

We had five vehicles all together, and two or three of them were buses. Ike Agbo drove me with his brother George Agbo's station wagon. It was packed with my mother and my closest relatives. My dad stayed home with my baby sister, Obiageli, who was only a tiny baby. I begged him to come with us, but he explained that it would be inappropriate or against our custom. I still have not understood why. People were already waiting for me at the airport. They explained that they had been waiting for a couple of hours.

We took many photographs. It was there and then that I realized that I would be leaving my closest friends and relatives for several years in America. I became sad, but I was able to hide it, especially from my mother. Everyone wanted to take a personal photograph with me but I had no time because my flight was scheduled to depart Enugu at 10:30 a.m. Thus, I chose to pose with friends over my family and I remember that when I turned down my sister's request for a photograph with me, I saw her weep bitterly.

It was my first time in an airplane ever! Luckily for me, Ms. Teresa Nnaji was there getting ready to fly to Lagos and then to London. She recognized that it was my first time on an airplane. She was very nice to me and made me feel at home. I wished that she could have followed me to the United States or even to London. Unfortunately, she had to spend a few days in Lagos before traveling to London. She switched me from the local to the international airport in Lagos. I sat there until 10:30 p.m. when we boarded British Caledonia Airline, which would take us to London. We landed at Heathrow Airport in London the next morning. They quickly provided us with a helicopter to take us to Gatwick Airport. I loved it. It was from there that we took off and flew for at least 8 hours on our way to O'Hare International Airport in Chicago.

I had mixed feelings during the flight. First, I was happy because I was finally on my way to the United States, finally. On the other hand, I was unhappy because of the beloved friends and relatives that I was leaving behind. I cried a lot. One man from Ghana that I met on the airplane from London to Chicago told me about racism, cold weather and a lot of strong wind in Chicago. It bothered me. However, the worst news was that I would not be able to find very traditional African food, such as garri, bitter leaf, egushi, ogbono, okra and so on in Chicago. I cried myself to sleep several times. My flight ticket between London and Chicago read from noon to 2:00 p.m. and I thought it was a two-hour flight. We flew for six hours and kept on flying. I started to panic a lot, but when I looked at the other passengers they appeared relaxed; having fun, eating and chatting.

Finally, I arrived at O'Hare International Airport. Father Emmanuel Edeh and Franka Anih were both there waiting for my arrival. I went to the city with them, and they took me to an apartment that they had found for me. It was the 30th of December, 1979. The next day was New Year's Eve. On January 2, 1980, DePaul University resumed after Christmas vacation. Father Emmanuel took me to DePaul, where I met Mr. James Van Linden, the international student's advisor; Mr. Stephen Goldberg, my advisor, Father Munster in the admissions office, and Dr. Patricia Ewers, the dean. I had talked to some of them on the phone from Nigeria, so it was quite an intriguing experience to meet them in person for the first time. I registered for classes, and Franka led me to the bookstore where I bought the textbooks. I came back for classes the next day, and soon I obtained a bachelor's degree in thirty months with a 4.00 cumulative grade point average, graduating Summa Cum Lauda. A year later, I got a master's degree, and I added a Ph.D. two and a half years later and the rest is history.

Chapter 3

The Role of Women in Africa

Pre-colonial Africa was, in most parts, matriarchal, matrilineal and, in some parts, matrifocal. Women had leadership roles in abundance. A dual-sex political system in which each sex managed its own affairs prevailed. The males were governed by queen-mothers known as *Omu* by the Igbo, *Kentake* by the Cush, *Nandi* by the Zulu, *Lyalode* by the Yoruba, *Ohemaa* in Ashanti, *Indlovukati* in South Africa and *Candmu Kulu* by the Bemba. Women's interests were represented at all levels. Women in pre-colonial Africa achieved recognition and distinction. They were queens, elders, priestesses, and titled elites. They were independent. They controlled the market, the farm, and ultimately the economy.

Things began to fall apart starting with the Western Colonization of Africa. Europeans were patriacrchal, hence they canceled out the female institution and replaced female leaders with males. Women fought back in various ways, the most outstanding of which was the Igbo Women War of 1929.

Rather than go back to the earlier ways of doing things, post-colonial and independent Africans decided to "disafricanize" and to "Westernize" themselves. In other words, they continue to cherish and prefer Western values over African values. Today very few African nations are governed by women.

The European administrators who came to Africa were almost all males and brought with them European sexist ideas. They taught farming to the men and embroidery to the women, even though African women farmed. They appointed male chiefs where formerly Queens and female leaders had positions of power.[1]

There are lots of miscconceptions here in the United states about Africians. The African woman is not an exception to these misconceptions. Some of the greatest misconceptions in the Western world regarding Africian women are: they are subservient to males; they never had as many leadership positions as males; they are economically dependent on males; their place is in the kitchen; they inherit nothing from their families; through dowries men buy them like cows; women have no rights; a single man can marry many women at the same time (polygyny) whereas a woman cannot be accorded the same or similar priviledges by marrying several males at the same time (polyandry); sexism was much worse in Africa before, rather than after, the European colonization of Africa; Western feminists need to liberate African women from their barbaric, primitive, and oppressive patriarchal coustoms; men's wishes are their command; African men are so arrogant that they are trained to believe from childhood that they are God's gift to women. I refer to these as misconceptions because there is not an iota of truth in any of them. Instead, there have always been both matriarchal and leadership roles of women in Africa. If anything has diminished the leadership roles of women it has been European colonization of Africa. I plan to prove this point in this chapter by examinating the status of African women in three different ephochs, namely: pre colonial, colonial and post-colonial Africa

Pre-Colonial Africa

This is the era during which matriarchy and "romantic primitivism" reached their apogee in Africa. Prominent queens ruled and governed African ethnic groups and empires from north to south, east to west. Africans never questioned that because to them it was natural for women to govern wisely, courageously, and justly. Europeans, on the other hand, were surprised to see African women in leadership roles. For example, British anthropologist Dugald Campbell was shocked to learn that the ruler of the whole tribe of Luena in Angola was a woman. He indicated this in his book, *In the Heart of Bantuland*, when he wrote:

> The Queen of the whole tribe was a woman of remarkable ability and personal character named Nyakatolo. The history of her springing into power, conquering the country she occupied, and subjugating the surrounding tribes is very interesting reading [. . .] for the purpose of conquest, she got together an army and fought her way through the countries intervening between the Luena River and the Kuvungu stream.

> She scattered every force that opposed her and established villages at the head of which she put women chiefs. She instituted a system of women chiefs all over the countries she conquered, who were tributary to her and sent in regular caravans of tribute each new moon.[2]

Some other ancient pre-colonial queens of Africa are:

- Cleopatra of Egypt, 51 BC
- Nefertiti of Egypt, 1365 BC
- Hatshepsut who ruled the 18th dynasty of Egypt, 1505 - 1485 BC
- Makeda, the Biblical Queen of Sheba, 1005 BC
- The four Cush Queens, Amanirenas, Amanishakhete, Nawidemak, and Malegereabar, around 300 BC
- Candace of Meroe, 3rd and 2nd century BC
- Kahina of Mahgreb, 575 AD - 702 AD
- Amina of Hausa Land, 1536 AD - 1573 AD
- Ais kili Nquinanaramama of Bornu (date uncertain)
- Helena and Sabia Wangel of Ethiopia, 16th century AD
- Nzinga of Angola, 1581 AD - 1663 AD
- Dona Beatrice of Kongo, 1682 AD - 1706 AD
- Mmanthatisi of the Sotho, 1781 AD - 1835 AD
- Ranavalona I of Madagascar, 1828 AD - 1861 AD
- Muganzirwazza of Uuganda, 1817 AD - 1882 AD
- Nehanda of Zimbabwe, 1863 AD - 1898 AD
- Yaa Asantewa of Ashanti, 1860 AD - 1921 AD
- Nyamazana, the Warrior Queen of the Shona
- Empress Taitu of Ethiopia, 1908
- Zaiditu, Empress of Abyssinia and grand daughter of Warrior Queen Taitu

Now, let us compare such ancient African queenship to the United States on the threshold of the 21st century. There has not been one woman president, or even vice-president. What is most alarming is that this is not likely to change in the near future.

The Dual-Sex Political System

Besides having women as chiefs of a whole society, many African groups had traditions in which power was shared so that women's issues were handled by women leaders, while men handled their own affairs. An example would be the Yoruba, who had the custom of having a *Lyalode,* or "mother of the town," to whom all women's quarrels were brought for arbitration.[3]

In many African societies the concept of a dual monarchy—which recognized the need for female as well as male rulers—was natural. This is because there were many dual associations for men and women with different initiation rites, social duties and religious obligations in many African communities. Therefore, many African societies had a dual-sex political system, a method through which the king and queen mother ruled simultaneously. The king was usually empowered to oversee all matters affecting the male population, while the queen was charged to oversee all matters affecting the female population. Take, for instance, the most admired queen of Africa, Nefertiti of Egypt. She ruled at the same time as her husband, King Amunhotep IV, around 1365 BC. At the age of 18, Cleopatra became the queen of Egypt and ruled with her brother, King Ptolemy XIII, around 51 BC. The Cush (Ethiopia) had *Kentake,* also known as Queen Mothers. In Rwanda, the king's biological mother was "Queen Mother." In Swazi, the Kom (Western Cameroon), the "Queen Mothers" were similarly the biological mothers of the kings. In Mossi, the "Queen Mother" was the king's first daughter. In Barotse, a sister became the "Queen Mother" and a brother became the king at the same time. Even Shaka Zulu, a self-proclaimed patriarch, put his wife, aunt, and sister in charge of military *kraals*. His mother was the "Queen Mother" known in Zulu as *Nandi*. The Igbos referred to the "Queen Mother" as *Omu*. The Yorubas called her the *Lyalode*. In Ashanti, she was known as *Ohemaa*, which translates as the king's female counterpart. She was the person who had the power to insult the King. She had her own court and she officiated at religious ceremonies. In South Africa the "Queen Mother" was called *Indlovukati*. Among the Bemba of East Africa "the Bemba princesses and the chief's mother held direct power. The chief's mother or Candamukula ruled over her own territory. The Princess Royal or Mukuamfuma held her own sub chieftainship and all the princesses had important roles in religious ceremonies."[4]

In her book, *An African Aristocracy*, anthropologist Hilda Kuper compared the "balance of power" between South African kings and "Queen Mothers" to that between the executive, the judiciary, and the legislature in the modern European (and American) system of government.

Those queens were not mere figureheads. They administered wisely and they fought fiercely in battles. John D. Omer-Cooper in his book, *The Zulu Aftermath*, (Evanston: Northwestern Univ. Press, 1969), described a woman warrior regent of Tlokwa, who by her own courage and ingenuity created a victory out of defeat in the following way:

> Only the quick wit of Mantatisi saved the day. Forming all the available men into a single rank, she made the women line up behind them waiving the handles of hoes instead of spears and holding up sleeping mats to look like shields. Faced with what looked like a compact body of warriors drawn up in a combat formation, the Hlubi hesitated and as they did so Sikonyela, the (woman) military leader, came upon them and inflicted a severe defeat.[5]

Western women, on the other hand, are not allowed to participate in combat as much as their male counterparts. In the 20th century, African women took part in anti-colonial actions in Kenya and in the wars of independence of Angola, Guinea-Bissau, Mozambique, and Zimbabwe.[6]

In European history, an English queen had to be either the wife of a king or the reigning daughter of a king who died without a male heir. An African queen did not derive her status in any way from an attachment or relationship to a king.

Priesthood

In several denominations of Christianity, such as Roman Catholicism, women are not permitted to become priests, bishops, cardinals, or popes. Only males can qualify for such honorable leadership positions. The Church gives several reasons for this, including the fact that Jesus Christ chose twelve apostles and seventy-two disciples, all of whom were men. African traditional religion, in contrast, has female priests and religious leaders. Priestesses, as a matter of fact, are accorded more respect because they are considered to be more clairvoyant than male priests. Many priestesses, such as Nobela of Zulu, became as popular as their kings or queens because they were both diviners and healers. Many of them were rainmakers and the people's lives were in their hands since they needed rain to grow their crops to avoid drought and famine. Diviners also uncovered witchcraft. They were said to tell the future. They presided over religious sacrifice and worship. They prescribed cures for illnesses, and most importantly, they made up an entire branch of any

African traditional government. The other branches were usually the council of elders and that of the titled men and women.

As a little boy growing up in Africa I remember when my aunt Mgbeke Nwatuoko Nnamani of Ihuokpara told me stories about the Queen of Sheba. What I recall the most is not her encounter with King Solomon, but the fact that she founded Ethiopia (the land of the burnt faces), and yet the major church in Addis Ababa was named after Mary. Moreover, no women are allowed in the Coptic Christian Church, Mariam Church of the Virgin.[7]

Marriage

Western Europeans and Americans seem to think that polygamy is synonymous with Africa. They think that polygamy means the marriage of a man to several wives at the same time. They also believe that an African male can marry several women at the same time; whereas, an African female cannot marry several males at the same time, even if she is capable and willing. These are misconceptions which stem from (a) ignorance of basic African traditions and culture, and (b) lack of respect for Africans as a people. Yes, Africans have always been polygamous. However, polygamy means a combination of polygyny and polyandry. Polygyny is a marriage between a man and several women at the same time. Polyandry, on the other hand, is the marriage between a woman and several men at the same time. Because polygyny is more common than polyandry, Westerners have always mistaken polygyny for polygamy. One of the reasons that polygyny is more common is a result of the transatlantic slave trade, wars and riots, through which Africa lost a lot more males than females. Hence, there is a ratio of only one male to several females.

More astounding to westerners, however, is that customary African marriages give more rights to females than males in multiple ways.

Whereas men are not allowed to marry any other male in any part of Africa, several tribes, such as the Igbo ethnic group, permit women to marry other women. Many people of African decent, especially the ones who were born and raised in modern cities, may not be aware of such aspects of African culture. As a matter of reference, Dr. Victor Uchendu, a professor of Southeastern Nigeria, described his life as a child growing up in a family where his biological mother was married to another woman, Ezigbo:

> My mother was a "big" trader and she needed someone to help in our house and so she "married" one wife after another. . . . Of all my mother's wives (she married them serially), I loved Goodness most. She was my mother's first wife and was ten years my senior. She helped me to prepare for school. . . . "Women marriage," a recognized institution among the Igbo, enables female husbands to acquire rights in other women (who become their "brides.")[8]

Further, the Lovedu have had the custom of female to female marriage, in which the queen "marries" the daughters of many of the chiefs' families.

Many tribes were matrilineal, and names were traced through the mothers' side of the family. Married women not only kept their family names, but children also took the mothers' names. Compare and contrast this with the Western world, where the mother, the wife and the children take the husband's name.

In the West, a woman is given the title "Mrs." if she is married and "Miss" if she is not married. The males are addressed with "Mr." whether they are married or not. This double standard is a legacy of patriarchy. By contrast, a majority of African languages are gender neutral. That is, there is only one word for the personal pronouns "he" and "she," and that single pronoun is definitely not masculine.

One summer, I attended a Dominican Colleges' Colloquium at Sienna Heights College in Adrian, Michigan. I met Chukwunenye Duru, a Nigerian professor of economics at Ohio Dominican College. He was planning to visit Mbano, his hometown in Nigeria for a grand celebration known in Iboland as *Ihe Onyima*. This celebration is so elaborate that it requires the return of people from other states, countries, and even continents as in the case of Dr. Duru. *Ihe Onyima* is a special thanksgiving ceremony performed once in a lifetime by a child to his mother in recognition of her sacrifice through his birth, childhood, and upbringing. As I discussed this with Dr. Duru we realized that Africans have no celebrations equivalent to *Ihe Onyima* for fathers. However, it was our questioning that is unusual, not the practice; Dr. Duru and I raised such questions only due to our Western influence.

Umuada is a grouping of women in the Igbo ethnic group. They have an extraordinary amount of spiritual and political power. For example, their prayers are believed to go straight to God and it could be disastrous to be cursed by them. There are several male associations, but none of them is this spiritually unique or effective. Politically, *Umuada* make rules that govern other females within the society. Every female is automatically a member by the virtue of her birth within the clan. It is a lifetime membership so she comes from outside to participate in this association if she is married from out of town, clan, tribe, or community. Women married into any community from outside cannot become members since that bond is that of sisterhood. As a matter of fact, *Umuada* have power over their brothers' wives and other women who are not qualified to join them. I realized how powerful they are for the first time in my youth when I witnessed them ostracize a woman for beating up her husband. They also have been known to punish by fines and I have seen them go on strike until they have gotten what they wanted. Obviously, *Umuada* are considered to be very powerful.

Colonial Africa

> Colonial rule in Nigeria in the first decade of this venture marked the beginning of the end of equality of the sexes in villages as well as in national politics. . . . What is often overlooked is that under colonialism women in Southeastern Nigeria suffered the greatest loss of power. Men could boast of some measure of participation because the British chose them to fill the newly created posts . . . the only monarch the British recognized was the male monarch, the Obi. He alone received a monthly paycheck. His female counterpart, the Omu, was relegated to the background, where her only role was to serve as the intermediary between the Obi and the women of the town. She could no longer make policy but had to take orders from the Obi.[9]

Africa is considered to be one of the oldest matriarchies in the world. The Europeans, on the other hand, are known to have always been patriarchal. As Europeans colonized Africa, they brought their patriarchal mentality with them, and it was strange and shocking to the Africans. The Europeans equally found the African matriarchal system to be very unusual and primitive; hence, they vowed to stamp it out of existence. They did that and more. They replaced *omu* with *obi*. Males were sent to Western institutions from where they returned as lawyers, doctors, teachers, political scientists, economists, and more. Women were expected and encouraged to stay home, cook, sew, bear and raise children. African women in some parts kept quiet and calm due to the Muslim influence on them. Those who have never been affected by the spread of Islam took it with qualms and without equanimity. Igbo women could be considered to be a good example of the latter. They were not used to being told what to do by men, not even their husbands. Kings could not order them to do anything. Each community had an *omu*, a woman leader, a queen or its equivalent. However, the colonialists ignored, disrespected and trampled upon them. This is the second of the issues that gave rise to the Igbo Women's War of 1929. The Europeans reported it in their history books as Aba Riots of 1929. They called it a "riot" because they did not believe that women had "inherent vitality, courage, self-reliance" and enough organizational ability necessary to stage a war. This Igbo women's war was an eye-opener for the Europeans. The Igbos call it *Ogu Umunwanyi*, which means "women's war" or "women's fight" for the right to be consulted on matters that affect them. Many of the women lost their lives, yet the war did not end until the British promised to listen to them. They made their point. The British kept their promises, but only for a while. Eventually, the British wore Igbo women out with all kinds of systems, including indirect rule plus divide and conquer.

When Igbo women forced the colonial administrators to recognize their presence during the women's war, their brief visibility was insufficient to shake these assumptions. The British failure to recognize the women's war as a collective response to the abrogation of rights resulted in a failure to ask whether women might have had a role in the traditional political system that should be incorporated into the institutions of the colonial government. What Westerners have not seen is that for African women actual autonomy, economic independence, and political power did not grow out of Western influence but existed already in traditional "tribal" life. To the extent that Igbo women have participated in any political action, whether anticolonial or nationalistic struggles, local community development, or the Biafran civil war, it has been not so much because of the influence of Western values as despite that influence.[10]

What became the most effective weapon in the hands of the Europeans was the concept of *dis-Africanization*. Ali Mazrui gives that name to the tactic used by Europeans to Westernize Africans. First, Europeans introduced Christianity at the expense of African traditional religion. They then introduced Western schools, in which they were able to brainwash Africans into picking Western values at the expense of African values. Also, those Europeans helped Africans to develop Western tastes without acquiring Western skills. That perpetuated African economic dependency on the Europeans. When a people's economy is controlled, their entire livelihood is controlled. Therefore, the Europeans at this juncture had gotten a full grip of the Africans and consequently were capriciously able to stamp out virtually every aspect of the African culture that had anything to do with matriarchy. By the early 1960s, many African countries had regained their political independence. However, they did not know what to do with it. Whereas they were politically independent, they were economically, psychologically, and spiritually dependent on the Europeans, thanks to dis-Africanization.

Post-Colonial Africa

Dis-Africanization, Westernization, brainwashing, and indoctrination of the Africans by Europeans during colonization continued to haunt and ravage Africa even in the post-colonial era.

Economically, Africans are dependent on foreign materials and foreign food products because they have been taught to believe that African-made goods are inferior to imported ones. An African alcoholic beverage known as "palm wine" is very scarce because it is not considered to be as good as foreign made beers, wine, whisky, or brandy. In the same way, Western-made clothes are preferred over the indigenous ones. Educated Africans seldom listen to African music. Instead, they elect to pay a lot more for American or European music. Other Africans prefer Western hairstyles, food, language, and culture in general.

Politically, the European separation of church and state, which was imposed on the Africans during colonization, continued to exist even in post-colonial Africa. The effect has been devastating. By not separating church and state, African rulers governed with the fear of the wrath of God, ensuring fairness and justice. Today, people do whatever they want without the politics, religion, and morality mixed with their politics. This explains why African nations are more corrupt today than ever. In the past, priests, elders, and titled people governed African traditional society. No one usurped power since the curse would ruin him, his children, and his children's children. Today, the government is foreign; therefore, "might is right" and the rule is "survival of the fittest." That explains why the military rule/regime and constant *coups d'etat* are the order of the day in Africa today.

Recommendation: Africans must study their history with pride and passion. This way they will be able to identify what has worked for them in the past in order to improve on it today. Many African ways of life must be revived (a) because they are good, (b) because they are African and so they suit Africans, and (c) because they are not inferior to Western or any other foreign style. For example, whereas a patriarchal society, according to Cheikh Anta Diop, tends to look down on females, "matriarchy is not an absolute and cynical triumph of woman over man, it is a harmonious dualism, an association accepted by both sexes."[11]

Notes

1. S.H. Gross and M.W. Bingham, *Women in Africa of the Sub Sahara Vol. II*, (Wisconsin: Gary McCuen Publications, Inc., 1989), 54.
2. D. Campbell, *In the Heart of Bantuland.* (New York: Negro Universities Press, 1969), 163-164.
3. Gross and Bingham, *Women in Africa*, 25.
4. Ibid., 21.
5. John D. Omer-Cooper, *The Zulu Aftermath*, (Evanston: Northwestern Univ. Press, 1069), 88.
6. Gross & Bingham, *Women in Africa*, 36.
7. Ibid., 42.
8. V.C. Uchendo, *The Igbo of Southeast Nigeria,* (Chicago: Holt, Rinehart and Winston, 1965).
9. Green, M., *Igbo Village Affairs,* (London: 1964), 66.
10. K. Okonjo, ed: Nancy J. Hafkin and Edna G. Bay, *Women in Africa*, (California: Stanford University Press, 1976), 55.
11. Diop, C.A. *The Cultural Unity of Black Africa: The Domains of Matriarchy and of Patriarchy in Classical Antiquity*, (London: Karnak House, 1989), 108.

Chapter 4

Matriarchy

Women In Africa: The Year 2000 and the New Decade

> Colonial rule in Nigeria in the first decade of this century marked the beginning of the end of equality of the sexes in village as well as in national politics. . . . What is often overlooked is that under colonialism women in Southeastern Nigeria suffered the greatest loss of power. Men could boast of some measure of participation because Britain chose them to fill the newly created posts.[1]

> The European administrators who came to Africa were almost entirely male and brought with them European sexist ideas. They taught farming to the men and embroidery to the women, even though African women farmed. They appointed male chiefs where formerly queens and female leaders had had positions of power. Although they sent African men off to colleges like Oxford or the Sorbonne, generally, they made few attempts to similarly encourage women as potential leaders.[2]

The thrust of this chapter is that besides Mesopotamia, Africa had the oldest matriarchy in the world. Africa was not only matriarchal but many of its societies were matrilineal. The leadership role of women in Africa was obvious. Even Western scholars such as Susan Hill Gross and Marjorie Wall Bingham recognized this African matriarchy. They went on to say that this matriarchy came to an abrupt end with the European colonization of Africa.

The Europeans looked down on Africans and their institutions. They vowed to replace them with European values, and they succeeded. African languages were replaced with English and French. African traditional religion was declared paganism and replaced with Christianity. The African matrilineal system was replaced with patriliny. African matriarchy was replaced with patriarchy.

How and why were the Europeans able to accomplish such havoc? They were able to achieve this through the disafricanization and Westernization of Africans.

Disafricanization

The disappearance of matriarchy from Africa was made possible by a process that Kenyan scholar Ali Mazrui referred to as disafricanization. What is disafricanization? It is the process through which contemporary Africans, to the dismay of their ancestors, chose Western institutions, values, and ways of life over, and above, African culture. There have been many theories as to why "reasonable" Africans engaged in such a disgraceful action. However, the one that stands out the most is that when a rumor, gossip, or even a false statement is spread about an individual or a group of people for a very long time, even they begin to believe it. This is a well-known psychological fact. For many years, Europeans have put Africans down. Africans have been considered to be sub-humans. They have been called monkeys, gorillas, savages, natives, bumpkins, yokels, and certainly inferior to Europeans. The devil is painted black and angels white. At weddings, brides dress in white garments, and at funerals, they dress in black garments. Whiteness is a symbol of purity, and blackness a symbol of mournfulness. This superiority complex of Europeans is found in every expression of the English language. Such expressions include: a black sheep in the family, to blackmail a person, a black day, a black market, a pot calling the kettle black, to be blacklisted, black magic, to be blackballed, the black cat crossing one's path, the bogeyman is black, villains have black hats and evil is black.

All of these strategies have been used to keep the African mind and body inferior to those of the Europeans. Unfortunately, it started to work over a number of years. Africans began to Westernize and disafricanize themselves as an inferiority complex set in. Today, disafricanization of Africans by Africans is manifested in various forms, namely:

a. African hairstyles are being abandoned for "jerry curl."
b. Africans in the Diaspora spend a lot of money each year on plastic surgery in an attempt to make their noses and lips thinner, like white people.
c. European suits and American jeans are preferred in Africa over traditional African wears.
d. Western brewed beer is preferred over fresh palm wine.
e. Foreign music is chosen over local ones.
f. Africans choose foreign names.
g. Christianity is preferred over traditional African religion.
h. English and French are the official languages chosen by most independent African nations.
i. Foreign foods are imported at the expense of the local food crops.
j. The African democratic style of government is being foregone in an attempt to embrace the Western style of government, which is plagued by coups, corruption, and maladministration due to its separation from morality and spirituality.
k. Most remarkably, the European patriarchal system is being chosen over the African matriarchal system. If patriarchy works in the West, it does not work in Africa because, according to the sheik Anta Diop, power tends to corrupt men more than women.

Looking at an elder's mouth, says an African proverb, one can never comprehend that it was once used for breast-feeding from the mother. Similarly, an African society today appears as if it was never ever matriarchal, but it was. Only a good historical review can show that African queens ruled tribes and some governed empires. They were not only effective but many of them were better than kings. A British anthropologist, Dugald Campbell, described Nyakatlol, the ruler of the Luena of Angola, in his book, *In the Heart of Bantuland*:

> The queen of the whole tribe was a woman of remarkable ability and personal character named Nyakatolo. The history of her springing into power, conquering the country she occupied, and the subjugating of the surrounding tribes is very interesting reading . . . for the purpose of conquest she got together an army and fought her way through the countries intervening between the Luena River and the Kuvungu Stream.

> She scattered every force that opposed her and established villages at the head of which she put women chiefs. She instituted a system of women chiefs, all over the countries she conquered, who were tributary to her and sent in regular caravans of tribute each new moon.[3]

This was a time when their women counterparts were not allowed to vote in America. American women could not run for offices. They could not even cast votes before 1920. After 1920, American women could run for the highest position in the land, yet, no woman ran for president until 1984, when Geraldine Ferraro did an unsuccessful bid for the highest position. Compare this to the African society where women presided over empires before Christ was born. We are now into the 21st century and America has never had a woman vice president. England has always had queens, but that has been only when there were no males to inherit the throne. An English queen had to be either the wife of a king or the reigning daughter of a king who died without a male heir. An African queen did not derive her status in any way from an attachment of relationship to a king. Africans were not sexist. An African woman who had brothers could still ascend the throne by inheritance, by age or most of the time, by achievement.

Umuada

> The *otu umuada* included all the married, unmarried, widowed, and divorced daughters of a lineage of village group. These women acted as political pressure groups in their natal villages in order to achieve desired objectives. They stopped quarrels and prevented wars. So powerful was their reputation that their natal villages had to reckon with them and their possible reaction to every major decision.[4]

Otu umuada as I pointed out in chapter three, is an association of women in many African societies, such as in the Igbo ethnic group. They have an extraordinary amount of spiritual and political power. For example, their prayers are believed to go straight to God, and it could be disastrous to be cursed by this group. There are several male associations but none of them are this spiritually unique and effective. Politically, they make rules that govern other females within the society. Every female is automatically a member by virtue of her birth within that community. It's a lifetime membership so she comes from outside to participate in this association if she is married from out of town, clan, tribe, or community. Women married into any community from outside cannot become members since the bond is that of sisterhood. As a matter of fact, they have power over their brothers' wives and other women who are not qualified to join them. I realized how powerful they were for the first time in my youth when I witnessed them ostracize a woman for beating up her husband. They punish by fines and I have also seen them go on strike until they got what they wanted. Umuada are considered to be significantly more powerful than "Uyomdi," a political pressure group made up of the wives of the lineage exclusively.

Polygamy, Polyandry, and Polygyny

Further, the Lovedu have had the custom of woman-marriage in which the queen "marries" the daughters of many of the chiefs' families.[5] Most people in America understand polygamy as a marriage of one man to more than one woman at the same time. That's not the correct meaning of polygamy. As a matter of fact, that is the exact meaning of the third term, polygyny. Polygamy, on the other hand is a combination of polygyny and polyandry. What most people do not know in America is that Africa is also polyandrous. Polyandry is the marriage of one woman to several males the same way a man can marry several women. If there are more cases of polygyny than there are of polyandry, it is not that women do not have as many rights as men. Instead, it is simply due to the fact that there are more women than men in Africa. There are several reasons why there are more women than men in Africa, but the greatest reason is that Africa lost a lot more males to slave trade than women. There is a ratio of about three males to one woman.

Besides polyandry, there is another marital privilege enjoyed by women in Africa that the males would die to enjoy. Women can marry other women in Africa whereas no male is allowed to marry another male. Can such a right be granted exclusively to women (without males) in any other part of the world? Suppose males could marry other males and women were denied such a right?

Uzi

This is a nurturing period for women before marriage. It is an unusual privilege for women. This tradition is believed to have been instituted by women for themselves. Such a privilege, scholars remark, could only have stemmed from a matriarchal society. It is a process whereby a newlywed, the groom to be precise, toils and labors to take care of his bride who is kept in seclusion for about six months. It is a nourishing period for her, during which time she is not allowed to lift a finger to work. Instead, she is surrounded by the groom's relatives, volunteers or people hired by the groom who wait on her and cater to her every whim from morning to night, seven days a week. They give her a bath, weave her hair, and give her a pedicure and manicure. They smooth her body daily with "*ufie*," calm wood, and "*odo*." And they decorate her body artistically with "*uli*" and sometimes with "*agalo*." She is fed well with the best diet. On the last day, she is paraded around the market squares and public places proudly exposing her half-covered body as "evidence of good living." People come out to see her. They shower her with gifts, ornaments, and money. Males cannot wait to put an end to this institution today because they consider it unfair.

Leadership Role

When he realized the dominant role of women in the Ashanti Kingdom of Ghana, a British officer wrote:

> Today the Queen Mothers are unrecognized by us and their position and influences are rapidly passing away. Many of us have only been made conscious of her presence by her "troublesome" activities in stool palavers [political arguments]; some of us may have been in the habit of going out of our way to speak to the old lady, feeling rather than knowing she was a power to be reckoned with. Official recognition she has none.
>
> I have asked the old men and women why I did not know all this—I have spent very many years in Ashanti. The answer is always the same: "The white man never asked us this; you have dealing with and recognize only the men; we supposed the European considered women of no account, and we know you do not recognize them as we have always done." . . .[6]

Besides chiefs, "*obas*," kings and queens, there are three other groups of leaders in most African communities. They are known as the council of elders, titled people and the priests. They are to African traditional democratic governments what the Judiciary, the Executive, and the Legislature are to the American government. It is very important to note here that African women are not only allowed to become priestesses but they can equally take titles like men and join the council of elders too.

Other signs of matriarchy could be seen in African names and proverbs. For instance, one of the commonest Igbo names is "Nneka" which means that motherhood is superior. Many African proverbs illustrate the role of women in Africa. One proverb for example, states that a project or an undertaking is never successful unless there is a woman behind it. Another states that a woman is like a flower garden and the man is the fence around it.

The Year 2000 and Thereafter

To understand the situation of African women in the immediate future and the decades thereafter, one must first seek to examine their past (pre-colonial) and present (post-colonial) situations. We have examined the past or the pre-colonial situation of the women in Africa and found it to be matriarchal and perfect for Africans. We have also examined the present or the post-colonial situation of women in Africa and concluded that it is patriarchal, patrilineal, European and alienating to Africans. Now, let us use this information to analyze, and understand, the role of women in Africa that began in 2000.

The Essence of African Women Lies in the Past

If the past has worked then we must learn from it. Africans are pragmatic and utilitarian by nature. They do things because they are practical and they work. They do things out of expediency. Empty theories and bureaucracy do not entice Africans. An Africanist once said to me that a ship that sails backwards does not see the sunrise. "Going back" to embrace matriarchy and respect for women as we had in the pre-colonial days is not backwardness. It is progress because it is an improvement. In my book, Jurisprudence, I made a similar point about the "non-transferability of the law." A legal method, I wrote, which works in Europe, does not necessarily work when it is transplanted to Africa. I made a similar argument in the chapter on "Afronanism" and in the paper I presented at the 18th Annual Third World Conference in Kingston, Jamaica. Today, I am making a similar appeal, but this time concerning the preservation of the matriarchal system in Africa.

Hegel, the German philosopher, made a similar point when he argued that people make progress by combining thesis and antithesis to reach a synthesis. Africans can only stay progressive by retaining whatever is originally African which is good and which we understand the most. That is the thesis. The synthesis could be achieved by accepting what the Europeans have to offer that is better than ours. This way we become receptive to change but not to erosion. Virtue stands in the middle between two extremes. A change is good as long as it is in the midway point. An erosion of everything African is extreme. It is not healthy for the Africans; the synthesis is a combination of the best of the African and the best of the European. Everything European, we have seen, cannot be good. Africans have a lot to offer to the world too. We can have the best of both worlds by retaining the best of the Africans and emulating the best of the Europeans. Many have done it and so can the Africans. The Japanese copied American technology and added it to their work ethic and begot one of the most progressive nations on the face of the earth today. The Japanese did not bother to emulate the American style of violence. Africans, on the other hand, have copied the American style of violence, thanks to Hollywood, and left their technology either because we do not know what we want, or because the former is easier and the latter is harder.

In addition, people of Jewish heritage have equally taken advantage of the American economy and the Western system of science and technology in a positive way. At the same time, they have been able to avoid European and American infirmities or ills such as violence, consumerism and secular fundamentalism. In spite of the holocaust and other atrocities that the Jews have suffered in history, they always have been able to retain what makes them unique and genuine, such as their religion and other ways of life. A Jewish rabbi, for example, stands out in any crowd whether he is in Africa, in Europe or in America. He does not care about what people think of him. He does not compromise his cultural identity even if he is being persecuted for it. But he knows when and what to learn from others. And with this, the Jews have been able to have the best of both worlds. They have been able to combine thesis and antithesis to formulate a synthesis. They have been able to maintain what is today one of the most enviable and progressive ethos on earth.

In America, the Jews rank among the most educated group of people. Professionally they are chiefly lawyers, doctors, engineers, writers, scientists, college professors, etc. They are also the most successful businessmen and women in the country. They are extremely wealthy, generally speaking. They own newspapers, television stations, magazine publications, schools, and real estate properties in the most affluent section of big cities. They have a lot of judges, people in the house of representative and the senate on both state and federal levels. In other words, they are as American as apple pie. They know how to enjoy capitalism and the American dream, yet they are the most ethnic group of people on earth. They tend to live together in Jewish neighborhoods. They build Jewish schools where they learn Jewish customs and Hebrew language. They build temples and they abide by the rules of Judaism including what they eat, how they dress and how they keep Holy the Sabbath day. Finally, Jews, regardless of where ever they are, never forget Jerusalem. "If I forget you Jerusalem let my right hand whither." I implore Africans to do the same. It is wonderful to learn from the Europeans but we must not let jettison our essence. We must retain that which makes us unique and that is our culture, our heritage-our Africanness.

Even the Europeans have been able to do it. They went into Africa and; a) copied the architectural pattern of our pyramids; b) learned from the Egyptian style of writing in hieroglyphics; c) copied the Egyptian form of irrigation and farming by crop rotation; d) learnt from the best of ancient African philosophers and scholars; and e) took diamonds, gold, and other precious arts and crafts, particularly from the Benin. To their credit, the Europeans knew what to take and what to leave behind. They did not copy whatever would retard their society. They even took our innocent men and women whom they brought here in the form of "slaves" and with their labor, blood, and sweat; they have built themselves the most formidable "civilization" and technology on the face of the earth today.

Therefore, to improve the situation of Africa in the new millennium, Africans must learn from the Japanese, the Jews, and from the Europeans. Africans must stop the inordinate disafricanization of themselves. Africans must learn to be proud of their identity: their color, their physical, psychological, intellectual, social, and spiritual features. They must realize that there is so much of their culture that the world can learn, such as African hospitality and family values.

Female Circumcision, Human Sacrifice, Slavery and Twin Killing in Africa

In 1992, I had an interview with Chief Azik Okenwa Nnamoko. He was the leader of the council of elders, as well as the eldest person in

Akpugo, a populous town within the Igbo tribe. The interview was on matriarchy, matriliny, and the leadership role of women of Nigeria in Africa before, during and after the European colonization of Africa. At the end of his astounding, but long, speech I asked him one question, which took him by surprise. I asked "If Africa had so much respect for women why do they involve themselves with that brutal and shameful practice we call 'women circumcision'?" After clearing his throat he preceded calmly by saying, "What do you respect more than anything else in your clan?" "Human life," I replied. "Then why did you participate in those brutal and shameful practices of human sacrifices, slavery and twin killing?" I was speechless. He then said, "Human beings make mistakes. Human beings miscalculate. It is a part of what makes us human. God saves us the way he made us. Our actions become unforgivable only when we become too proud to correct our mistakes. And let he who has nothing shameful in his own culture cast the first stone."

Africans are natural laws theorists, who believe that it was not natural for humans to deliver more than one child at the same time. Dogs, cats, and other animals did such. Delivering more than one child at the same time by a human being was considered a bad omen or a sign of an impending danger from God. Hence, twins were not only killed but a number of sacrifices were performed to placate, atone, pacify or make peace with the gods and goddesses. As time went on Africans reasoned differently about twins. They reasoned that if a child is a blessing then a twin must simply double the blessing. Today, twins are needed, wanted, and desired so much in Africa that, at the sight of twins, a pregnant woman touches them and touches her womb simultaneously. This might seem superstitious but women believe it makes them give birth to twins. In Igboland, most twins are named, "Ngozi," which means, "blessing." They are "doubled blessings," because they are not only human gifts from the gods but also they bring good luck and fortunes to their parents, communities and to their "extended families" in general.

As for human sacrifice, Africans believe in reincarnation. Therefore, kings and queens were buried along with their servants and material wealth to enable them to continue their lives of Queenship and Kingship in the next life. As time went on, Africans reasoned that it is in their nature to be royal and they will always end up royalties regardless of whether they are buried with their possessions or not. Hence, they discontinued burying royalties with humans, diamonds and gold. Human sacrifice was discontinued, but Africans still believe in reincarnation.

What about slavery? It is a taboo for an African to shed blood, especially that of a tribesman. That is why "Okonkwo," the hero of Chinua Achebe's *Things Fall Apart*, was banished for seven years. His action was inadvertent but he was considered to have soiled the soil with a tribesman's blood. His punishment was the only way to clean the soil and appease the gods. Precaution was taken by each side not to even hurt anyone, let alone shed blood. People's wealth was taken from them and captives were brought home to remain as servants. Eventually, the captives regained their freedom partially but they still pay tribute to their captors or masters for the rest of their lives. They were considered slaves. Therefore, slaves were people who could have been killed during wars, were it not for the strictness of African laws against shedding of blood. "Slaves" were also descendents of royal families, because Africans made it a point of duty to bring home the entire ruling families after they were defeated. Without that they would reorganize themselves, being warriors, to seek revenge. Thus, African Americans, the descendants of "slaves," should be informed of African history and hold up their heads high as descendants of kings and queens. Secondly, I do not understand the reason why Westerners refer to Africans as savages when they were the ones who killed each other during Europe's savage wars. Today Africa is becoming westernized. They kill each other like westerners and with western guns too. African religion is not there anymore to appeal to our conscience. The African's religion was viewed by westerners as paganism. Today, a 14 year old Somalian youth, who has not a single penny to his name, has an automatic rifle with bullets worth thousands of dollars with which he runs up and down the streets chasing his fellow Africans. Whereas twin killing, human sacrifice and slavery have not existed in Africa a long time before my great grand mother was born, female circumcision, unfortunately, still exists to a certain degree. What's the nature of female circumcision and why do Africans do it? There are three types of female circumcision performed in Africa. One is very mild and entails the removal of the foreskin of the clitoris just like in the males, my mother said. The second is the mutilation on which the western tabloids focus. The third is in between the first and the second, not as mild, but not mutilation. What the tabloids and the self-imposed or so-called Western experts fail to show is the percentage of Africans who practice the first, second and the third kinds of circumcision. Less than 5% of Africans practice the worst kind of circumcision and over 50%

practice the mild type. This is not to justify circumcision of males or females because they are terrible no matter how mild.

Why do Africans circumcise girls? They circumcise girls for one primary reason, religion. Circumcision is to the African Traditional Religion what baptism is to Christianity. It serves as the single ritual that initiates one into manhood or into womanhood even though over 95% of all Africans are circumcised during their first year of birth. In Igbo tribes, for instance, one is circumcised when one is eight days old exactly, just like the Bible dictates. Therefore, circumcision is simply a rite of passage to Africans. Women claim that it would be chauvinistic if they were denied this rite. As a matter of fact, circumcision is said to have started long before Africa was either Arabized or colonized, that is, when Africa was matriarchal. There is what I call secondary reasons, or what African women consider the benefits of women circumcision. The first claim is that it makes childbirth easier. The second claim relates to hygiene or cleanliness. Whether the above reasons are true or false, I still contend that female circumcision should be stopped once and for all. Western experts and tabloids, on the other hand, maintain that Africans are male chauvinists who practice female circumcision as a form of chastity belt meant for a single purpose of preventing the women from enjoying sexual intercourse. African women refer to this as a preposterous argument because no man forces them to be circumcised.

I do believe that Africans had only a limited comprehension of the nature of the anatomy of a woman's reproductive system. Hence, they equated the clitoris to the male's foreskin. In other words, this problem stems more from biological ignorance than from male chauvinism. A Western dominant religion, Catholicism, still or once considered masturbation sinful because it was once believed in the Western world that "little men" swam in the semen and so to "spill one's seed" was virtually equivalent to murder. Recent scholars have shown this to be bad physiology; yet, the principle of this aberration still applies in Western churches today. That's why most Africans think that westerners complaining about circumcision in Africa should read their Bible and do themselves a favor by removing the logs in their eyes in order to see well while removing the speck in other peoples' eyes.

Why should Africa, the cradle of matriarchy, be accused of male chauvinism by a patriarchal society known for its degradation of women? Today, women still cannot become popes, bishops, cardinals or even priests in some Christian denominations. In Africa, on the other hand, women priesthood is as old as humankind itself is. America's founding fathers wrote the American constitution. What about the mothers? The founding fathers wrote the American document when empires were being run by queens in Africa. Women were not allowed to vote in the USA until 1920. There has never been a time that women could not vote in the history of Africa. The United States gained its independence in 1776. Still today, America has never had a woman president, not even a woman vice president. In Africa, men could never have gotten away with that. African women were known to be much more assertive and aggressive about their rights as evidenced in the Aba women war of 1929.

In the United States, as well as in many countries of the Western World, women are not allowed to participate in combats regardless of whatever ranks they may have in the Army, Navy, Air Force or the Marine's corp. In Africa, Queens led their soldiers to war even before Christ was born. Obviously it is the westerners who have the backward view that females are inferior to males. That view, like female circumcision, is infested with an overdose of biological and physiological ignorance. It is the west that is chauvinistic. An average female lawyer earns only about 85 cents per $1 earned by her male counterpart and this is the twenty first century.

Notes

1. Okonjo, K. *Women in Africa*, (California, Stanford University Press, 1976), 55 (Edited by Nancy J, Hafkin and Edna S. Bay).
2. Gross, S. H. and Bingham, M.W. *Women in Africa on the Sub-Sahara Vol. II,* (Wisconsin, Gary McCuen Publications Inc., 1982,), 54.
3. Campbell, D. *In the Heart of Bantuland,* (New York, Negro Universities Press, 1969), 163-164.
4. Green, M. *Igbo Village Affairs,* (London, 1964), 66.
5. Gross, S. H. and Bingham, M.W. *Women in Africa of the Sub-Sahara Vol. I,* (Wisconsin, Gary McCuen Publications Inc., 1982) , 21.
6. Ibid., 22.

Chapter 5

Religion

African Traditional Religion (Omenani)

There are three major religions in Africa today: African traditional religion, Islam, and Christianity. Almost every African is deeply involved with one of these religions today because Africans, by nature, are deeply and incredibly religious. They are so religious that many of them border around fanaticism superstition.

African traditional religion is definitely, without a doubt, monotheistic. Unfortunately, many foreign authors have described it as a polytheistic religion. The reason is simply that they mistake the minor gods and deities as major. These minor gods/goddesses and ancestors are to African traditional religion exactly what the saints or sainthood is to many denominations of Christianity, especially Roman Catholicism. Another major misconception about African traditional religion is that the members worship the ancestors. The truth is that they worship their ancestors no more that the Roman Catholics worship the Blessed Virgin Mary.

African traditional religion is the only known religion that Africans always had before the introduction of the foreign ones, much later, such as Islam and Christianity. African traditional religion is so indigenous that it is impossible to separate it from the African culture. As a matter of fact, the African traditional religion is not considered a religion in Africa; instead, it is a way of life. In Igboland, it is known as *omenani,* which loosely translates into culture, custom, and traditional philosophy. It has no separation between church and state because the religion determines the politics, the economy, the festivals, the music, the laws, and the philosophy of the people.

African traditional religion has no scriptures or bible. It does not believe in either Mohammed or Jesus Christ. Every member inherits it simply by chance of birth. That is why it does not proselytize or attempt to win converts. Foreigners and outsiders are not expected to join.

First, there is a Supreme God, *Chukwu*. He is neither male nor female. I refer to him as "He" due to a lack of neutral gender in the English language. *Chukwu* is the creator of heaven and earth and all that surrounds it and within it. He is *Summum Bonum* (highest good) and all merciful. He is ubiquitous or everywhere at the same time. He is omnipotent or all powerful. He is omniscient, or all knowing. He is a king/queen who lives up in the heavens and whose regal loincloth sweeps the land below. *Eze chitoke abiama. Eze binigwe ogodoya nakpu nana.*

Next to the Supreme God are the ancestors, minor gods, goddesses, oracles, and deities. They care for, protect, guide, and guard the creations of the Supreme God. They cannot create, and they are not considered to be supreme. Be that as it may, they are considered to be ubiquitous. They are usually male or female. Among them is Ani, the earth goddess, who is responsible for conceptions, human growth and development, vegetation, earth fertility, agriculture, crops, and the harvest. Others are the oracle of the cave, the oracle of the hill, river deities, and market day deities; *nkwor*, *orie*, *afor* and *eke* the four days which make a week.

On the third hierarchical level are the ancestors. Like the Christian concept of sainthood, these are people who have lived what is considered to be righteous lives, as we know it in Africa. It is very common and every family has several of them. The difference is that in Roman Catholic tradition, for instance, the honor of sainthood is reserved only for exceptionally righteous ancestors who have undergone several papal recognitions, the last of which is known as canonization. In *Omenani* (African traditional religion) everyone who is righteous enough to get into the spirit world is righteous enough to become recognized as an ancestor. Ancestors, like minor gods, goddesses, oracles and deities, are not worshipped. They are only highly honored, respected, and reverenced. In African traditional religion, it is only the Supreme God that is worshipped, and that is why it is a monotheistic religion.

On the fourth hierarchical level are the priests and priestesses. Africans are the oldest matriarchal people in the world; hence, it is not uncommon to find male as well as female priests. Actually, priestesses are generally believed to be more clairvoyant than priests, their male counterparts. The priesthood is a special vocation, and those who are called are revealed through one type of divine inspiration or another. After they are chosen, they undergo some kind of preparation or tutelage, after which they become full-fledged priests or priestesses. They preside over prayers and over all religious worship, libations, and sacrifices. They also serve as fortunetellers, diviners, herbalists, and healers. On the same fourth level are the council of elders and titled men/women. Many authors have referred to this as the three branches of government. The priest makes the law, the council of elders interprets the law, and the titled men and women enforce the laws. The priests, known as *ndinze*, make the laws because they have the divine inspiration and spiritual power and guidance necessary to determine the rules, which would be favorable to the will of God and the ones that would be in opposition to the Divine Will. The elders, known as *ndi ickie*, on the other hand, interpret the law because that they have age, longevity and experience in their favor. With the experience they are able to go very far backwards in time examining, illuminating and citing how similar cases were decided, determined or ruled in the past, using the rule of stare decisis. This is the laws of precedence. Finally men and women with titles otherwise known in Igbo as *Ndi Ozo*, have the duty of enforcing the law. This is because they tend to be the most youthful, the wealthiest and they tend to have the political power of leadership from the community. They are usually the most ambitious of the three branches of leadership because title is by achievement, whereas the others are just bestowed on the individual either by nature in the case of age or by vocation (divine calling) in the case of priesthood.

The fifth and lowest level belongs to the indigenous African worshippers. For them there are only two worlds: that of the living and that of the spirit. Every African has a common goal in life, and that is to rest in peace in the spirit world after death. If one fails to rest in peace, his/her soul remains on Earth forever as an evil spirit, otherwise known as a ghost. Ghosts are souls of bad people who fail to make it into eternal life. They remain condemned on earth forever. That is why ghosts are not only evil but they are also constantly angry, haunting people and gnashing their teeth. When any of them goes too far haunting people and causing people incessant nightmares, fortune tellers are contracted to destroy them permanently by digging them out, burning them, and scattering their ashes in an evil forest often reached after crossing seven rivers or seven seas. This means that cremation of the dead is a destruction of his/her soul in *Omenani* (ATR).

Oftentimes, on the other hand, an Igbo realizes his goal in life by making it into the spirit world. There are precisely three criteria or conditions necessary for realizing this purpose in life.

1. Righteous life
2. Righteous burial
3. Righteous funeral

Righteous life entails living and abiding by a long list of rules. They include the following:

- Never steal, particularly yams or palm-wine from a palm tree
- Never kill
- Never gossip
- Never disrespect an elder, a titled person or priest
- Never commit adultery especially in the marital home
- Never harass a sacred animal, object or relics
- Honor your parents
- Never destroy or abuse a food crop
- Never mistreat a stranger
- Always abide by the community or group decision
- Never fail to correct a child
- Never unmask a masquerade
- Never be cursed by a parent, an elder, a priest, a titled person, or by umuada
- Never abort a child intentionally
- Never commit arson
- Never commit incest

Righteous burial and righteous funeral cannot be determined by an individual, but only by his family and by his community. This means that two-thirds of one's fate is in the hands of one's community. One can control only a third of one's chance of resting in peace. That is why we have interdependency and communal responsibility in Africa. One cannot afford to be individualistic. One has to be his brother's or sister's keeper. That is why the Igbos describe life as a big boat with everyone sailing along, but in different rooms. If one in a far end of the boat begins to drill into the sea/ocean, do you ignore him saying, "After all he is in his room?" Or do you stop him, realizing it is one and the same boat, and that once he sinks, you will sink too? That is why they say that sin has a pancosmic effect. Each one's evil affects us all. When one finger is soiled by oil, it affects the rest. In Africa, what you do is my business whether you like it or not!

Reincarnation

Reincarnation is a belief or process through which one comes back to life again and again after one dies. African traditional religion maintains that reincarnation is inevitable for everyone. The number of times that one can come back to life may vary from one tribe to another. The Igbo, for example, believe that people come back to life exactly seven times. In other words, one has seven times or chances to make it into the spirit world successfully. The sequence is usually unknown to the individual. That means that people do not usually know whether it is their first, second, third, fourth, fifth, sixth, or seventh time around. No one comes back to life as an animal or as a tree. As a matter of fact, people come back with the same gender and names. This is the most important criterion that traditional Africans used for determining the name to be given to a baby.

When a child is born, the parents consult a fortuneteller, who reveals who it is in the family that has come back to life again. This is usually within the family and the parents are often aware of the relative who has come back to life. The child would name the baby accordingly after the reincarnated relative.

Ogbanje

Instead of living a full life seven times, some individuals choose to live short times. The *ogbanji* choose their fate when they are in the spirit world before birth. They die after only a few minutes, hours, days, weeks, months, or years at the longest. They are wicked and evil children because their objective is usually to come and tease or torment their parents. Since this is far too common in Igboland, parents have discovered a few ways to make the children live. One of them is to trick them to stay since they are usually children. Another way is to coax or promise them their demands. The third and the most prevalent method is to make them reveal their *iyi uwa*. This is a special white stone that is usually buried very deep on the ground. It is usually so deep that a little child could not have put it physically there. *Iyi Uwa* must be dug out and destroyed by a priest, but first, it must have been revealed by the *ogbanje*. It is only an *ogbanje* that knows the location of one's *iyi uwa*. So, how do parents and priests talk an *ogbanje* into revealing the exact location of his/her stone? It is more difficult than pulling a tooth. This is because they do not even usually admit that they are *ogbanjes*. People only suspect them because they are usually sickly, exceptionally intelligent, and smashingly/ravishingly beautiful or handsome. If revealed, a priest digs the stone out and destroys it and that is usually the end of the parents' anguish. Parents become sure that their child is no longer *ogbanje* only when *iyi uwa* is destroyed or after the *ogbanje* gives birth to another baby. An *ogbanje* never procreates. If a female *ogbanje* becomes pregnant, she would die before, during, or right after delivery, along with the baby. If a male *ogbanje's* wife becomes pregnant he and/or the baby will die before she gives birth.

Punishment

African traditional religion, like Judaism, is an Earth-centered religion. That means that this religion does not only prepare for life after death; it also prepares for life on earth (*hic et nunc*). Besides life in the spirit world, this religion determines how one should live a worthy life while alive or simply a "good life" on the Earth through:

- Just laws,
- Just punishment,
- Good families,
- Good marriage,
- Good government,
- Good community,
- Righteous burial,
- Righteous funeral,
- Festivals,
- Wealth,
- Title taking,
- Just wars,
- Trade,

- Farm,
- Harvest,
- Work and Play.

This is why there is no separation of church and state in traditional African societies that there is in the Western world. Punishments are applied religiously since they are determined by religion. There are quite a few reasons why Africans punish offenders. The first reason is deterrence, the second is rehabilitation, the third is retribution, and the fourth is purification. The last one needs further elucidation. Every sin, offense, or taboo pollutes the land, and through sacrifice and punishment, the community is cleansed once more.

The most severe type of punishment, according to the African traditional religion, is banishment or being exiled for life; that is the reason why it is very seldom given. Actually, it is so rare that most Africans have neither witnessed nor heard of it. The second and certainly less severe type of punishment is capital punishment. That, in this context, is better known as the death penalty. Why is the death penalty considered far less severe than banishment? The answer is simple in African traditional religion: The death penalty is not even a destruction of one life out of seven lives. With a righteous burial and funeral, a victim of the death penalty may still gain the spirit world if he had lived a righteous life altogether. Banishment, on the other hand, automatically ruins both body and soul. It ruins one's life on Earth because one is condemned to live in a foreign land until one dies. The soul is equally ruined because a burial and funeral in a foreign land can never be considered righteous. Hence, the exile serves a complete annihilation of one life out of seven whereas the death penalty in not.

The third type of punishment is not only the most deterrent, but it is also the most effective from both expedient pragmatic and utilitarian points of views. It works. It is known as ostracism or excommunication. This is a punishment through which everyone else in the community punishes individuals by total and complete exclusion. Put simply, no one is allowed to speak to him, sell to him, buy from him, pray with him, dance with him, eat with him, or even greet or be greeted by him. The exception is a member of his immediate family. Outside of his immediate family, anyone else found communicating with him becomes ostracized himself; hence, everybody avoids him like a plague. Africans thrive on communal responsibility, and to be excluded from one's society is comparable to taking a fish out of water and expecting it to live on.

This type of punishment is usually given to defiant members of the society to force them to become compliant. For instance, if a member refuses to pay taxes, which is necessary for the efficient functioning or operation of the community, the member would be imprisoned in any Western country. There is no concept of prison in African traditional society, so an individual who refuses to pay his fair share of his community tax or levy would simply be excommunicated. This excommunication would continue as long as the individual chooses to prolong it. It would continue until he gets fed up, crawls, begs for forgiveness, and if pardoned, pays his tax. It works 100% of the time and unlike imprisonment, it neither corrupts the individual nor costs the taxpayers any amount to house, feed, or maintain the defiant criminal. It may not work everywhere, but it works for the Africans. In fact, the percentage of recidivism is zero.

The fourth, most prevalent and most common type of punishment dictated by the African traditional religion or *Omenani* is payment of fines. It ranges from about a single dollar to up to a million dollars, depending on the offense. No one is employed permanently to repair the roads, for instance. Everyone in the community repairs them on certain days. Anyone who fails to show up surrenders an equivalence of a day's wage, plus interest and fees. Another example is that the idea of home loans and mortgages is totally nonexistent in Africa. The idea of apartment rental is also nonexistent. Since everyone is left with only one option of owning his own home without mortgages and unpaid loans, people have to strategically devise a means of making that possible. In other words, they take turns to build one another a home as a group and according to hierarchy within an age grade. When everyone shows up to build one a home, carpenters among them work with woods, brick layers work with bricks, masonries work with cement, and those without special or highly needed skills fetch water, lift objects, run errands and perform menial tasks as might be needed. In a few weeks, someone becomes a homeowner. What happens if I help to build you a home, and you fail to show up to build mine? You are simply punished with an adequate fine payable to the peer group; this is another typical example of how this most popular type of punishment is applied.

The fifth and final type of punishment is "*akaja.*" It is next to banishment in the category of unpopularity. *Akaja* is, however, the most bizarre, strange, and weird. It is so highly humiliating that it is equally deterrent. *Akaja* as a type of punishment is a method of tying an object of theft on the thief, on the stealer or on the robber and parading him all over the town singing songs of mockery and making him dance to it. The humiliation is so unbelievably shameful that the culprits have been known to have never repeated the crime. People who witness it have equally been known never to commit the crime.

Since traditional Africans have no lawyers and Western-Style judges, magistrates, or justices, who then determines whom to punish and the type of punishments?

Cases are decided and punishments determined by peer groups, the entire community, or the council of elders for the most serious cases, such as murder. Any decision could be appealed until it gets to the highest level usually presided over by a group of masquerades believed to be ancestral spirits, as clearly depicted by Chinua Achebe in Chapter 10 of his classic book, *Things Fall Apart*:

> "We have heard both sides of the case," said Evil Forest. "Our duty is not to blame this man or to praise that, but to settle a dispute." He turned to Uzowulu's group and allowed a short pause.
>
> "Uzowulu's body, I salute you," he said.
>
> "Our father, my hand has touched the ground," replied Uzowulu touching the earth.
>
> "Uzowulu's body, do you know me?"
>
> "How can I know you father? You are beyond our knowledge," Uzowulu replied.
>
> "I am Evil Forest. I kill man on the day that his life is sweetest to him."
>
> "That is true," replied Uzowulu.
>
> "Go to your in-laws with a pot of wine and beg your wife to return to you. It is not bravery when a man fights with a woman." He turned to Odukwe, and allowed a brief pause.
>
> "Odukwe's body, I greet you," he said.

"My hand is on the ground," replied Odukwe.

"Do you know me?"

"No man can know you," replied Odukwe.

"I am Evil Forest, I am Dry-meat-that-fills-the-mouth, I am Fire-that-burns-without-faggots. If your in-law brings wine to you, let your sister go with him. I salute you." He pulled his staff from the hard earth and thrust it back. ~ (Achebe 93).

African Christianity

Christianity is sweeping all of Africa today. Although up to 50% of Africans are now Muslims, Christianity has been growing at a much higher rate in Africa. The most important reason for this increase is that Christianity is often associated with Western civilization, Western education, Western industrialization, Western urbanization and Western development. The above association tends to make the rest of the Africans look down on non-Christian believers as backward and primitive. The history also goes back to when the European missionaries first arrived in Africa (excluding areas such as Ethiopia where Christianity has existed from time immemorial) and described members of African Traditional Religion as yokels, pagans, and barbarians.

Though Africans rushed into Christianity as a fad, they tend to practice Christianity in the form of African Traditional Religion. They also view the God of Christianity the way they used to perceive the Supreme God of African Traditional Religion. In other words, Africans now have another version of Christianity, which I call African Christianity. What is the nature of African Christianity? It is the type of Christianity in which people worship the Christian God as if it were the God of African Traditional Religion. For example, charismatic, Christian priests—regardless of denomination—have not only been popularly heralded in Africa, but recently they have been deified. Why is that? It is simply because of the old and natural laws of supply and demand. Those priests, pastors, ministers or preachers have finally understood the psyche of the African worshippers. In other words, they are finally giving their African brethren a chance to be "cool" and still do it the African way. It is a chance to worship in an African way without being called a pagan, primitive, or backward.

Some instances that illustrate the above observation are as follows:

1. Worshipping as extroverts: The earliest missionaries taught African Christians to be quiet, soft spoken, and solemn when they worship. Charismatic ministers, on the other hand, indeed encourage worshippers to shout, cry, laugh, dance, fall down, or gesticulate during worship. This is exactly how Africans worship the God of their traditional religion.

2. Earth Centeredness: Western Christianity views the earth only as a place of preparation for the next life—heaven. The Christian catechism asserts that God made us "to know Him, to love Him, to serve Him in this world and to be happy with Him forever in the next life" Hence, the world is only a means to an end, not an end itself. After all, the Christian Bible asks, "What does it profit a man if he gains the whole world and suffers the loss of his own soul?"

In African Traditional Religion, life on earth is not only a means of getting to the next life. Life on earth is very important and God, religion, and priests are all supposed to help make life on this earth much better. That is why they have the goddess of fertility, who helps barren women become fertile. That is why they have the goddess of health, who heals and restores health to the sick. That is why the African Traditional Religion has the goddess of justice which the Igbos call "*Offor*" and which strikes one dead for swearing a false oath. That is why they have a god of wealth, which gives wealth to the faithful and poverty to the unfaithful. And that is why they have the earth goddess which blesses and multiplies our harvest in abundance.

African Christianity is designed to copy this pattern. The childless couple is promised children if they continue to pray. The infirm is promised health through a direct miracle of God through the priest. One who swears falsely in the Bible is guaranteed to die here and now. The faithful are promised wealth, progress, success, and general well-being on earth and not necessarily in the next life. It is lack of miracles and lack of emphasis placed on the affairs of this world that make Christian converts to continue to go back to African Traditional Religion (Omemani). To find both of the above in Christianity is to have the best of two worlds and African converts embrace it. This is what is known as African Christianity. The Christian preachers, pastors and the Roman Catholic Priests who carry them out, such as Father Edeh Cssp at Ehele and Father Mbaka at Enugu, are very famous and they attract a thousand times more followers than their colleagues.

3. Healer, miracle performing and omnipotent priest:
   Africans have a popular parlance that states that the priests are known for never admitting that they have limitations (*dibia ekwe na ife yilu ya*). One of the greatest attributes of African Traditional Religion priests is that they are healers or native doctors. They use herbs and charms to heal people. Another important characteristic of theirs is that, like the prophets of old, they are clairvoyant and therefore can predict the future. The new charismatic leaders of African Christianity claim to perform miracles through the power of God. They claim to heal the sick, make the blind see, make the lame walk, make the deaf hear, make the barren fruitful, make the poor wealthy, and have the lost found.

4. Quid Pro Quo: Followers of African Traditional Religion always give something to God in return for which He grants the giver his wishes. The worshipper offers this gift as a libation or in the form of sacrifice or worship. Every sacrifice or worship is made using cows, goat, chicken, palm wine, or kola-nut. In their prayer, they say, "Please take this ram and heal me." The new African Christianity tends to emulate this method because they sacrifice or donate a lot of their wealth to God and the priest in thanksgiving for their fortune. That is why many of those ministers are able to build and own universities, high schools, banks, churches etc.

5. Vindictive God: Members of African Traditional Religion believe that their God is vindictive, jealous, and retaliatory; therefore, oath taking is extremely rampant because the guilty one is usually struck down by God's wrath within a year. Members of African Christianity are becoming exactly the same way. They expect the sinners to suffer most on earth and the faithful to be more successful on this earth. They

often go to their priests for oath administration, various covenants and different types of arbitration.

6. Pragmatism: Worshippers in African Traditional Religion work with concrete, tangible, or visible relics through which miracles could be performed and with which they are always fighting the devil. Such relics include like items as "offor" stick, palm fronds. In the same way, members of African Christianity are often seen carrying plastic bottles of holy water, picture images of the Holy Spirit from Hele in Nigeria, the crucifix, the cross and most of all the Bible with which they fight the evil spirit.

Omenani and Confucianism: A Brief Compare and Contrast

Like Confucianism, the Igbo traditional religion has some basic relationships, which it stresses as more important than others do. As a matter of fact, the Igbo Religion has six relationships while the Confucianism has five.

1. Father and Son. The Confucians regard the relationship between the father and his son as the most important but it is not so with the Igbos. For the Confucians, the father should always manifest mercifulness or kindness to his son. The son should always manifest filial piety and between them should his affection exist. This is similar to the Igbos, but Igbo religion includes something more. Both parents are included—father and mother. In this relationship, the daughter is also involved.

2. King and Subjects: the Confucians maintain that the king owes benevolence to his subjects always and the latter owes loyalty to the former. Between them integrity should exist. This is exactly the same with the Igbos, except that one owes loyalty, not only to his king, but also to his elders, priests, titled men and women.

3. Husband and Wife: According to Confucianism, the husband should be upright with his wife, the wife obedient to him, and between them should be a proper distance. This is quite similar to that of the Igbo Traditional Religion. For the Igbos, the wife should always show concern for her husband. The husband is supposed to protect his wife always. Between them should be abundant respect for each other.

4. The Elder Brother and Younger Brother: Among the Confucians, the elder brother should show nobility to the younger brother, while the latter shows respect to the former. The Igbos likewise consider the relationship as immensely important. Indeed, they emphasize here the relation between father-in-law and son-in-law. The son-in-law owes dutifulness to his father-in-law. This duty is concretely manifested annually during each rainy season when he goes into the company of hired workers to work for his father-in-law. To the son-in-law, the father-in-law owes constant blessing without which his daughter would not be prosperous. Between them should exist justice.

5. Elder and Younger Friend: The Confucians contend that the elder friend should show humaneness to his younger friend, while the latter shows difference to the former at all times. Between them should exist faithfulness. Here, the Igbo's theme *enyi* does not simply mean friends but "neighbors." One's enemy, for example, is included in this relationship. This is precisely why one is not always free to harass even one's enemy in Igbo society. When this relationship is interpreted further, one finds that the guest is referred to as the elder friend, while the host is the younger. There is a saying in Igbo society that a guest is greater than the host is, as a master is. No wonder there is a great amount of hospitality shown to strangers, visitors, and foreigners in Igbo-land.

6. God and Man: This is the most important relationship as far as the Igbos are concerned. The Confucians do not even include this in their five relationships. The Igbos maintains that we owe food to God. He gets this food from our sacri-

> fice, worship, and work in His garden. This is implied in one of their songs: *"Ibem riom oru okikem riom oru meburo uzo Jeelu okikem olu, biko, Udele Bekewalum nisi."*
> God Himself owes us long life, health and good luck. Between God and us should exist compliance.

The Confucians stress the non-violation of these relationships for the attainment of true human welfare. The Igbos, on the hand, believe that the land would be desecrated unless everyone complies or plays his role efficiently. Hence, evil befalls every one in the community when one goes against one's role. The evil is corrected by performing the ceremony for the appeasement of "ala" (the earth goddess).

Chapter 6

Islamic Influence

Islam In Africa

More than 50% of all Africans are Muslims. There are over 300 million Muslims in Africa today, which means that about 20% of Muslims live in Africa. This makes Africa the continent with the highest concentration of Muslims on Earth. Islam, however, did not originate in Africa. It came into Africa around the ninth century AD through one of Mohammed's three Caliphs or successors known as Othman. Other Caliphs were Omar and Abu Bakr.

Islam is one of the three major religions in Africa. The oldest is the African Traditional Religion, which is indigenous to Africa. The Europeans once knew it as paganism, but that was a mistake. The most popular religion in Africa today is Islam. The second is Christianity, which began to gain its strong foothold in Africa around the eighteenth century A.D. With the exception of some African regions, such as Ethiopia, which has been considered by many as the cradle of Christianity, it has gotten a strong tap root in Africa since then, not only because Africans are religious and deeply spiritual people but also because Christianity, so far, has been able to attract followers through their flamboyant or Western ways of life. However, today Islam is the single most populous religion in Africa. Over 40% of all Africans practice the Islamic religion, and that percentage is still growing.

What is the Nature of Islamic Religion?

Islam is known as one of the youngest of man's greatest universal religions. It is also very clear-cut and simple. Muslims are monotheists, the one God is called Allah, and Mohammed is his greatest and last prophet. The Muslims recognize the prophets of Christianity and Judaism; they range from Abraham to Jesus Christ himself. They are so monotheistic that they do not believe in the Christian concept of the Trinity, even though it means three persons in one God: the Father, the Son, and the Holy Ghost.

The Christians have the sacred book known as the Bible, Islam has its own sacred book called the Koran. The Koran gives a clear and "sufficient" guide to man's behavior on earth and without which he cannot win or spend an everlasting life in the paradise. The Muslim scripture, the Koran, equally contains some of the basics of the Islamic teachings; for instance, the believer must help the poor; avoid alcohol, pork and gambling; honor his parents; protect orphans; be just and honorable in his dealings; and most importantly, be humble before Allah.

The word "Islam" means "submission" to the will of Allah. Hence, a Muslim is simply "One who submits to God's will."

Mohammed was born in 570 AD in the city of Mecca. Kaaba (cube) was the highest of shrines in Mecca, and Mohammed's tribe acted as its custodian (priest). His family had a business of supplying drinking water to the pilgrims of Kaaba, the black rectangular meteorite, with its various idols.

As a young man, Mohammed developed an aversion to his people's idol worship and felt similarly toward the overall concept of polytheism. He seemed to admire the Christian and the Jewish sense or practice of monotheism. Oftentimes, he wandered into the mountains, forest and hills to fast and meditate. One day he was on a hill, hungry and meditating, when the Angel Gabriel appeared to him and said, "RECITE!" Then Mohammed recited, "In the name of Allah, the Beneficent, the merciful . . ." This recitation is believed to be the earliest verses of the Koran. He quickly rushed home to Khadija, his wife, who became convinced that her husband had been truly chosen by Allah to be his spokesman.

The priests of Kaaba and others began to plan to take away Mohammed's life because they depended on Kaaba for their livelihood, and Mohammed had spoken against the worship of idols. As a result, Hegira, the famous flight of 622 AD from Mecca to Yathrib (which was renamed Medina) had to take place in order to safeguard his life. It is said that all Muslim calendars are dated from Hegira, the flight. (AD minus 622 is an A.H. date).

Mohammed's supporters launched a number of serious armed attacks and encounters against his challengers while at Yathrib (Medina). Eventually, it turned into a full-blown war, which ended in 630 AD when Mohammed entered Mecca again, but this time triumphantly. He destroyed all of the idols in Kaaba, with the exception of the black stone, or the meteorite. He, in addition, quickly declared the Kaaba the sanctuary of Allah! Henceforth, Muslims from every part of the world, at prayer, face toward the Kaaba in Mecca as they kneel. Since then, Mohammed tried to reestablish himself and strengthen his position as a religious leader in Arabia and all over the world. He formed a formidable army with which to conquer the world for Allah. Like an active volcano, this new faith became unstoppable. It erupted and continued to advance and proliferate even after Mohammed's death in 622 AD.

The Law and the Prophet

The sacred scripture of all Muslims is known as the Koran. The words of Allah revealed through his prophet, Mohammed, are believed to be in the Koran. It contains a total of 114 chapters known as Suras. The Suras were all revealed to Mohammed by God and from God. For the Muslims, there are two kinds of messages from Mohammed. The first kind is made up of the words that he received through revelation from Allah and which is held holy by all Muslims. The second is known as the "Hadith." It is not considered to be holy. Instead, these are classified as other remarks made by Mohammed that are kept as part of the tradition. The former is read today as the Koran, and the latter is read today as the Hadith.

It is not certain that Mohammed, like Jesus, could read or write. Soon after Mohammed died, his followers wrote the Koran from a collection of what he recited, The Koran has been translated into many languages today, but it was originally written in Arabic. The Koran forms the "foundation stone" of life in the Muslim world. It also determines the laws, ordinance, rules, or regulations that govern all Muslims. These Muslim laws, as determined exclusively by the Koran, are known as the Shariah.

The first Sura, as in the Christian Bible, is called the Lord's Prayer of Islam. It has been popularly referred to as "the essence of the Koran" like the Christian "Our Father," it is one of the most important "prayers" in the Muslim faith. No Muslim worship (private or public) and no solemn transaction are considered to be complete in the eyes of the Muslims without the recitation of the Lord's Prayer, which appears below.

The Lord's Prayer of Islam

In the name of Allah, the Beneficent, the Merciful!
Praise be to Allah, Lord of the Worlds,
The Beneficent, the Merciful,
Ruler of the Day of Judgment,
Thee alone we worship; Thee alone we ask for help.
Show us the straight path,
The path of those who Thou hast favored;
Not of those who have earned Thine anger
Nor of those who go astray.
—The Koran

The Five Pillars of Islam

1. Faith in Allah

To be a Muslim is to submit to the will of Allah, and a part of that submission is to proclaim from heart "La ilaha illa llah; muhammad rasulu llah." It means that there is no God but Allah, and Mohammed is his messenger/prophet. Muslims all over the world have a lot in common and the greatest of all is the belief that Allah is the one and only God and that Mohammed is his greatest prophet. Even Jesus Christ is considered to be only a prophet.

2. Prayer

One of the key observances prescribed by Mohammed to all Muslims is to pray five times each day. It is one of the five pillars of Islam. There are beautiful prayer carpets, which the Muslims use to mark the sacredness of their prayer sites. The call to pray is usually summoned by a "muezzin", not by a bell or anything else. For prayer, Islam has no altars or images, no organized priesthood or sacraments. Instead, they have an imam or an officer of the mosque who delivers the sermons and presides over the worship, even though most worship is individual.

3. Almsgiving

Almsgiving or charity for supporting the poor and the mosque is highly imperative for all Muslims. A certain percentage of one's income is usually donated. The Red Crescent, like the Christian Red Cross, is a charity organized by the Muslims. Right below is what the Koran says about charity:

> Whatever alms ye spend or vows ye vow, Lo! Allah knoweth it. Wrong-doers have no helpers. If ye publish your alms giving, it is well, but if you hide it and give it to the poor, it will be better for you, and will atone for some of your ill-deeds. Allah is informed of what ye do . . .
>
> —The Koran

4. The Fast of Ramadan

By the "Night of Power," the Angel Gabriel appeared to Mohammed and revealed his divine calling to him for the first time. This Night of Power took place during the ninth month of the Muslim year, called Ramadan. In remembrance of this calling, Muslims all over the world must fast from sunrise to sunset during the month leading up to the night of Power when "the gates of paradise are open, the gate of hell shut, and the Devil is in chains." According to the Koran, Ramadan takes place only during the daylight hours. At night they eat and drink until dawn when a dark trade may be distinguishable from a white one. Ramadan itself lasts for a month exactly, and during it, people are supposed to refrain from, not only food and drink, but also unworthy acts such as lying, gossip, adultery, murder, since one such act can make a month's fast meaningless. The faithful are supposed to pray and meditate during the daytime at Ramadan, but most of them end up sleeping or working as they fast until the sunset when feasting begins. Finally, a festival of good will and gift giving, equivalent to the Christian Christmas, concludes the fast of Ramadan, the most observed of all Islamic religious duties.

5. Pilgrimage to Mecca

> Perform the pilgrimage and the visit for Allah—observe your duty for Allah, and know that Allah is severe in punishment . . . and whoever is minded to perform the pilgrimage (let him remember that) there is (to be) no Lewdness nor abuse nor angry conversation on the pilgrimage. And whatsoever good ye do, Allah knows it . . .
>
> —The Koran

Every Muslim has to make a hadj to Mecca at least once in a lifetime. This has ended up becoming one of the greatest forces binding all Muslims together today. First, the pilgrims dress up wearing seamless white garments, and then they run seven times around the Kaaba (three times quickly and four times slowly). At each lap, whether slow or fast, each pilgrim slows down to kiss or touch the black meteorite with his hand, staff or stick. Second, the faithful pilgrims trot seven times, this time, across the valley between the hills of Safa and Marwa. This is in remembrance of Hagar's dire search for water to feed her infant son, Ishmael, who is believed to be the historical father of all Arabs just as Isaac is said to be the father of all Jews.

First, there was Abraham, known to be the father of all nations. He was married to a woman called Sarah. She was barren and unable to become pregnant with a child. After several years of frustration and unsuccessful attempts conceive, she permitted Abraham to sleep with Hager, his maid, so he could have a child with her since that was what he was missing most in his life. He did, and Hagar became pregnant. Fortunately or unfortunately, Sarah also became pregnant just a few months after Hagar did. Hagar gave birth to Ishmael, who became the first son of Abraham. Then, Sarah gave birth to a baby boy named Isaac, who was the second son of Abraham. Isaac grew up to give birth to two sons: Esau and Jacob. Esau gave rise to the Edomites, who were later conquered. Jacob, on the other hand, became the father of the twelve sons, and together, they rose to become the fathers of the twelve tribes of Israel. Jesus Christ, himself, originates directly from one of those tribes, and that is how Jesus traces his genealogy to Abraham. Ishmael, the first son of Abraham, married an Egyptian woman, who gave birth to twelve children who multiplied to give rise to the Arabic world, through which Mohammed traces his genealogy. Hence, both Mohammed and Jesus trace their beginnings to a common father, Abraham. (Genesis Chapter 16, chapter 21 verses 8-20).

Towards the conclusion of the pilgrimage, the faithful proceed towards "the Mount of Mercy in the Plain of Arafat." There, they "stand before God" from noon to sunset. This period is known as "the greater Pilgrimage" and it is the most vital and highest point of the pilgrimage. Whoever misses "the Greatest Pilgrimage," is said to have missed the entire pilgrimage and whoever participates in "the Greater Pilgrimage" no matter how late, is considered to have made the hadj. Finally, the pilgrims proceed from the Plain of Arafat to an open area where they spend the night followed by a three-day feast. After the feast, they run around the Kaaba one more time. This final lap completes as well as concludes a hadj, the most joyful incident in a Muslim's life.

Muslim Beliefs

Muslims are not allowed to eat pork or swine flesh. They are forbidden to play a game of chance, and they are not allowed to take alcohol. It is also sinful to lend out money with interest. They can consider men to be a degree above women, yet men must treat women with kindness and justice. Sinners will burn in hell, and the righteous will enjoy the kingdom of heaven starting from the Day of Judgment.

Muslims have to fight hard in the holy wars. The Koran confirms that as follows:

Holy Wars

> Warfare is ordained for you, though it is hateful unto you; but it may happen that you hate a thing which is good for you, and it may happen that you love a thing, which is bad for you. Allah knoweth ye know not. . . . Persecution is worse than killing. And they will not cease from fighting against you till they have made you renegades from your religion, if they can. And whosoever become a renegade and dieth in his disbelief, such are they whose works have fallen both in the world and the hereafter. Such are rightful owners of the fire; they will abide there in. . . .
>
> Fight in the way of Allah, against those who fight against you, but do not begin hostilities. Allah loveth not aggressors. And slay them wherever ye find them, and drive them out of the places whence they drove you out. . . . If they attack you, then slay them. Such is the reward of disbelievers.
>
> —The Koran

One of the several misconceptions in the United States of America about Islamic Religion is that its followers are terrorists, war mongers, aggressors, and suicide bombers. From the above instructions, it is clear that the Koran insists that Muslims should never begin hostilities since Allah doesn't love aggressors. They fight holy wars. Mohammed did. He also made sure that his successors continued it. No one ever became as great as Mohammed did in Islamic religion. Nevertheless, there were three Caliphs who succeed him. They were Abu Bakr, Omar and Othman, otherwise known as Usman. The three of them continued with Mohammed's system of expansion through conquest. For instance, it took them less than twenty years to have Islam overrun Egypt, Syria, Iraq, Palestine, the entire Persian Empire, and many more lands. Put differently, between 635 AD and 650 AD, all of the above mentioned nations were converted to Islam. This Islamic conquest and triumph continued. They conquered as well as spread Islam eastward to India, across the Straits of Gibraltar into Spain, Portugal, and France, and westward to the Atlantic. Finally, they were halted at Tours in 732 AD by the Franks. This defeat saved Europe from Islam and for Christianity. They still moved on to spread Islam to China and to the islands of the Pacific. With this, Islam is today more than 500 million strong and this makes it one of the seven most populous religions in the world.

The holiest and the most sacred Islamic city is Mecca, the second is Medina, and the third is Jerusalem, which has remained with the Muslims since its conquest in 638 AD by Caliph Omar. Omar helped to build the "Dome of the Rock" in 691 AD. Muslims believe that Noah's Ark sailed around it seven times, that Abraham almost sacrificed his son, Isaac, on that stone/rock, that all the great prophets from Elijah to Mohammed came there to pray, that it was from that rock on which Mohammed ascended to heaven, and that is from there that Angel Israfil will sound the last trumpet on judgment day.

Beneath the Caliphs were the Viziers, each of whom was delegated with an empire to control. Slightly lower than empires were provinces governed by Emirs. Finally, an Imam is an officer of the mosque who only presides over the worships and delivers the sermons.

Regarding women, the Koran says:

> And they (women) have rights similar to those (of men) over them in Kindness, and men are a degree above them. . . . When ye have divorced women, and they have reached their term, then retain them in kindness or release them in kindness. Retain them not to their trust so that ye transgress (the limits). He who doeth that hath wronged his soul.
>
> —The Koran

Like many Christian nuns losing their habits, many Muslim women are equally losing the purdah (veil) today. The practice of keeping women secluded in their homes is also becoming like the purdah. Modern Muslim women are becoming physicians, lawyers, professors, engineers, and a lot more today. It is hard sometimes to distinguish the rules depicted by the Koran from those that develop over time through traditions. For example, it was Mohammed's idea to permit men to marry as many as up to four wives at the same time "if they could treat them equally."

Like Christianity, which has many denominations, Islam has many sects. The Sunnis have the vast majority of Muslims today. The Shiites are over 30 million strong, and it is said to be the largest minority sect. The Ahmadiyya sect has one of the most active missionary programs in the world. It is unbelievably huge in Africa. Fifty percent of the African population is Muslims today. Ahmadiyya sect is credited for much of that.

In contrast to Christianity, Islam has no altars, no images, no sacraments, no organized priesthood, no ten commandments, only the five pillars. There is no predominant group worship; but instead, most worship is individual.

The Importance of Islamic Law in Muslim Life

The Shariah is of paramount significance, value, and importance in the life of any Muslim. Before I delve into the core of this topic, I would like to explain or introduce some issues worth knowing or which are very fundamental to Islamic Law.

Literally, "*Shariah*" means "a clear path." It is more or less law in any European sense. In fact, Shariah could be said to be a rule of conscience. Shariah has been defined (in Encyclopedia Britannica) as "a system of duties that are incumbent upon a Muslim by virtue of his religious belief." Its principal teaching is a total submission to the will of Allah.

The Islamic law has four major sources:

1. Koran: This book contains the revealed words of Allah.
2. Sunnah: This is the practice or the lifestyle of the prophet.
3. Ijma: This is a consensus or a unanimous agreement by the people.
4. Some degree of human reasoning.

Another great aspect of Shariah is the five pillars:

1. The Creed of Islam: (*La ilaha illa Allah*) "There is no God but Allah and Mohammed is his messenger".
2. Prayer: It is generally a custom that Muslims pray five times everyday.
3. Almsgiving: This is done annually to aid the poor and the actual percentage differs from place to place.
4. Fasting: This is done at the Muslim month of Ramadan. (*zakat*)
5. Pilgrimage: (*HAJJ*) this entails going to Mecca for some religious celebrations at the proper season at least once during one's lifetime.

Shariah differs from the Anglo-American laws in two chief aspects:

1. The law of Shariah is much wider in scope because it does not only deal with man's relation with his neighbor and the state, but it also includes man's relation with God and his own conscience.
2. Being an expression of God's will, Shariah is static unlike a secular legal system that could be changed or altered to suit the developing or growing circumstances of society. All of these imply that the Shariah is an exhaustive or detailed Muslim code of conduct that extends to both private and public activities.

The importance of Islam on the life of any Muslim depends on the school of thought to which he/she belongs. For instance, there were the Malikis School of Law in Medina and Hanafis School of Law in Al-Kufah. These were named on behalf of two famous scholars of the respective localities, Malik ibn Anas & Abu Hanifah. There are also the "Shiite" Muslims and the "Sunni" ones, and they are different in many aspects.

Though each of these groups of Islam differs in their observances, some factors of the Islamic Law still remain common.

Six crimes have also had their punishments fixed for both men and women. They are:

1. Highway robbery, which is punishable by death
2. The same punishment goes for apostasy

3. Theft is punishable by amputation of hand
4. Extramarital relationship is punishable by being stoned to death if the offender is married, or given a hundred lashes if unmarried
5. A proven act of unchastity, which is punishable by eighty lashes
6. Drinking of any intoxicant, which is equally punishable by eighty lashes

The authorities (court) could determine the rest of the measures.

All of these measures, in addition to the conscience, help every Muslim abide by Islamic Laws. His conduct is so influenced that he cannot but be distinguished from non-Muslims. In Northern Nigeria, Shariah came along with a change in social conditions and exposure to new cultural ideals, which caused disputes and offenses that involved deviation from traditional rules of conduct. Moreover, certain verses in the Koran such as, "You will not attain piety until you have given that which you cherish most" (III, 85) tend to influence the faithful to make his/her religious life "an inward one."

Nevertheless, it is important to underscore the value of Islamic Law in building the society by improving the conduct of the people therein. One can rarely overemphasize "the mutual assistance, hospitality, generosity, fidelity, the faithful keeping of promises made to other members of the community, moderation in one's desires, sobriety" and other virtues. All of these characterize the Muslims even today. Being "a divinely ordained path of conduct that guides the Muslim towards a practical expression of his religious conviction," the Shariah is definitely one of the main factors responsible for these virtues. It has succeeded in giving the Muslim a sense of personal dignity that was unknown to the Arabs of the "Jahiliya" (J.M. Abd-el-jalil).

Yes, there is no denying the fact that real virtues are practiced within the community of Islam, and above all, those virtues possess social values. Such virtues are thus defined in the following verse of the Koran:

> It is not righteousness that ye turn your faces to the East and the West; But righteousness is he who believeth in Allah and the last day and the Angels and scripture and the prophets; and giveth his wealth, for Love of Him to Kinsfolk & Orphans and the needy & the wayfarers and to those who ask, and to set slaves free And those who keep their treaty

when they make one—such are they who are sincere. Such are the God fearing. (II, 172)

The Importance of the Koran and the Bible to their Respective Religions and Why They Were Revealed

God entrusted every one of the prophets with a copy of the one divine book, which Muslims believe actually exists in heaven. However, the books of previous prophets were either lost or corrupted by later generations. The same case is applicable to the Torah of Moses and the Injil ("good news") of Jesus. The Holy Koran is, therefore, the only correct copy of the "heavenly book" existing now. Christians and Jews are still "people of the book" who are entitled to special professions in Muslim states, according to the Muslim belief. Mohammed received revelations from God throughout the years of his active career. These were transmitted to the prophet through the agency of the Angel Gabriel. These revelations were sometimes short and other times long. They governed almost every aspect of religious, public and private life. All of them were delivered in a kind of rhymed Arabic prose, which is difficult to capture in English translation. However, it has a powerful effect when recited to Arabic speakers. Its ability to move the hearers is expressed in the description of the recitation as "Lawful magic." Some years after the prophet had died, these revelations were collected in the Koran, literally meaning, "the reading" or "the recitation." When referred to by Muslims, some adjective is usually added so that it is always called the "Holy Koran," or the "Noble Koran." Although the revelations found in the book are very complex, there are certain teachings and practices, which Muslims of all sects consider to be essential to the faith of Islam. The Koran thus gives guidelines to what it is to live as a Muslim.

The Christian Bible

To the Christian, the Bible is the basis of revelation. It is also called the revealed word of God. An average Christian would regard the Bible as the ultimate text of basic Christian faith. The Bible depicts the story of Salvation History, and this is one of its most important functions to Christians. The Christian Tradition expresses itself in two principal ways, the Scripture and the continuous teaching of the Church. Every word in the

Bible could be said to be inspired but it is not every word there that is revealed. The passage from the Bible, for example, where it is said that women should always cover their hair in the church, I believe, must not have been revealed. Many scripture scholars have written that such themes, though inspired, were chiefly influenced by what they called "sitz em Laben." The importance of the Bible to Christians, therefore, should be seen in the light of

1. Its (the Bible) role as a witness to the faith of the church.
2. Its role as a revealed word of God,
3. Its depiction of the story of salvation History
4. Its normative pattern.

I have already discussed all of the above briefly except the normative pattern. The Bible in some aspects tends to be normative while playing its roles. In this respect, the Christian reads the Bible as a source of guideline to his faith. The Bible, of course, is not the only guideline to this pattern. The teaching of the church is sometimes normative too; for instance, the Pope's encyclical.

The Bible and the Koran

In Africa, both Christians and Muslims believe in one God who is supreme, the creator, eternal, just and loving. How did they come to know all these characteristics of God? The two possible answers are either that God is a creation of their mind, or God has revealed Himself to mankind. If the first position is correct, then it could possibly be said that God is a fabrication, an absurdity, and therefore non-existent. However, if the second proposition is true, then the revelation of God becomes extremely important.

If we accept the second proposition, then God had to reveal himself to man in a human way; otherwise, we wouldn't comprehend the spiritual with our limited intellectual faculties. This then creates a need for the infinite God to enter the sphere of man, space, and time in order to reveal Himself to man.

The belief in the existence of God therefore entails certainly a point whereby divinity emerges with humanity. This contact point for the Christian, though expressed in the Bible, lies in the person of Jesus Christ. For the Muslim, it is the Koran. The knowledge of this relationship is very essential; otherwise, one would often be led to the mistake of thinking that Christ is to Christianity what Mohammed is to Islam. It is in this perspective that one can understand the weight or the importance of the Koran to Islam and that of the Bible to Christianity. The Koran being a divine communication to man is on the same level with Jesus of Christianity. This means that the Bible and the Koran, though generally accepted as holy books, occupy different positions in the minds of their respective adherents. This accounts for the reason why the Bible was produced through the medium of many different kinds of persons over a long period, while the Koran was produced through the medium of one person and within a very short period of time. Hence, we say that every word of the Bible was written under the influence of divine inspiration, while every word of the Koran was written under the influence of divine revelation.

Chapter 7

Law

Offense In Igbo Ethnic Group

The Igbos have several levels of offenses ranging from "*mmehie*" (negligence) through "*alu*" (crime) to "*nsoani*" (abomination). Whereas an offense is a violation of civil law in America, it is a sin against the earth goddess (Ani) in Igboland. Hence, it is the duty of the Ani priest to make sure that those who violate the land by committing an offense be not only punished adequately but also made to undergo some appropriate rituals necessary to appease the land. The people of every community take seriously the obligation of being their brother's keeper, because anyone's transgression could bring the anger of Ani against the entire society "*ofu mkpulu aka luta mmanu ozulu ora.*" "*Nsoani*" is of two types: advertent and inadvertent. The former includes incest, voluntary manslaughter, and homicide induced by a married woman. The latter includes giving birth to twins, a child cutting the upper teeth first, a breech delivery, or giving birth to a crippled baby. Though they are not malicious, they are offenses that require purification, because the Igbos believe that they are a sequel to the sins that either or both of the parents might have committed in secret.

The idea of suffering the consequences of one person's sin by all of the people is a powerful principle in Nigerian legal reasoning today. Undoubtedly the principle in origin was tribal. We find it, for example, among the ancient Israelites who, like the Igbos, attempted to avoid evil even though they were not attracted by good. Because sin, for them, violated the will and law of the Lord, an offense was not simply a legal infraction but also a rupture of piety, of the hesed, which the law formulated and expressed. Just as an Igbo woman in her menstrual period is not clean enough to cook for her titled husband, so too the holiness of the Israelites, a people consecrated to God, could be violated without the performance of any immoral act. The women of ancient Israel, for instance, had to make guilt offerings after childbirth.

Since we do not live in a tribal society, the concept of shared guilt is largely on us. The idea that the consequences of an act can be visited on us because in some sense a wonderful act continues to exist in its consequences is alien to the more individualistic thinking that characterizes our era. Only of late has the notion of corporate responsibility been thrust upon us.

The Igbo term "*mmehie*" (mistake) is used in the same way as is "*hattah*," the Hebrew Bible word for sin, literally meaning, "missing the mark." One does not always miss the mark in a moral sense. For example, a pilot might miss the controllers' signal due to bad weather, which is no fault on his part but an act of God. Nonetheless, he missed the mark and must do all that is necessary to get back to his route or else destroy the lives of the innocent people aboard.

The Igbos are known to perceive life as an adventure (*oriri*). They navigate the world as if in a big canoe on the ocean (*orimiri*), with every individual taking part in paddling the canoe. Everybody in the canoe, including each of the domestic animals, is capable of sinking it. Most of the laws are intended to promote the safety of the passengers and the safe sailing of the canoe. Thus, most of them figure as laws of common sense, laws perceived by our natures or laws of nature.

Most African laws are similarly reasoned because they stem from a "natural law" perspective. In the United States, a court would authorize the mother to keep the children. I do not claim to know all the reasoning substantiating such a law, but it has to do, I am sure, with the fact that in the United States legal reasoning springs from a utilitarian or pragmatic point of view.

The Igbo term "*alu*" (crime) is equivalent to "*pesha*," a Hebrew, Biblical term that means "to rebel." The term "*alu*" is generally used for an advertent attempt by an individual to do any deed that might contribute to the sinking of the "canoe" such as maliciously taking away the life of any one born in it. It is less of a crime to kill outsiders. Indeed, sometimes doing so is, as Mr. Nnam Agu, an Enugu Nigerian based education officer stated, "gallantry." I do not mean to imply, of course, that all that is required by Igbo customary law is simply the avoidance of wrongdoing. On the contrary, it is the duty to care for others that confers on one the right to be the object of solitude. In Igboland, duties and rights, as we shall see later, complement each other. This reciprocity is taken seriously. How seriously is exemplified in the case of the repeatedly defiant son who vowed never to comply with the mores of Igbo society. He was sold into slavery, banished without remorse. "*Alu*," therefore, includes both commission and omission.

A parallel to the Igbo "*alu*" is found in the Prophet Amos who spoke of the good deeds, that God required of Israelite tribes (Am: 6, 12). We have a clearer idea of what these are when we understand what the prophet included in transgression, a term which appears repeatedly in Amos 1, 3-2, 8. It embraces, as Bruce Vawter has pointed out, inhumanity, cruelty, social injustice, the violation of a contract, the acceptance of a bribe, a violation of public trust, greed, lust, and hypocrisy.

"*Nso Ani*" ("taboo" or "abomination") is a far more grievous offense. It is classified as follows:

a. The taboos that violate the law of nature or what the community accepts as the normal "rhythm of cosmic life." Such violations are the delivering of twins, dying without an attendant, the climbing of a palm tree by a woman, a breech delivery, a child's cutting the upper teeth first, and suicide by hanging;
b. Unnatural behaviors on the part of animals, such as a cow bearing two calves, a hen hatching only one chick, a dog delivering a single whelp, a she-goat suffering the pains of parturition while tied by a rope, a dog crossing a corpse, and a goat climbing the top of a roof;
c. The taboos that regulate and protect the economic life of the community, the violation of which is a defilement of Ala. This category includes the purloining of planted yams and "*ikwo nkwu*," the stealing of palm wine from a palm tree;
d. The taboos that regulate the sexual life of the community, such as those against incest and bestiality;
e. The taboos that safeguard the reverence due to the invisible segment of the community, such as the prohibition against killing a sacred animal that has been dedicated to the spirits, ancestors, gods, and goddesses;

f. and finally, the taboos that regulate the domestic life of the community and ensure harmony in the home, such as those against adultery, patricide, matricide, a willful abortion by a married woman, and pregnancy during the first year of a husband's death.[1]

Punishment

What is punishment, and why is it in the Nigerian customary law? Punishment or sanction is the act of repudiating an offender for his non-observance of the law. Offenders are punished in Igbo traditional society for a number of reasons.

1. Retribution: (Ometalu Bulu)

Expiation is solely the purpose here. A person is punished because he deserves it.

2. Deterrence

With this in mind, Igbos punish an offender not only to prevent him from repeating his offense, but also to use him as an example to the entire community of what will be done to any mischievous son of the land who attempts to emulate him. Thus criminals who were sentenced to death, for example, during the last military regime in Nigeria were made to face the firing squad in a public place so that their executions might be public spectacles.

3. Spiritual Reparation

The Igbos picture their relationship with the spirit world as a kind of string that is strengthened by the good moral behavior of anyone from their community. This relationship, in similar fashion, is made weaker and weaker by "*alu*" and "*nsoani*." Therefore, each time one weakens this string through incriminating behavior, no time is wasted in offering a sacrifice of atonement. The bond with the spirits must be restored, and the polluted land must be cleansed through an expiating sacrifice. Such rituals can be regarded as punishments in the sense that the offender provides the sacrificial lamb, cow, goat or chicken, depending on the gravity of the offense. Whenever an individual is too poor to provide the animals of sacrifice, it is incumbent upon his kindred to do so. The principle of collective responsibility is enshrined in African traditional law. So closely bound together in brotherhood are the members of an extended family "*onye anyana nwanne ya*" that all are responsible for the conduct of each member. In fact, it used to be, and still is, in some localities, that for murder, the responsibility is not just that of the individual, but for the entire family, unless the family performed some necessary rituals of denunciation to isolate themselves from the crime. In some communities it is the custom that the murderer's local group or family be forced into exile with him lest rioting result. While they remained in exile the kinsmen of the murdered person conducted a raid on the compounds of the murderer's family. During the raid the compounds were burnt to ashes, their yams were uprooted and their other vital economic crops, for instance, palms, were cut down.[2] In most localities these goods were destroyed and not appropriated because they were considered "blood wealth." Whoever secured these goods for himself was considered callous, inhumane and even cannibalistic.

The principle of collective responsibility was not unknown to English law in bygone days. In the feudal period the institution of the frankpledge made every member of a tithing responsible for the conduct of the rest.

Today, with the introduction of Anglo-American law into Nigeria, collective has given way to individual responsibility. Now, everybody speaks and answers for himself, at the expense certainly, of social cohesion. We are experiencing the gradual disappearance of slogans like: "*i gwe bu ike*" (In union is strength) and "*onye ayana nwanneye*" (Be your brother's keeper), expressions rooted in the idea of collective responsibility.

4. Remuneration

One of the principal characteristics that distinguishes Nigerian tradition from Anglo-American criminal law is the role played by compensation to the victim in equivalence for the injury, loss or privation sustained. In the United States, a criminal law violation, such as murder is regarded as an offense against the state to which the victim serves merely as a witness. Most African ethnic groups frown upon Western criminal law because they view a criminal offense as perpetrated against the victim as well as the state. Thus if a murderer is neither banished nor compelled to hang himself, he is made to spend almost the rest of his life laboring for his victim's family, performing the services or tasks which the deceased would have done were he alive.

At Nengwe, in Enugu state of Nigeria, a thief is made to compensate his victim with three times the worth of the stolen goods. At Ugwueme in the same state, compensation is for the exact value of the stolen article. At Isu, yam is considered so sacred that the owner had the option of either receiving compensation for it or calling "on the thief to hang himself."[3]

Jurisprudence

For centuries Africa was known to the Western world as the Dark Continent. It was so called because the collective mind of the rest of the world had yet to be enlightened about Africa: its diversity, its history, and its culture.

The awareness of the need to study Africa with the same degree of insight and understanding that we study Europe, Asia, and other continents is growing and continues to expand, especially in the United States. This is because African-Americans, who constitute about 12.5% of the American population, have begun to realize the need to understand the genesis of their cultural heritage; the importance of this awareness was demonstrated by Alex Haley's *Roots*. *Roots* was one of the first, and certainly the most successful literary attempt not only to understand Africa, but also to link the black Africans to the African-Americans. The message of *Roots* transcended race and spurred a heretofore-unparalleled interest in genealogy. However, for African-Americans, its message served as the beginning of the end of a void in their collective consciousness. *Roots* gave a tremendous sense of pride in race and culture to a people emerging from the physical bonds of slavery and its psychological aftermath.

The Western political, industrial, and economical investment in the continent of Africa is on the rise, and the countries of Africa are ready to take their place as equal participants in world affairs. In light of these facts, it is impossible for one to overemphasize the need to understand the judicial processes on the continent.

This research is not comprehensive enough to study every aspect of the African culture. Instead, it is only tailored toward the African legal reasoning. In other words, this is a scholarly attempt to study African legal reasoning, that is, the source of their law and their rules of law, and then to compare and to contrast them with those of Anglo-Americans. I know from the extent of the research I have conducted so far that the sources of Anglo-American law include the common law, customs, judicial, and legislative intent. African law, on the other hand, stems largely from traditions (*Omenani*), proverbs, and most importantly, from allegories.

Allegories, in this context, are short stories, which contain some hidden meanings and are usually used for teaching morals. While the allegories seem simply like fairy tales, they are full of implied moral instructions, just like the parables of the Bible, most of which have allegorical meanings. Those implied moral meanings are hidden within the allegories (tales) in the form of proverbs to be used as rules of law. This explains why the traditional African concept of law is inseparable from ethics and morals, a basic contrast with Anglo-America, whose legal positivists are determined to maintain a sharp separation of law from morals.

Other major contrasts between the two legal systems include: whereas the ultimate goal of every case trial in Anglo-America is to find one party guilty and the other innocent, the end of every trial in Nigeria is solely reconciliation and pacification. If a legal reasoning is logic of reason in Anglo-America, that of Nigeria is logic of the heart. Obviously, a legal method that works in one of these countries does not necessarily work when it is transplanted to another. From our study of comparison and contrast, we should gain a clearer understanding of the "non-transferability of the law" from one culture to another.

It is truly remarkable that a majority of these rules of law are not only similar to, but also identical with some established *rationes decidendi* in the U.S. legal system. For illustration, we might note:

1. "*Ahia oma na ele onwe ya*" or "*eji anya ama oka chalu acha*." (Action speaks for itself.) The proverb expressed the Anglo-American rule of law: "Res ipsa Loquitur," *Miles v. St. Regis Paper Company*, 77 Wash 2d. 828, 467 p. 2d 307 (1980) and *Hillen v. Hooker Const. Co.* Tex. Civ. App. 484 S.W.2d 113, 115.
2. "*Oke Okuku Kwachuo akwa enwelu ya mechuo ife.*" This is equivalent to the U.S. rule of law concerning the standard of care for minors, which states that when a minor undertakes

an adult activity which can result in grave danger to himself and to others, he is held to the same standard of care as the average prudent adult. *Daniel v. Evans*, 107 N.H. 407, 223 A.2d 63 (1966).

3. "*Egbe belu ugo belu nke si Nwanne ya ebena nkwu kwaa ya nike.*" This is similar to the U.S. law of self-defense, which justifies an act prompted by the reasonable belief of immediate danger. *Baltimore Transit Co. v. Faulkner*, 179 Md. 598, 20 A.2d 485, 487.
4. "*Ndu ka akwu.*" (Life is worth more than property.) This is equivalent to the U.S. rule of law: Unless adequate notices are posted, deadly weapons like spring guns cannot be used to protect property. *Bird v. Holbrook*, 4 Bing. 628 (1825).
5. "*Ogo egbuna.*" (Let none die of his kindness.) This is the same principle of so-called: "Good Samaritan" law: that an attempt to save the life of another involves no negligence unless attempt is either rash or reckless. *Eckert v. Long Island R.R.,* 43 N.Y. 502 (1871).

In support of this view, Justice Cardozo wrote:

> Danger invites rescue. The cry of distress is the summons of relief. The law does not ignore these reasons of the mind in tracing conduct to its consequences. It recognizes them as normal. It places their effects within the range of the natural and probable. The wrong that imperils life is a wrong to the imperiled victim; it is a wrong also to his rescuer. (C.O. Gregory, Lanvin, Jr., Epstein, R.A., *Cases and Materials on Torts*, (Boston: Little Brown and Company, 1977), p. 311.)

6. "*Ani mmaa relu.*" The sense here is the same as an "act of God," an accident, namely, that could not have been occasioned by human agency but proceeded from physical causes alone. *Watts v. Smith*, D.C. App., 226 A.2d 160, 162; *Middaugh v. U.S.*, D.C. Wyo. 293 F. Supp. 977, 980.
7. "*Afu Ihe ka olu ato ogwu.*" This is equivalent to the U.S. case law that defines an emergency as an unforeseen combination of circumstances that call for immediate action. *State v. Perry*, 29 Ohio App. 2d 33, 278, N.E.2d 50, 53 *Sandberg v. Spoelstra*, 46 Wash. 2d 776, 285 P.2d 564, 568; *Hall v.*

O.C. Whitaker Co., 143 Tex. 397, 185 S.W.2d 720, 722, 723.

8. "*Afughi ka emelu, emee ka afulu.*" This maxim is similar to the case law of *Cooley v. Public service Co.*, 90 N.H. 460 (1940), which maintained that where danger to two classes of persons cannot be simultaneously guarded against, only the more immediate and injurious risk need to be protected.
9. "*Ihe nwa mmadu namaro adighi egbu nwa mmadu.*" This is the same as the Anglo-American case law: "*Ignorantia facti excusat.*"
10. "*Osisi kpalu eso na eso ga ana.*" This adage is similar to the U.S. case law, which assigns criminal sanction for an unlawful act without requiring a showing of criminal intent. *State v. Lucero*, 87 N.M. 242, 531 P.2d 1215, 1218. This is known as the strict liability cases, for example *Davis v. Gibson Product Co.*, Tex. Civ. App., 505 S.W.2d 682, 688. In Africa, on the other hand, strict liability applies to both criminal and civil cases alike.

Other questions raised here include: How does a judge make a decision? What are the factors that he examines or considers when deciding a case? To what extent should those factors contribute toward his decision making? How does he determine when and when not to use precedents? How far does he apply the rules of logic without losing touch with reality? On the other hand, at what point should a quest be halted by considerations of social welfare, customs, social justice, morals, or others stemming from a conscious or unconscious personal "underlying philosophy of life?" What factors do they consider as relevant? Are judges in fact legislators, not interpreters, of law? Given the *stare decisis* doctrine, how do they separate *ratio decidendi* from an *obiter dictum*? How do they determine when and when not to use "plain meaning," legislative intent, or precedence as a means of interpretation? How far do they apply the rules of logic, if at all, to statutes without losing touch with reality? From another standpoint, are decisions tempered by considerations of social welfare, custom, justice, prevailing morals, conscious or unconscious personal underlying philosophies of life?

Notes

1. Bruce Vawter, The Mystery of Sin and Forgiveness, "Missing the Mark," 25.

2. F. A. Arinze, *Sacrifice in Igbo Religion*, (Ibadan: Ibadan University Press, 1970), 34-37.

3. C. K. Meek, *Laws and Authority in a Nigeriean Tribe*, (New York: Barnes and Noble, Inc., 1937), 206.

Chapter 8

Tradition and Values

African Cardinal Values

Spirituality

Faith or spirituality for an African is simply a recognition that there is more to life than meets the eye. In other words, spirituality is when an African knows/understands himself and the source of what he is that he can look at the world and be convinced that there is a power greater than man.

Africans have little tolerance for agnostics and atheists because it is impossible to see how everything could have started with man and ended with man and the living world. Who in his right mind can take credit or blame for all creations? How can the ultimate cause of reality be traced to the world of the living (the physical world) and not to the spiritual world?

Natural Laws

The natural law is the second most honored value in African culture. It is only second to spirituality. Africans are natural law theorists by nature. They use the natural theory to determine the legality, the morality, and even the spirituality of whatever they do. Such a determination is so simple that all an African asks is whether something/an act is natural or not. Whatever is natural cannot be wrong. *Ka evuru meta abuho nso.* Telling a lie is always wrong because God did not create the mouth and the tongue for the purpose of deception. Abortion cannot be right since it is unnatural for humans to take others' lives, even if they are those of the unborn. Euthanasia must be wrong for the same reason. Homosexuality, they insist, is equally wrong since the acts cannot result in procreation. God created humans with reason and common sense, and all is good. We can differentiate right from wrong by asking if it is natural or simply by using our common sense. Similarly, a just law can equally be differentiated from an unjust law.

The natural law theory is the single criterion with which Africans have always decided their actions. For example, Africans have been known to kill twins right after birth only because they believe that it is only natural for dogs, cats, goats, and rabbits to give multiple births at the same time and for humans to give birth to only one child at a time. Hence, they killed twins because they considered them unnatural.

Family and Community

The family is the most important institution in Africa. Families are dear to Africans exactly in the same way that Americans are patriotic to their country. It is not unusual for an African to remain nonchalant or unconcerned when something unkind is said about his country and for him to be unforgiving when the slightest remark is made against his family. Families are almost sacred in Africa.

The family is the most cohesive unit in African tradition. It is the first and the last institution to which one is exposed. It is also the first and the most primary basic governing unit in the life of a young African. The family is a governing body that plays such a vital role in the life of an African that he cannot but embrace it. Like the late Chief Azik Okenwa Nnamoko put it during my last interview with him, "The family unit determines life (through marriage), and it equally determines death (through burials and funerals)."

No African couples, for instance, contract marriage alone. Marriage can only become a covenant between families. Death is equally in the hands of the families since they alone can give a righteous funeral to the deceased. Chinua Achebe showed a clear illustration in his novel, *Things Fall Apart*, where Okonkwo's family refused to bury him because he committed suicide. If an African must receive a righteous burial in order to rest in peace and if one's family can only give such a burial, then the family is extremely important to every individual. That is one of the reasons why every African is extremely close to his family.

There are two kinds of family: extended and nuclear family systems. The Western type is typically nuclear, and the African system is known as the extended family system. The latter includes nephews, nieces, uncles, aunts, parents, children, siblings, and first, second, and third cousins.

Extended families are very hierarchical, and leadership is usually bestowed on the oldest. It is usually very large and extensive, yet it is very organized and efficient. The family governs marriage, and the divorce rate is less than 20% in Africa. Nuclear family is non-existent in Africa as it is often only a couple and their children.

Hospitality

Like spirituality, Africans are very proud of their hospitality. Some of the virtues being explained here may be valued more in some parts of Africa than others. However, one particular value viewed alike in all parts of Africa, with the exception of the urban cities, is hospitality. Hospitality is simply an aspect of African tradition, that requires that one's guest may never be harmed under any circumstance. It requires that guests be treated with the utmost respect, kindness, and honor. It even calls for guests to be treated better than hosts.

Like Plato, Africans teach using short stories and allegories. There are stories told of hosts who opted to be killed themselves rather than have their guests decapitated in their own homes. They saw it as a taboo that cries to the spirit world for vengeance. African hospitality also calls for a host to give up his only bed to the guest and sleep on the couch himself.

Finally, African hospitality entails that one does not have to forewarn his host before appearing in his home as a guest. Care and hospitality are often so automatic that an African does not think of it. It is as though Africans believe that letting down a guest is often followed by retaliation from the ancestors against one, against one's children, and against one's children's children.

Life

Africans have a deep appreciation for life. It is considered so sacred that destruction of life pollutes or desecrates the land; the land would need some type of purification each time it is polluted intentionally or unintentionally.

In Igboland, a special type of sacrifice is offered once a human being is killed on the land. It is known as a sacrifice of purification. It is often followed with some type of punishment, depending on whether the killing is premeditated or inadvertent. The punishment is usually seven years in exile when it is unintentional and lifetime in exile when the killing is intentional.

Finally, life is so holy that during wars, the unwritten rule is that one must capture one's enemies alive. One can only kill at war if and only if one's own life is in danger. As I explained in an earlier passage in this book, slavery in Africa began only as a result of the Africans' reverence for life.

Justice (Ofor)

Africans have a wonderful sense of justice. They have many proverbs that reflect it. The following are some Igbo examples:

- *Oji ofo ga ana*
  He who has justice gets free (unharmed).

- *Egbe belu ugo belu nke si nwanne ya ebena nku kwaa ya*
  Let the kite perch and let the eagle perch and let he who tries to stop the other break his wings.

- *Idide si na ofo kaya ji awa ani*
  The earthworm said that he is able to dig through the earth only because he has justice on his side.

- *Ome if jide ofo*
  Let the actor better have justice on his side.

Africans give names to their children reflecting what is important to them. Justice is very important to them; therefore, many of their names reflect "*offor*," some of them are:

Ofodile – Justice works,
Ofobike – Justice is strength,
Ofor – Justice,
Ofoedu – Justice guides,
Ofoegbu – Justice never kills (it might hurt),
Ofoka – Justice is highest,
Ofodi – There is justice.

Finally, when Africans pray they evoke justice constantly,

- One has to be just in order to call on God's name,
- One has to be just in order to stand before God,
- One has to be just in order to win favors from God.

Seniority and Respect

Africans are very hierarchical, and every rank is determined by a single criterion called age or seniority. Seniority comes with deep respect, so everyone wants to be older.

Affirmative Action In Nigeria

Nigeria is divided into north and south. During the colonization of Nigeria, the British occupied the south much quicker and much easier than they were able to overrun the north. This failure to win the north by the British was due to a number of reasons, the most remarkable of which was due to the stronghold of the Islamic religion there. Another reason was the formidable leadership of the Hausa Emirs and several other northern empirical rulers. Meanwhile, the Igbos, Yorubas, and other southern tribes embraced Christianity, Western education, and foreign ways of life. The Hausas and Fulanis, on the other hand, continued to reject the Eurocentric way of life, including Western education.

As time progressed, the southerners gained a tremendous amount of advantage over the northerners. The most important companies were owned between the Europeans and southern Nigerians. The most advanced civil servants were the Igbos, the Yorubas, and people from other minor southern tribes. The Hausa tribe was, and still is, the most populous tribe in Nigeria, yet it had the least educated men and women, compared to the other major southern tribes like Igbo and Yoruba.

Whether the above advantage over the northerners was fair or unfair, whether deserved or undeserved, the northerners wanted to do something about it. Given their high population, they voted a type of affirmative action. That was a program carefully designed to bridge or close the gap between the two sectors. First, special emphasis was made to close the gap in education. For instance, qualified northerners were given more scholarships and financial support than the southerners. Many educators were specially trained and sent to the northern region to recruit uneducated northerners who were not interested in acquiring a Western education. A conscious effort was made to build more schools in the north.

The best teachers were paid better to teach in the north. Finally, educated northerners were rewarded better since they were given preferential treatment. Be it affirmative action, preferential treatment, or reverse discrimination, the fact remains that no Hausa, Fulani, or Tiv was offered a job for which he/she was not qualified simply because he/she came from the Northern region.

Many southerners resented this program as well as the northerners who took advantage of it. They were called stupid, foolish, and opportunistic. Personally, I resented the program with much passion. I felt that the northerners' refusal of Western education in the beginning was no one's fault. However, the fact is that southerners benefited from it. Nevertheless, I was adamant in my position, and I led a crusade of mockery against the northern students, especially against those on Nigerian government scholarships after I arrived in Chicago from Nigeria in the early 1980s.

Like Saint Paul of the New Testament, I had a change of mind as we debated and made fun of some students after a monthly meeting of the African Students' Union in Chicago, which I founded at DePaul University in 1987. A Hausa graduate student, Dan Almagiri, posed a question that astounded me. He said, "Suppose me Yusuf and me Abimbola agreed to a soccer shooting contest." It was a twenty thousand dollar bet from each of them. Being students, it was as though they had their entire livelihoods bet on it. The night before the contest a third party, unknown to either of the contestants, snuck into the stadium and changed the size of both the goal posts in favor of Yusuf and to the detriment of Abimbola. After much anticipation, the contest commenced. By the end of the first half, Yusuf had 50 points, and Abimbola had zero points. All of a sudden, it was discovered that Abimbola was kicking into a goal post that was less than its normal size. After a careful examination, it was further discovered that her opponent, Yusuf, was unjustly kicking into a goal post that was much more than its normal diameter. Yusuf was shocked, Abi was angry, the referees were embarrassed and the spectators were speechless! Meanwhile, the contestants had one more half to play. The officials deliberated over and over again. They were unable to reach a consensus or common agreement. One of them insisted that Yusuf must relinquish his fifty points since he gained them unjustly. The other referee disagreed, stating that two wrongs do not make a right. For a solution, he remarked that Yusuf should be allowed to retain his fifty points while Abimbola be automatically awarded fifty points as well. The third official became infuriated and furiously asserted that Yusuf did nothing to cause the unfortunate incident; therefore, it would be unfair to him if his opponent, Abi was automatically awarded any points whatsoever.

The third referee insisted that they should go on and play through the rest of the second half. However, Abimbola must be given a chance to score into the wider hoop for the rest of the second half; whereas, Yusuf gets to shoot into the smaller hoop as Abimbola did during the first half. Having both of them go through the same experience is exactly the only way to be just and fair. Needless to say, it is a competition and that is simply the fairest way to determine the just winner. Abimbola accepted the third decision as fair. Yusuf rejected each of them as unjust. He went to refer to them as reverse discrimination because, according to him, he was being punished for a wrong that was done by another and a wrong for which he was innocent. The referees told him that he was missing the issue. The issue, they said, was whether Yusuf benefited from another's wrong act, not whether Yusuf knew and consented to the act or not. Of course, he admitted to benefiting from another's unfair action. Sometimes, he denied benefiting from it. Whether he admitted it or not, the fact is that he had 50 points, and his opponent had zero.

Finally, Yusuf was asked to suggest the best way to resolve the problem or the way he would have resolved it if it were up to him. He said, "I thought you would never ask me," then he cleared his throat and went on to suggest the following:

> First, let the hoops be repaired and made equal, correct and legal regulation size, hence correcting the problem. Second, let them continue the second half with no cheating from either party, third, let each party retain the score from the first half. Fourth, let no one dwell in the past since the game will be played fairly henceforth.

If Abimbola is better, Yusuf continued, she will outscore her opponent now that the game is fair in the second half.

After telling me this story, Dan Almagiri, the student from Northern Nigeria, asked me what I would do if I were the referee. I asked him to give me one week to think about it. First, he told me that as a referee I did not have the luxury of thinking about it for an entire week. However, for the sake of peace among us and for the progress of our newly formed association, which was in the middle of all these, he told me to think about it until we came to our weekly meeting in seven days.

I thought about this all week and finally came to a conclusion. I agreed with the three referees and disagreed very much with Yusuf. The more I thought of it the more I realized that I was Yusuf in the analogy, Dan Almagiri was represented by Abimbola, and the Nigerian government was represented by the three impartial referees. Why is it that I was capable of being quite fair in the basketball analogy, but I could not be as fair whenever it came to the concept of affirmative action in Nigeria? Would Yusuf have chosen or favored his stance if the position/circumstances were reversed? The principles of justice according to John Rawls must be chosen behind "a veil of ignorance" to ensure that no one is disadvantaged, since no one is able to design principles to favor his particular condition. I had a veil of ignorance in the basketball analogy; hence I was unable to favor myself, unlike in the case of affirmative action in Nigeria where I had to design principles to favor my particular condition since I lacked the veil of ignorance there. That is why the symbol of justice in America is a woman who is blindfolded. That unbiased state that "appropriate initial status quo, where all fundamental agreements reached in it are fair, is what John Rawls called 'the original position' and this explains the propriety of his article entitled, 'Justice as fairness.' In other words, justice can only be gotten from a stipulation that is fair. In the case of affirmative action, it was unfair for me to be a judge in my own case Nemo *eudax in sua causa*. In other words, the best and only way to come up with a just and fair decision is to think of that to which rational, free and equal persons might have chosen or agreed if they were "mutually disinterested" in the issue—not taking interest in the outcome. Put differently, a decision is fair if and only if it would be agreed to in an initial situation of equality, under a "veil of ignorance," notes Rawls in his book, *A Theory of Justice*.

This is why a mention of affirmative action brings into mind such terms like, "evening the score," "a free swing of the ball," and "fair equality of opportunity," as opposed to such principles as meritocracy. Besides the fact that they have interest in the outcome, most people who argue against affirmative action, as I did indeed, tend to confuse "the opportunity to compete" with "the opportunity to win." Second, they fail to realize that affirmative action is meant to correct a problem and then stop! Third, Yusuf's position was unfair because he failed to realize that any competition in which the outcome will always be known in advance would always remain an unjust competition.

Work: A Basic Concept

One of the most traditional African values is work and one of the misconceptions about the people of Africa is that they are all lazy. However, that is the farthest from the truth. The Africans abhor laziness and they cherish work as a value. Laziness is an abomination. In his book, *Things Fall Apart,* Chinua Achebe depicted Obonkwo's father, Unoka, as lazy and that was shameful enough to haunt him all his life.

In Africa, work "*olu*" is different from labor which is performed in the form of punishment. Work, on the other hand, is performed in fulfillment of what it means to be human. Work edifies, work nourishes the human spirit and work dignifies the human soul. In other words, there is more to work than a means of making a living.

Many philosophers, such as Karl Marx and Pope John Paul II, have written extensively about work as a basic concept in Western philosophy. What they have written is not very different from the African concept of work.

When we see work as an activity permeating all areas of human life, we can wonder why so little attention was given to it prior to Karl Marx. However, several reasons for this can be suggested. Many people have regarded work as a kind of punishment, as an activity fit for slaves, as a necessity for daily bread or finally as simply a means to an end. In these perspectives, little or no importance was attached to it.

In his article, "Work and the Humanistic Society," Professor Gerald Kreyche indicated that scholars have long debated the origin, nature, and purpose of work. Even though the narrator of Genesis portrayed God's work of creation as a sort of playful activity, the story nonetheless makes the point that work is incumbent upon man because of the original sin of Adam and Eve. The Hebrews thus tended to consider work as a necessary evil.

For the Greeks, on the other hand, work was the task of slaves because it brutalized the mind. They made use of myths, such as that of Sisyphus, to teach that work is a curse of the gods. In contrast, the Romans had mixed feelings regarding work; was not Romulus glorified as a farmer? However, the ideal was not to work. Before the Reformation, Christianity accepted agriculture, but found the commercial world repulsive. The Catholic religious orders stemming from St. Benedict stressed the salutary character of work *laborare est orare, or* to work is to pray. On the whole, the Christian attitude prior to the Reformation can, perhaps, best be described as ambivalent.

In his preaching, Martin Luther took up this theme of the salutary nature of work and can thus be regarded as a leader in fixing the idea that work is basic to life in the modern mind. For him, work animated and controlled human beings in all facets of their everyday existence: spiritual, social, psychological, and intellectual. He emphasized that work is natural, so he encouraged all who could do so to work. For him, idleness and beggary were associated with the contemplative and monastic life, forms of life he branded unnatural because he maintained that they stem from egotism and lack of human sympathy. Monks became oblivious of social duties. For Luther, then, work was a way of serving God, and thus every work enjoys equal spiritual dignity, provided it is performed for the love of God and one's neighbor. To do most perfectly the work of one's profession was therefore the best way to serve God. This work ethic undoubtedly inspired Abraham Maslow's observation: "The only happy people I know are the ones who are working well at something they consider important."[1] For Luther, profession and vocation became synonymous, and the German word, *Beruf* retains this two-fold significance. Accordingly, as Adriano Tilgher noted in his *Homo Faber*, "Luther placed a crown on the sweaty forehead of labor."[2]

Closer to our own days, we find Mussolini's Fascists glorifying work. During their convention at Bologna in 1922, the following principles were enunciated: (1) Work constitutes the sovereign title that legally gives men full and useful citizenship in the social fabric. (2) Work is the result of efforts harmoniously made, to create, perfect, and increase whatever constitutes to the material, moral and spiritual well-being of man."[3]

Over the years, others have had their say about work. Litterateurs like Ruskin and Tolstoy have incorporated their views into their literary studies. Ruskin promoted the idea that every man ought to work with his hand; whereas, Tolstoy maintained that work, like food, is a necessity. Whoever capitalized upon the work done by others does so because of the mistaken notion that work is a burden. With Marx, however, we came to a full-fledged philosophical theory of work.[4]

In this chapter, I am concerned with that type of work labor which Engels said creates use-value. The use-value of any product is essentially its ability to serve the purpose for which it was made.[5] The German term "*Arbeit*" covers both meanings.

Before Marx, Hegel had indicated that work accounts for the dynamic nature of the world. In the celebrated "Master-Slave" dialectic, we come to the realization that the slave can achieve the self-recognition denied to him by his master through his work. The dialectic of work, therefore, is the dialectic of freedom: a freedom that is achieved because his work places in his hands more powerful, more sophisticated weapons. Alexandre Kojeve remarked in commenting on this transformation:

> Quite different is the situation created by work. Man who works transforms given nature. Hence, if he repeats his action, he repeats it in different conditions, and thus his act itself will be different. After making the first ax, man can use it to make a second one, which, by that very fact, will be another, a better ax. Production transforms the means of production; the modification of means simplifies production; and so on. Where there is work, then there is necessarily change, progress, historical evolution.[6]

Kojeve is offering us a Marxist reading of Hegel, for which, to be sure, there are grounds in Hegel himself. For Hegel, man remains in contact with the concrete and the real only by rising above given conditions through the negating or determining activity that is work. Such activity is characteristic of the truly human, for through such action is the real transformed and satisfied. The human value constituted by work is essentially particular and personal, which is to say that it is by work that the particularities, the personalities, and the differences, between men are established.

This Marxist interpretation attributes to Hegel the idea that the historical evolution of man is due to work. At the beginning, the future master and slave were not yet truly "human historical beings." Subsequently, the master raised himself above given nature by risking his life and becoming human. Then, he compelled the slave to work. Through work, the latter raised himself up; he changed himself by realizing a project. The slave accordingly changed along with the changed world that he affected. However, the master, because he does not work, remains unchanged, dependent, in effect, upon the slave both for acknowledgement as master and his nouriture. Marxists thus envisage the historical becoming of the human being as the work of the slave. "To be sure," Kojeve noted, "without the Master, there would have been no history; but only because without him there would have been no slave and hence no work. . . .The creative education of man and work (Bildung) creates history, i.e. human Time."[7]

It is not germane to our purpose to evaluate the justice or injustice of this Marxist reading of Hegel. Whatever the genesis of his ideas, it is clear that for Marx the history of the world is nothing but the begetting of man through human work (cf. his *Manuscripts*. p. 68). Both Marx's advocates and his critics are at one on this point. Tom Rockmore, for example, has pointed out that Marx's notion of human being is to be understood in terms of activity. Consequently, freedom, for Marx, the highest human ideal, is to be achieved through social relations, which is to say through work or relationships of production. A human being is to be adjudged free, therefore only when his work is spontaneous and autonomous. By nature, man has no instinct to work. It is material desire that prompts or evokes the work, which satisfies. However, for every need thus satisfied, a new need is begotten. The epitome of the new desire is universal freedom, a goal that can be achieved only through work. Because there is never a need without a corresponding power, it is evident that the proletariat, the working class, is of both political and economic potential.

In his third encyclical letter "on Human Work," Pope John Paul II, making use of Biblical sources, did his best to highlight the role of work as the lifeblood of humanity. The Pope placed the Church firmly within the camp of those who envisage work as a fundamental dimension of man's existence on Earth. This position is grounded in the basic metaphors of Genesis: that man, created in the image and likeness of God, is called to participate in God's creative activity by subduing the earth (Gen. 1:28). Within the limits of his own capabilities, he is to develop and complete creation as he advances further in his discovery of the values that suffuse the whole of creation (Gen. 2:2-3). Work, the Pope said, is man himself in the subjective sense, because man is the subject of work (*Homo Laborem exercens*). The human person seeks to fulfill his calling to be a person, to realize his humanity through work (Gen. 3:19). Evidently, it was of work in the broadest sense that the Pope wrote: industrial or agricultural, manual or intellectual, the provision of services or the toils of research blue or white collar. Having found in nature the resources that he needs, man, the Pope insisted, is not the creator of these resources but their transformer. Hence, entirety is the result of the historical heritage of human labor. Because everything at the service of man, the Pope noted, is a result of man's labor, we have solid reasons for stressing priority of labor over capital. Labor has always remained, in man's experience, the ultimate efficient cause of his endeavors, whereas, capital has ever remained an instrumental cause. Therefore, seen in his true perspective, man develops through his love of work even when this is accompanied by toil. Work, moreover, unites people, and its social power is the power to build community. In the final analysis, both those who work and those who manage the means of production or who own them must in some way be united in this community (cf. Pope Pius XI, Encyclical "Quadragesimo Anno." : AAS 23 (1931), pp. 221-222). For Pope John Paul II, the world of work is the world *en toto*—in totality.

Biblical creation stories present work as injunction. Man must work not only in order to live "in the sweat of thy brow shalt thou eat bread," but his relationship to the human race requires it as does his own humanity impose it upon him. Commenting upon decisions made in the faraway headquarters of multinationals about the lives and livelihood of individuals and peoples without taking into consideration the true nature of work, the Pope asserted that work enables each human being to live in dignity and enables the society to become more human. "Taking decisions on the sole basis of economic criteria is not only economically counterproductive, but it disregards the most fundamental criterion of all: the human person."[8]

There is literature, I do not know how vast, critical of the commonplace notion of work. Robert Armstrong's article, "The Rehumanization of Work" is one such. In it, he has proposed a "normative" concept of work, the application of which would obliterate or eradicate the prejudices surrounding the common concept. For him, the ordinary concept of work embraces three elements: necessity-especially where a living must be earned; respectability; and congeniality. These he has combined to form the two aspects of his normative concept: (a) work that enables the worker to develop or exercise his potentialities, abilities, talents and creativity in a humanly satisfying way; *fabricando fit faber*. (b) Work as instrumental to the realization of an ideal human society through its positive contribution to the whole community, including us. He reiterates the phrase, "positive contribution," as something socially worthwhile in order to differentiate it from negative ones such as theft and prostitution. In his conclusion, he argues that happiness is not actually found in play or "creative leisure." Rather, it is to be found in purposive work, which is personally, and socially satisfying, and which enables the worker to exercise his abilities. Of play he says, "If our systems of work should somehow provide more time for play . . . only the symptom of our discomfort would be alleviated, not its cause. For happiness or self-fulfillment, we would still have to look to work that requires all the abilities, talents, intelligence and creativity and that contributes to the welfare of the whole human community."[9]

Evaluation

Together with Armstrong's argument, I find myself persuaded by the fact that we work for acceptance and human dignity, which leads me to support the idea that work should be conceived as a primitive concept, deserving our fullest attention. Like Marx, I am convinced that work is intrinsically rewarding, an end in itself, expressive of individual personality. If we are to come to a better understanding of work, we have to develop concepts that reflect the realities of modern civilization and not allow ourselves to be bamboozled by a dream of a world without work.

Any understanding of work results from its misconception as arduous, numbing toil or as the consequence of a curse. More fruitfully, we must conceive it is a normal expression of human nature: an activity, which aims at its further development. Something is lacking to our humanity if we have never known the joy of creative production. My contention is that work can only be inhuman or alienating if, and only if it is carried out in ways or conditions that are brutalizing. Work, for example, that is forced has little or no humanly liberating effects; nothing, as we know, when misused remains good, not even the four cardinal virtues.

Another African Problem

In Western solutions for African problems, Kwame Nkrumah had two objectives, unification of Africa and the development of Ghana. By development he meant industrialization—the Western style. That was a mistake that led to his failure. He did not have to attempt solving an African problem with a Western solution. He trusted the United States and got into the business of having them install a hydro-electric dam for his country, Ghana. The failure, they claimed, was due to a miscalculation. Personally, I have no doubt that it failed due to many more reasons than that.

The central African country, formerly known as Zaire, made a similar mistake with its steel mills project with the West in an attempt to solve its economic and social problems. African countries have a tendency of picturing civilization as building western monuments, Western gadgets, skyscrapers, and automobiles. To make matters worse, maintenance of these monuments is usually and absolutely out of the question. That is what I call "Western style monuments without maintenance." A good example is Muritala Mohamed International Airport in Lagos, Nigeria. It was built like O'Hare International Airport in Chicago. It was built with escalators, elevators, and a central air-conditioning system. Today, none of the above mentioned amenities works. I was in Nigeria a couple of months ago, and I felt so hot that I wished they had installed simple ceiling fans. Airport tax is collected from travelers leaving that airport, and only God knows what they do with the revenues collected. In the words of Ali Mazrui, "Drink deep or taste not the western spring because a little modernity is dangerous."

Besides airports, African countries spend quite a lot of money building good roads but they would spend little or no money for the road maintenance. They even collect tolls along roads as Westerners do, but they fail to utilize the collected funds for road maintenance. Officials embezzle a lion's share of the collected funds. A few years later, the road falls apart, and it gets even worse as years go by. There is a saying in Africa, "Show me a man who drives along a straight line and I will show you a man who is drunk." This is another clear example of "acquiring western taste without western skills."

Notes

1. Abraham Maslow, *A Theory of Human Motivation: The Goals of Work*, in Fred Best (ed), *The Future of Work*, Englewood Cliffs, Prentice Hall, Inc., 1973, 26.
2. Adriano Tilgher, *Homo Faber*, tr. Dorothy Fisher, Chicago, Henry Regnery Company, 1930, 50.
3. Tilgher, *Homo Faber*, 119.
4. Karl Marx, *Capital*, trans. Samuel Moore and Edward Aveling, vol. 1 Moscow, 1958, 183-4.
5. Marx, *Capital*, 42.
6. Alexandre Kojeve, *Introduction to the Reading of Hegel*, New York, Basic Books, Inc. Publishers, 1969, 51.
7. Kojeve, *Introduction to*, 52-53

8. Cf. "The Social Teaching of the Church," presented by Jan Schotte, C.I.C.M., Secretary Pontifical Commission "Lustitia et Pax" Vatican City at the Centennial Conference "Ethics and Economics" College of Business Administration, Marquette University, Milwaukee, Nov. 1-4, 1981, 43.

9. Robert Armstrong, "The Rehumanization of Work," *Social Theory and Practice*, vol. 2, Fall 1973, 473.

Chapter 9

Government

Afronanism: The solution to the problem of the post Cold War Era in Africa.

Afroanism is an ideology that emerged from the African philosophy of an *Oba*, an altruistic and prudent leader. It seeks to help people uphold the values they cherish most. What are Africa's problems in the post Cold War Era?

Shifting of Western funds from African needs towards the needs of Eastern Europe and the Soviet

Since the dissolution of the Soviet Union, there seems no longer to be any compelling reason for the West to send aid to African nations. Africa appears to have been forgotten because the United States, for example, no longer cares whether Africans threaten to turn to the Soviet Union for aid.

Dis-Africanization of Africans

This is another legacy of colonialism. This is a process through which the Africans have been conditioned to believe that they are inferior to the rest of the world. This mentality is concretely manifested today in several aspects of their lives, for instance, more Africans dress wearing Western attire than their own clothes. Foreign-made foods are more acceptable than the locally-made ones; it is much easier to find an American apple pie and Budweiser in a four star hotel than it is to find African foofoo and palm wine. Also, now a disc jockey is much more likely to play records by Michael Jackson and Madonna than the African juju records from either Sunny Ade or from Ebenezer Obey.

To put it bluntly, Africans are becoming westernized at such an alarming rate that little or no aspect of their culture may survive the 21st century.

Neo Colonialism

There is a new form of colonialism in Africa which is very subtle and more covert than it is meted on African people in disguised manner. The West usually comes up with some seemingly noble institutions through which they surreptitiously run the lives of people without their consent. Many African nations today are run indirectly by the western power through the United Nations, foreign aid, and most significantly the International Momentary fund (IMF). Why is there a tendency for former British colonies to hold tenaciously to the common law, equity and statutes of general application even after they have gained their independence? One might note that the British, for instance devised a strategy of making their colonies continue to depend on them despite their autonomy. Obviously, a legal method which works in some of the Western countries does not necessarily work when it is transplanted to Africa. From one study of comparison and contrast, they (the West) should gain a clear understanding of the "non transferability of the law."

Africans against Africans

Under this heading I try to ascertain the validity of the parlance, "Africans are their worst enemies." Have Africans learned to love each other? Are foreigners still able to instigate Africans against Africans? Regrettably, "divide and conquer," still takes place there even at the present century. The Whites in south Africa have been able to sustain the dreadful apartheid regime for such a long time because they kept inciting one African faction against another particularly the African national Congress (ANC) against the Inkatha group and vice versa. Therefore, whereas foreigners are mining their mineral resources and gaining political and economic advantage South African blacks are busy engaging each other on inter-tribal wars and rioting. In other parts of the continent we have brain drain, a system whereby the most educated members of every community are living abroad primarily because they cannot obtain adequate and befitting positions in their own homes.

Bribery and Corruption

This is the most devastating of all problems facing Africa today. Africans are not traditionally corrupt. It was considered heroic to steal from the government because it represented Western imperialism. The Africans unfortunately, have failed to realize that the government is now in their hands for them by them. They still take from the government as though it is still foreign. For example, the ibo word for the white person is *oyibo*. Their term for the "government job" is still called *oluoyibo* which means literally "white man's job." It is this askant view of government that causes instability, corruption and incessant coup d'etats.

> This Republican ideal can exist only so long as the people remain uncorrupted. They must be trained in civic virtue, in love of country; else the natural tendency of human beings to maximize their self-interest at the expense of the whole society will become dominant. In these conditions, Republican ideals will become hollow and, people, will eventually lose their liberty. For once the political sphere becomes corrupted by selfish interests, control can be maintained only by the strong leader who is waiting to yield power in the manner recommended to Lorenzo in *The Prince*.[1]

In addition to bigotry and corruption are embezzlement, mismanagement, nepotism and constant coup d'etats. These are the worst of our problems because no country will ever make it politically and economically unless corruption is reduced to a minimum. Machiavelli once remarked that corruption is to a government what a hole is to a sack; nothing accumulates. What good is a great economic plan in a country where the president and his ministers are so corrupt that the country owes billions of dollars to the IMF? Ironically, the country's money is stashed in Individual accounts in Swiss bank. Hence what we need is not the greatest economic plan. What we need is instead a change of attitude.

Definitions

"Afronanism" is defined as an ideology, that emanated from African Philosophy with an *"Oba"* (an altruistic and prudent leader) to help the people to uphold the values, that they cherish most.

African philosophy is a particular *modus cogitandum*, which simply stems from the African way of life. It has several sources, the major of which are Religion, Proverbs, Folk Tales and Mythology.

Religion

If the African way of life is inseparable from traditional religion, what is that religion in a nutshell?

The first point to keep firmly in mind regarding the African concept of religion is that it touches every aspect of the culture. The natives, for instance, refused to accept the official Christian religion because of the fact, they said, that Christians worshipped God on Sundays and spent the rest of the days forgetting about Him. Even the Hausa and Fulani ethnic groups in the northern region of Nigeria who later inherited the Muslim religion from the Arabian countries of north Africa now have their religion so interwoven into the fabric of their daily lives that one cannot separate the religious from the secular.

Due to an exceptionally keen sense of the unknown, and a deep appreciation of the ultimate mystery of life on the part of the Yorubas in western Nigeria, religion permeates the legal and, indeed, every other facet of their existence.

By the same token, the Africans are said to be so religious that they work religiously, dress religiously, eat religiously, converse religiously, think religiously, and observe rules and regulations religiously. Religion pervades all circuits of their life so fully that it is difficult, even impossible, to isolate it.

That the first European missionaries in Africa lacked insight into this religious character of the African is clear from their reference to the people as pagans or heathens, and beyond that as rustics, yokels, and bumpkins. Religion plays such an indispensable role in the life of the African that it is, in fact, the most vigorous and hardiest element in his background. It dominates rules of law, judicial processes, and whatever one does consciously or unconsciously. The Africans have no scriptures, dogma, or any other kind of religious formalization. They do not clamor to win converts because everyone is born into it; everyone lives by it and dies within it. Traditional religions are thus viewed as part and parcel of people's way of life. It is so natural that it does not claim a founder, a savior, or a prophet. The Hausas, on the other hand, have Mohammed as the founder of their religion. He is also the prophet of Allah, the Muslims' one and only God. The Koran is their law. *Shari'ah* translated literally means the "prescribed path."

The God of the traditional African religion is very great and transcendent. He is the God of creation (Chineke). He is so superior that no one is worthy to have any direct communication with Him. However, there are minor gods, goddesses, and righteous ancestors through whom one may communicate with Him. This, of course, does not make African religion any less monotheistic than the canonization of saints does to the Christian religion. The minor gods and ancestors are reverenced, not worshipped:

> We make sacrifices to the little gods, but when they fail and there is no one else to turn to we go to Chukwu. It is right to do so. We approach a great man through his servants. But when his servants fail to help us, then we go to the last source of hope. We appear to pay greater attention to the little gods but that is not so. We worry them more because we are afraid to worry their Master. Our fathers know that Chukwu was the Overlord and that is why many of them gave their children the name Chukwuka-Chukwu is Supreme.[2]

It is not every one of the ancestors that is venerated. Usually, a person's way of life on Earth has to meet certain expectations in order to merit reverence. Very seldom is a man who has been convicted of any serious theft, murder, rape, and other grievous crimes revered.

The religion of any African people is part and parcel of their heritage; it dates far back as their origin. This heritage is a fabric woven out of historical, cultural, legal, and religious principles. It is also said to be a product of the thinking and experiences of forefathers who observed religious ceremonies and rituals, inaugurated festivals, formulated religious beliefs, recited proverbs and myths that have religious meanings, and enacted laws based on customs that regulated community life. For the African, religion is the usual way of looking at and experiencing life *per se*. Religion is, indeed, so intermingled with a people's *modus vivendi* that many of the African languages have no word for it. Their words are for religious objects, principles, places, practices, and ideas. In the

Igbo language, for example, the word *omenani* meaning "tradition" covers religion, law and morality.

In summary, Africa is traditionally a religious society with the accompanying contemporary normative patterns. A careful study of her people will reveal the active role of religion in all phases of life and customary law.

Proverbs

The proverb is a very important literary form. It is an esoteric statement, a succinct assertion, or an evaluation of a situation, an epigrammatic remark that could be prognostic in its import. "It is an unflattering commentary on society that also provides a rule of thumb for predicting a people's attitude to a given situation."[3]

Africans have an extraordinary number of proverbial sayings and regard knowledge of them as a mark of a true "son of the soil." Proverbs are also a proof of great wisdom and religiosity, hence the saying, "A priest (also a counselor) who understands proverbs soon sets matters right. When the conversation droops a proverb revives it."

Africans love wise sayings, proverbs, adages or idiomatic expressions. They have a saying that proverbs are the palm oil (spice) with which words are eaten. For them, to speak in a literal and direct manner is to be childish. *Atuolu omalu omalu, atuolu ofeke ofeba nofia.* This means that proverbs are used so that the wise might read more meanings into a word and so that the fool might wallow in ignorance.

Folk Tales and Mythology

It is interesting to note the predominant role of the tortoise, as the intelligent trickster, and the crafty, though sometimes well-meaning superstar. What influence does his success have in the peoples' values and ethos?[4] Well, they are a very important source of African philosophy/ epistemology.

What then is African philosophy? It is hard to fit it into a system. It is pragmatic because Africans are very practical. Their philosophy is an offshoot of utilitarianism, which relates the good or the truth to the useful. However, an appeal is often made to both faith and reason. Reality is constituted by various principles, For instance, in African philosophy, recognition is given to an extra-mental world on one hand and a supernatural order on the other.

African philosophy has been described as existentialist because of the emphasis it gives to man and the concrete meaning of human existence. To some it is dualistic due to its explanation of reality in light of two worlds: the world of the living and the world of the spirit. To others, African philosophy is equally teleological in the sense that every agent has a goal, an end, or a purpose in life. It is sometimes determinist because every event is explained from without to a point of sometimes ruling out the possibility of free will. It is also occasionalist because God causes everything; whereas, man only provides the opportunity for God to exercise that causality. It could even be seen as mystical because man can acquire a special super-knowledge beyond what reason or the senses convey to him. This is achieved by some kind of communion (for priests, priestesses, and diviners) or inspiration with the divine or some fundamental cosmic principle. Such knowledge, which is moral, religious in nature, is restrictive, individual, incommunicable, and esoteric.

Chukwu

This means a shared apprehension of the divine. This is precisely where the Africans recognize that religion is the most important institution in politics. Many modern and contemporary Western political scientists, Machiavelli for example, have reiterated this point. "If God did not exist, said Voltaire, it would be necessary to invent him." According to Machiavelli, religion gives a divine sanction to the laws without which the people would have no reason to obey. He continued:

> The observance of divine institutions is the cause of the greatness of Republics—the disregard of them produces their ruin; for where the fear of God is wanting there the country will come to ruin.[5]

This is pertinent to what is taking place in Africa today. We have a disregard for the divine institutions and morals, both of which give divine sanction to the laws without which we have no reason to obey. We also copy the Western styles, for instance, the separation of Church and state, without realizing that these two forms of institutions have not taken root in Africa. The most recent arrival, Western culture, seemingly has had the most profound effect on African life; colonial boundaries and Western-style states, armies, and bureaucracies are found throughout the continent. In reality, these institutions have neither taken root nor produced stability in Africa. Western borders have served mostly to enclose battlegrounds; Western-style army military corps and bureaucracies are corrupt; roads, railroads, and factories stand unfinished, in need of repair, or in disuse. Hence, imperialism transmitted capitalist greed to Africa without capitalist discipline.[6]

Ezinuno

This has a lot to do with the concept of the extended family, life, and hospitality. The extended family is such a part of typical African life that one without his family is like fish out of water. That is why banishment and excommunication are to the African jurisprudence the most severe form of punishment, comparable to the death penalty in the Western jurisprudence. The *Oba* recognizes this fact and respects it. Several African proverbs, that underscore the importance of communal responsibility include:

a. When one finger is soiled with palm oil, it affects the rest.
b. A fly without a kin (advisor) enters the grave with the corpse.
c. Group is power (strength).
d. When people urinate together, it foams.
e. A rational man never bets against his own family.

Amamife

This simply means wisdom. Africans value wisdom greatly. In Igboland of Nigeria, the proverb is much related to *Amamife*, and that is why the wise ones in the communities use proverbs most. As a matter of fact, another phrase for "proverbs" is "wise sayings."

Values are also deeply recognized all over Africa but more so in West Africa than other parts. In East Africa there are other related values that are known as the seven pillars or principles. These values are:

1. *Umoja* (Unity)
   To strive for and maintain unity in the family, community, nation and race.

2. *Kujichagulia* (Self-determination)
   To define ourselves, name ourselves, create for ourselves and speak for ourselves.

3. *Ujima* (Collective Work and Responsibility)
   To build and maintain our community together and make our sisters' and brothers' problems our problems and to solve them together.

4. *Ujamaa* (Cooperative Economics)
   To build and maintain our own stores, shops, and other businesses and to profit from them together.

5. *Nia* (Purpose)
   To make our collective vocation the building and developing of our community in order to restore our people to their traditional greatness.

6. *Kuumba* (Creativity)
   To do always as much as we can in the way we can, in order to leave our community more beautiful and beneficial than we inherited it.

7. *Imani* (Faith)
   To believe with all our heart in our people, our parents, our teachers, our leaders, and the righteousness and victory of our struggle.

Checks and Balances

To act as checks and balances on *the Oba's* power is his cabinet of ministers, namely:

- *Nze*—Priests/Priestesses
- *Ozor*—titled people *Ichie*—Council of elders

Each branch prevents the other from monopolizing power, and they all exercise restraint on the *Oba's* power.

The political system that I am describing would have the African people governed by leaders in the place of rulers. This is not new. For Africa today, it would be a reintroduction to an old system because this is the best government that Africans knew before they were colonized. It worked. For verification, look at how British imperialism derailed the

Oyo Kingdom, which was at its apogee right before the British arrived in Nigeria, in the 18th century AD. The Oyo Kingdom was governed by an Aladdin, whom Frank Willet called "a supreme monarch" in his "Interim Report." For checks and balances Aladdini's power on Alafin had *Oyo Mesi* which was a group of seven counselors headed by the Bashorun (Prime Minister). The composition and nature of *Oyo's* army, it is said, best illustrates the general administration of the Oyo Empire. The *hari* or *Ona Kakanfo,* was in charge of the army.

However, *Afronanism* was best illustrated in the Benin Kingdom under Eweka I, who assumed the throne as *Oba* of Benin in about 1300 AD. The *Oba* conducted affairs through *Uzama* and through the town chiefs known as *Enojie,* who acted as checks and balances on the *Oba's* power. The council of chiefs was directed by the *Iyase,* who was also the special chief advisor to the *Oba.* Caution was taken to make sure that each *Enojie* had his area of jurisdiction so laid out that it was impossible to construct a power base from which revolutionary activity could be launched. Such an arrangement likewise impeded the possibility of succession by an *Enojie* who acted as an administrative local chief of remote towns of the empire. No doubt, this administrative strategy contributed to the Benin Kingdom's extremely long duration in peace and tranquility, in sharp contrast to the post-colonial African countries that repeatedly have been undergoing outbursts of revolution and *coup d'etats.*

The problem with most of the solutions that have been proposed to the African problem so far is that they tend to be superficial. They fail to begin from the roots of African problems. They seem to focus more on the symptoms rather than on the cause of the sickness itself. A physician, first of all, studies his patient's medical history in order to get to the root cause of the illness. Most of the solutions that I have seen make little or no reference to African history. Such scholars study Africa the way it is today and begin to define and dissect its political and economic problems without a historical context.

Many factors contribute to the problems that we have in Africa today, but the most devastating of all is the corruption of rulers. Naturally, Africa is not a poor continent. It can be self-sufficient if the leaders were not corrupt and selfish. Zimbabwe has proved this notion right.

Former British Prime Minister Margaret Thatcher once stated that the International Monetary Fund must not be compassionate with Nigeria because she claimed to know of two or three Nigerians who could settle the Nigerian debt from their personal bank accounts in London. The irony is that one of those Nigerians was Imaru Dikko, our former Finance Minister, who ran away from Nigeria to England with over two billion dollars. He captured the world news headlines when the Nigerian government captured him and put him in a crate in an attempt to smuggle him back home to face questioning. Unfortunately, British customs officials aborted this plan. It was a national disgrace to Nigeria; however, the incident brought a special awareness of corruption as the main cause of African problems during and after the Cold War.

It is not that Africans are innately corrupt. Instead, corruption is a legacy of Western colonization. Africans have always reacted so negatively to the foreign administration that they cannot stop even after their independence. In other words, nepotism, corruption, embezzlement, and coups have always been the African ways of fighting the foreign government that have alienated them. Therefore, Africans need an African system that is receptive of contemporary progress yet purely African. The tradition and custom is that any true African with African blood cannot abuse Africa deliberately. An African proverb states that sin has a pancosmic effect, which means that the citizens would all encourage each other to abide by the rules and regulations since one man's sin could ruin the entire land.

If *Afronanism* has worked for Africa in the past, it can work today, provided that we take into consideration the complexities of life today. I mean that Africans must continue to be as innocent as the dove but as wise as the serpent. Since no man is an island, the Africans must decide what to assimilate from the rest of the world and what not to. Africa cannot afford to compromise our precious and unique values. The African concept of the family has been cited as the best in the world and it is already being copied by foreign cultures. The *Oba* realizes this because he is very prudent. He is also selfless; thus, emptying the national treasury into his personal Swiss Account is out of the question. He is what Chinua Achebe describes as "a man of the people." His subjects love him. Therefore, coups are very rare and in most cases nonexistent. The *Oba* is advised by three groups of people, the priests, the titled people and the council of elders.

With this system, Africans will neither worry about who lobbies on their behalf in Washington, D.C., nor about corruption in their seemingly foreign governments any more. Instead, they will begin to manage what is rightfully theirs for the benefit of their own people. Africa can prosper without foreign aid. Africans can trade natural resources (not blood) in exchange for Western technology. They can buy Western expertise as the Japanese did. The only difference would be the fact that Africa has more resources, friendlier climate, and harder-working people. Most importantly the rest of the world has so much more to learn from Africa.

I recognize that all of Africa is not equally blessed with natural resources; hence, the next task of the *Obas* would entail a unification or cooperation of different African regions for economic purposes under the guidance of O.A.U. An example of such economic cooperation of some African countries in existence already is the Economic Community of West African States. My theory indicates that the latter would have been more successful than it is now had it re-introduced *Afronanism* before the economic unification of those West African countries. Today, the ECOWAS is like the Biblical "pouring of new wine into an old wine skin."

Conclusion

What Africa needs in this post-Cold War era, when every other continent/country is being liberated, is not any sort of dependency in the form of foreign aid. Africa has enough to be economically and politically independent, if only Africans do not mismanage these resources and if African leaders are not corrupt. However, corruption will never cease in African nations until Africa rediscovers *Afronanism*, a political system that is not only indigenous to Africa, but is in our blood. If Michael Jordan excels in the way that he plays, why ask him to abandon his style and play like Larry Byrd? African forefathers handed *Afronanism* to their ancestors, and true Africans would consider it abominable to abuse it. Like one African proverb says, "The dog does not eat a bone that is hung on his neck."

We have been following the school of thought known as Romantic Gloriana, whereby the African concept of civilization is determined by the Western standard. I am, on the contrary, calling on the Africans to join the other African school of thought known as Romantic Primitivism, which insists that African ways of life be determined according to the traditional African values.

The most direct example of the failure of western ways in Africa is Nigeria. Like Saudi Arabia, Nigeria is one of the major suppliers of crude oil to the USA. Nigeria is the seventh largest oil-producing nation in the world after (1) Saudi Arabia (2) Norway (3) Iran (4) Russia (5) United Arab Emirate and (6) Venezuela. Ninety percent of Nigeria's export is oil. Nigeria is one of the leading OPEC countries. Nigeria has exported oil for up to thirty years, yet it does not have much to show for it today. Nigeria exports over 1.69 million barrels of oil per day, yet it has nothing to show for it. Why? What happens to the money? Why are the citizens so impoverished? Why is Nigeria so backwards that annual per capita income is only about $200?

To make matters worse, Nigerian citizens, especially in the south, face perpetual fuel scarcity. A majority cannot afford fuel at all. Why is there such a fuel scarcity in one of the leading petroleum-producing countries of the world? The answer is that the leaders are so inefficient, so inept, so ignorant, so selfish, and so corrupt that they cannot provide it. The reason why the masses are so impoverished, in spite of the huge daily oil sales, is because the leaders are so corrupt and so insatiable. They continue to embezzle and stock the oil wealth for themselves in major banks around the world at the expense of the impoverished citizens.

Ken Saro-Wiwa, a prominent Nigerian activist from the Nigerian oil delta area, was hung "for spearheading tribal protests against oil development." Oil workers and employers are often taken hostage even very recently. At one point, "more than 20 Ijaw youths protesting for greater control over their oil wealth were shot down by soldiers." As I said, "peace, unity and tranquility will not be found in that part of the world," until a "fair share" of the oil proceeds goes to the area from which oil is drilled in Nigeria.

To make matters worse, affirmative action has been going on in Nigeria from independence to the present day. That is a process through which the oil money from the south is used to give a lot more jobs and scholarships to the northerners at the expense of the south in order to compensate them for the number of years during which they (the northerners) were less likely to go to Western schools than their southern counterparts due to the Arabic/Islamic influence.

Instances abound of how greed and corruption have been the bane of Nigerian life. General Sani Abacha, a Nigerian head of state for about four years, died suddenly in June of 1998. A few weeks later, his widow was arrested at the airport while attempting to leave the country with twenty-three suitcases of cash. Her husband, General Abacha, is said to have funneled not less than $2 billion into his foreign bank accounts.

In the mid 1980s, some Nigerians were arrested in one of London's airports because they were trying to smuggle Mr. Umaro Dikko, another Nigerian fugitive, by crate back to his country. Further investigations revealed that the fugitive was once a Nigerian federal minister who took a total of about $3 billion from the Nigerian government into Great Britain for himself. He got away with it. He went back to Nigeria after a few years, and he was forgiven without being asked to replace the money that he stole. He has even run for public office since then.

The majority of African countries are very poor and small. For example, there are more black men in American prisons than there are people in Gambia, a West African country. A majority of African nations are so poor that many American corporations such as GM, IBM, Coca-Cola, and many more, have more money than many of them. However, the heads of state of those African nations rank among the richest people in the whole world. As a matter of fact, many African leaders such as the late Mobutu Sese Seko of Zaire had more money than several African countries. *Afronanism* will certainly eradicate corruption in Africa. Another political system that will surely function as effectively as *Afronanism* in Africa is "an amalgamation" of the church and state. This is not new. Africans have always had it and it has always favored them. It is a type of theocracy, but not exactly the kind that one would find in most Moslem countries. It is unique. It is purely African. It is described in most African history books. The chosen political leader must serve as the people's religious leader at the same time. This gives divine sanction to the law. When divine sanction is genuinely found in the Laws, Africans will obey them because they rank among the most religious people on earth. I repeat, without God, religion or divine sanction, Africans would have no reason to obey the laws and desist from corruption. I am not the first to make this point, and I will not be the last. Voltaire made a similar point a long time ago. Machiavelli similarly observed in *The Prince* that observance of divine institutions is often the cause of greatness of Republics and their disregard produces destruction. Where the fear of God is wanting, he continued, there the country will come to ruin.

The Burkean Critique of the British Destruction of Nigerian Institutions

Who is Edmund Burke?

Edmund Burke (1729-1797) was educated (partially) at Trinity College in Dublin and ended up as a member of the British Parliament from 1759 until 1794. He was a great advocate of natural law theory and of human rights. He criticized vehemently the English destruction of foreign institutions, especially the legal and religious institutions of English colonies. Like John Locke, Burke believed in each individual's basic and inalienable rights to life, liberty, and property. According to Burke, the government's role is to ensure these rights. Burke advocated the political equality of all men and women and held that ultimate political authority should reside with the people.

Nigeria was an English colony until 1960. The English destroyed a great number of Nigerian institutions, including the country's religions, laws, and family-structures.

I will be presenting here Edmund Burke's critique of the British destruction of Nigerian institutions with a particular reference to legal institutions.

Estrangement of the Nigerian Legal System

There is a problem in British Africa: a problem peculiar to many of the former British colonies. This problem is the tendency of these countries to hold tenaciously to the common law, equity, and statutes of general application even after they have gained their independence. One might note that the British devised a strategy of making their colonies continue to depend on them despite their autonomy. The law has been no exception, especially since the law and politics move *pari passu.*

In a nutshell, legal decisions in Nigeria prior to the advent of the Europeans to the interior of West Africa at the beginning of the 19th century were customary and traditional. Things began to fall apart from the first moment of colonization. Lagos, the former capital of Nigeria, became an extension of London and thus in great part subject to and under the jurisdiction of England.

The Nigerian traditional judiciary was ignored and for survival became depressingly influenced by colonial masters. The country's independence, sad to say, brought little or no drastic change, not in the least because the country lacked the schools in which indigenous lawyers could be trained. Lawyers and judges went to England and returned home with English values and attitudes.

Burke proposed the Natural Law Theory as the Best Rule of Law

As a strong natural law theorist, Edmund Burke acknowledged people's possession of natural rights. The rights of men, he wrote, are indeed sacred things, and if any public measure is proved mischievously to affect them, the objection ought to be fatal to that measure (*Inork* 11, 437). He adhered to the Aristotelian-Thomistic doctrine of the state as a natural and divinely sanctioned institution. He seriously opposed the English adherence to legal positivism because, he emphasized, it dissolves the bonds of civil society. It is not a return to nature but instead, an action against nature. In his *Letters on a Regicide Peace* (*Inork* 11, 407), Burke wrote concerning the natural law, "Never, no, never did nature say one thing and wisdom say another."

Burke advocated and respected as authoritative "the judgment of the most poor, illiterate, and uninformed creatures upon earth." Politics should be adjusted not only to human reasoning, but also to human nature, of which reason was but a part and by no means the only part.

Similarly, Nigerian traditional rule of law stems primarily from religion and natural law. This traditional law has always clashed with legal positivism for a number of reasons, especially its separation of law from religion and morals.

Natural Law

> There is a law, not written, but born within us, which we have not learned or received by tradition, or read, but which we sucked-in and imbibed from nature itself, which we were not trained in, but which is ingrained in us.[7]

Edmund Burke implied that the natural law is connected with religion, but it is not always so. Natural law theory can be described as a school of thought that maintains that law is reason, or rather, that we can identify the law (or what it means to be human) through human reason. However, how can we agree on what is reasonable in a pluralistic era where there are no shared fundamental premises for critical judgment? A concrete example is the case of abortion, *Keeler v. Superior Court* (1970) 2 Cal. 3d 619, 470 p. 2d 617, in which there is no reasonable means of determining when life begins or what it means to be human.

Another reason why people question the idea of "follow your reason," which is encouraged by the natural law theory, is that it leads to subjectivism, a theory of knowledge that claims that it is impossible to know anything for certain and consequently there can never be an absolute and objective method of testing the truth or falsity of any standard.

For many ethnic groups in Nigeria, the main application of natural law is to seek good and avoid evil. That everyone wants happiness is a law ordained by nature, even though different people have different ways of seeking it, for example with suicide. This is the reason, as we shall see, why a plea of social background, like the insanity defense in the West, exonerates some criminals in many African countries. Most Africans believe that no one seeks evil consciously because man's nature is basically good. *Mma-du,* the Igbo term for man, means, "let there be goodness" or "there is goodness." The same Igbo word means "person."

Some Anglo-American natural law theorists distinguish three main levels of inclination that are the roots of natural law precepts. First, the inclination to self-preserve, expressed in the natural tendencies to eat and to defend oneself. Second, the inclination shared with animals to preserve one's offspring. Third, Man's natural attraction to the good.

> The observation of external things reveals in nature a hierarchy of orders: the mineral, the vegetable, the animal order, each serving its own and, at the same time sub-serving each higher order

In his fifth argument for the existence of God, St. Thomas makes a similar point: we see inorganic objects operating towards an end, but they have no knowledge or intelligence, which means that they cannot tend towards an end unless directed by one who is intelligent as "the arrow is directed by the archer." Therefore, there must exist an intelligent being by which "all natural things" are directed to their appropriate ends: a being, he concluded, that Christians called God.

The natural law, therefore, is not for man alone but also for both animals and vegetative life. The only difference is that man has reason and free will to choose either to abide by the laws or not. Animals act by instinct. Inanimate beings fulfill their functions by "chemical attractions and physical propensities." The important thing to stress in this idea of natural law is that it is not made known to us by feeling or moral sense. Natural law, for us, is promulgated by what is specific to our nature, reason.

The misapplication of natural law to legal decisions is exemplified by a statement made in the mid 1700s by Johann Friedrich Blumenbach, a German anthropologist that was quoted in 1958 by the original trial judge in a Virginia case:

> Almighty God created the races white, black, yellow, malay [sic] and red, and he placed them on separate continents. But for the interference with his arrangement there would be no cause for such marriages. The fact that he separated the races shows that he did not intend for the races to mix.
>
> —*Loving Et Ux. V. Virginia*, 388 U.S. 1 (1967).

Legal Positivism

Legal positivism is interpreted to hold that a law is a rule laid down by those in power to control the behavior of people. When are the commands of one in power supposed to be obeyed, asked Africans, according to this school of thought? What are the criteria for determining when the authority's commands are laws? What about the case in which a ruler gives directions or orders to his/her teammates on a soccer field, to the members of his/her household in the dining room, or even from a washroom? These are some of the problems yet to be resolved by this school of thought before winning Burke and Africans to its side.

Burke maintained that natural rights have their origin independent of positive law. Conversely, positive rights can be seen as stemming from the positive law itself. These rights are part of a system in which a sovereign or his agent promulgates regulations that establish rights and duties.

Legal positivism is associated with modern liberalism. One of its major proponents is Thomas Hobbes, who wrote that strong power in the state should be absolutely invested in the sovereign. Hence, the validity of any rule is in the declaration of it by the sovereign, and this makes the will of the sovereign the only source of law. Hobbes tried to prove this by indicating that there is no law in the state of nature where there is no ruler. Customary laws, he maintained, are good insofar as the sovereign recognizes them. Judges and legislators are both subject to the sovereign. Why, then, do judges, for example, interpret laws instead of the sovereign?

Burke, on the other hand, focuses most on natural right. He opposed the "divine right of Kings." He was also opposed to Hobbes' claim that subjects have no rights unless they are given them by the sovereign. For him there should be limitations to the power of government. Individuals have the right to realize themselves and relate to others. He considers it rather inconsistent with the law of nature to enslave oneself or not to have any power at all. He believes that everyone has inalienable rights. The colonized man, for example, has got the right not to be sold into slavery by his masters even when the masters may wish to do so.

Revolution is encouraged whenever the government decides to interfere with the subjects' inalienable rights. Every government must have procedural limits, publish them to the people, require judges' decisions to be in accordance with existing laws, and use force solely to enforce laws or to defend against a common enemy.

David Hume, a proponent of legal positivism who is also associated with modern skepticism, attacks the natural law theory. He even sees reason as subservient to passion because reason confuses the following factors: particularity and universality, cause and effect, and the claim by natural law theory that there is necessary truth about human nature. That the sun came up this morning is not a necessity, but a mere contingency. There is nothing that makes it absolute. Reason is a slave of passion and should serve it. Reason, therefore, cannot be the source of moral good since the latter is supposed to be derived from the moral sense, which enables us to feel satisfaction. Hence, we should always obey the law, neither as a matter of reason nor as a matter of obligation but as a matter of self-interest, since obeying the government is to everyone's advantage.

Any description of legal positivism is incomplete without a mention of analytical jurisprudence, which is mostly associated with John Austin, who emphasized or echoed the following aspects of analytical jurisprudence: that laws are commands of human beings, that there is no necessary connection between laws and morals, that we should be concerned with the analysis of legal concepts independent of historical and sociological contents, that there are pre-determined legal rules, and that moral judgments being assertions can never be established as true. Austin's fundamental stance is the substitution of the command of the sovereign for justice. He defined law as a rule to be followed reasonably and set forth by one who has power. This means that even the customary law, for example, is only so when it is enforced. It also means that we should never relate law to goodness or badness.

For Austin, there are only two kinds of law: the first is what he refers to as "law properly so called." This is the law set by a political superior or by such an authority as the legislature. "Laws properly so called" also includes any rules and regulations set by private individuals, for instance, making an enforceable contract with another. The second kind of law is called "law improperly so called." This includes any rule that is not commanded by superior, say scientific laws. Even international law falls within this category since there is no one to enforce it. Every law that deals with morals and ethics should not be studied as an integral part of the law but rather as official sanction. Hence, there are four main qualities of any true law: command, duty to follow the command, sanction, and sovereignty.

Austin disagrees with Wesley Hohfeld's statement that there is right where there is duty. The sovereign has no limit except when he is acting as an individual. Thus, Austin does not only analyze law "as it is" (which tends towards neglecting law as good or bad) but he also attributes preeminence to sovereignty.

One of the most controversial features of legal positivism is its separation of law from morality. Among all of the schools of thought supporting the separation of law from morals, legal positivism appears to Burke as the most persistent, vehement, and outstanding advocate whose influence has greatly affected the entire field of law and the judicial process in particular. With this system, only the civil law is recognized as law, and once a given rule has gone through the law-making process, it acquires all of the validity of a law even without any moral consideration or perhaps public consent. For the legal positivists, law has no moral, ethical, or religious connotations. "Law is what it is in practice, and not what it ought to be in principle." Thus, they argue for the separation of law and morals.

On the other hand, Nigerian traditional law is quite inseparable from religion and morals because they all intertwine and coalesce to constitute life and fundamental human values. Burke argued for the latter repeatedly.

One of the natural law theorists who attempted to reconcile natural and positive law was Pufendorf. In his view, natural law was a supplement, a support not a source, of positive law. His contribution lies in the development of a systematic natural law based on the relationship of law to human action. He regarded human action as a composition of moral and natural actions. The moral includes actions for which we are responsible. The natural embraces the rest. He differed with Burke and Aquinas by maintaining that natural law is not a matter of divine ordinance. It is simply human reason issuing imperatives like, "do well," or "treat others as you would want them to treat you."

Pufendorf s guides for formulating laws are "self-preservation" and "the need for assistance from others." Our laws are expression of these because everyone has a natural drive for self-preservation and the achievement of the common good. The natural law, he agreed with Burke, is such because it reflects basic principles of our nature: self-defense, honoring obligations, equality, restitution, the necessary rule of action (choosing the lesser of two evils), and the development of human beings.

In order for natural law to qualify as law, its proponents have singled out its characteristics. Consequent upon their understanding of reason, they regard the natural law as universal, perpetual, immutable, easily knowable, and innate. As is the case with most people who talk about reason, natural law theorists concern themselves with "normal" individuals in "normal" conditions.

Ex Pluribus Unum

Prior to the "creation" of Nigeria by Great Britain, Nigeria had about 250 ethnic groups with as many languages and ways of life. Every "tribe" had its own legal system and moot trials according to its culture. For example, *Shar'ah* courts prevailed in the Muslim areas (North). Pragmatically speaking, it worked!

In the name of unity, Britain, all of a sudden, abolished indigenous legal institutions and introduced one centralized legal system with its source as the British Common Law, Equity, and Statutes of General Application. This, of course, was contrary to Edmund Burke's repeated argument for the position that each of the British colonies should be allowed to exercise its inalienable human right in a reasonable way. This, Burke realized, could entail making their own laws in accordance with their own ways of life. A law does not have to originate from the sovereign or from the queen since, according to St. Thomas Aquinas, one of Burke's most favorite philosophers; law is simply an ordinance of reason.

Has the removal of the criminal law from the jurisdiction of the customary courts really helped in the unification of Nigeria? No! Nigerian ethnic groups do not have to have much in common in order to be faithfully united under one government. Rather, disintegration and resentment of the central government has occurred as the government has stripped every ethnic group of its institutions. Unity thrives where ethnic diversity, individual peculiarity, and uniqueness are respected. That is unity in diversity. Unity does not mean uniformity. Rather, because unity entails an entering into union by people with differences, it is characterized by tolerance, accommodation, and the freedom of individuals to be themselves. This is the profound sense of the motto: *ex pluribus unum.*

The removal of criminal matters from the jurisdiction of the customary courts was nothing short of an attempt to integrate the English adapted law and the Nigerian indigenous law. Undoubtedly, there is a host of problems that stem from the differences among "tribal" laws. However, these rest upon more fundamental questions: How much unity can a nation have and still have diversity? How much diversity can a nation have and still have unity? Clear-cut answers to these questions are lacking, but one thing is certain from experience: any integration sought at expense of the legal plurality in Nigeria is bound to cause more harm than good. The underlying reason is that Nigeria, with its 250 languages and cultures, is one of the most heterogeneous nations in the world. Diversity, therefore, is of the country's essence, an integral part of its nature culture. Consequently, the suppression of diversity in the name of ideological unity is bound to be dangerous, just as an over-emphasis upon ethnicity can endanger a national consciousness. In the United States, a national poll indicated that well over 50% of Hispanics considered themselves to be Hispanics first and American second. The irony, of course, is that their loyalty is not to a country that employs and protects them, but to a culture. There is no nation of Hispania. Further evidence of this trend is the refusal of many whose native language is not English to learn the country's official tongue. My former professor Kreyche once wrote that: The partisan pushing for bilingual programs where English and our general culture take second place seems a travesty. This is now pretty well regarded as a hindrance to the education of children. In Chicago alone, well over 60 percent of the Hispanics who enter high school never finish. This is scandalous. Many ought to examine their consciences and ask: which comes first, preservation of what is now a foreign culture or the well being of children in a newly adopted land?

In our world where mobility is a way of life, cultural problems of this kind are endemic. In Nigeria, it is different; there is no homogeneity. In Nigeria we are not dealing with an influx of immigrants and aliens into what is a country already unified by language and law. On the contrary, because Nigeria itself as a country is a latecomer, built upon tribal loyalties and customs, it cannot abolish customary law without serious upheaval. Most African leaders know this. For this reason, almost every African country has a pluralistic and mostly dualistic system of law—countries as diverse as the Republic of South Africa and the sub-Saharan and North African lands. A professor of law at New York's Columbia University, A.A. Schiller, pointed to this fact when he wrote that Africa is certainly not the only continent where presently there are states with a plurality of legal systems, but it is clearly the one where this fascinating type of legal structure ought to prevail.

The Case of Congo

Colonization, CIA, Capitalism, and Christianity

The former Republic of the Congo serves as a good example of the nature of the European colonization of Africa. I use Congo for this illustration not only because of the five "C's" for which Congo is known, but to explore the Belgian model of colonization, the perfect application of the method of divide and conquer in Africa by Europeans.

During the scramble for Africa, Europeans partitioned Africa and Belgium colonized Congo. Eventually, a number of African countries began to request and gain independence. This was partly due to inspiration from anti-colonial leaders, such as Kwame Nkrumah of Ghana who preached Pan-Africanism, a belief in the unity of all African peoples.

The Republic of Congo became independent from Belgium on the 30th of June, 1960. Patrice Lumumba (1925-1961) became its first Prime Minister and Joseph Kasavubu was the first President. These two nationalists did not get along with each other, to say the least. As a result, they led different and opposing anti-colonial movements.

Just a few days after independence, the Congolese Army started to revolt against their Belgian Commanding officers. Belgium, as a result, decided to evacuate all Europeans from Congo. Such a move on the part of the Belgians left Congo with no technicians, administrators, or professionals of any kind. Congo had urbanization without technicians or administrators. "Western tastes without Western skills" brought only confusion and tension to the new government.

To make matters worse, Belgium advised the mineral-rich Katanga providence in the Southeast to secede. Led by Moise Tshombe, Katanga proceeded as advised, and there was confusion everywhere. Chaos, rioting, and civil unrest took possession of the entire Congo, just as Belgium had planned it. The United Nations (UN) sent in peacekeeping forces to restore order, to no avail. Lumumba then appealed to Ghana for aid. After that, Lumumba made the most costly mistake of his entire life. That mistake was to appeal further to the Union of Soviet Socialist Republic (USSR), a communist government, for help. Though Lumumba never described himself as a Communist, that last move brought him under the attention and microscope of the United States and the CIA who viewed him as a communist sympathizer. Concerning Lumumba's flirtation with the USSR, CIA director Allen Dulles wrote, "Consequently, we conclude that his removal must be urgent and prime objective." Westerners became pro Kasavubu and quickly advised him, as president, to dismiss Lumumba from office. In September 1960, Kasavubu followed Western advice and dismissed Lumumba as Prime Minister. Lumumba returned that favor by lobbying the legislature to dismiss Kasvubu from his own position as the President. The government was deadlocked. Western governments, especially Belgium and the USA, did not get their ways, so they had to try something else. This time, they went to the brim. They advised Army Chief of Staff Joseph Desire Mobutu, later known as Mobutu Sese Seko, to overthrow both Lumumba and Kasavubu. On September 14, 1960, Mobutu did and quickly placed Lumumba under house arrest. Lumumba escaped from house arrest but with tips from foreign secret agents directed by Harold Aspremont Lynden, Belgium's African-Affairs minister who was monitoring his every move, was recaptured and taken to Katanga, which was still under Belgium's control, in January 1961. It is still not known who gave the order, but it was announced in February 1961 that Lumumba was brutally murdered and his flesh mutilated beyond investigation. The next step was to destroy the evidence. Four days later, Belgian Police Commissioner Gerard Foete and his brother cut up the body with a hacksaw and dissolved it in sulfuric acid. In an interview on Belgium television last year Foete displayed a bullet and two teeth that he claimed to have saved from Lumumba's body.

With Patrice Lumumba gone and Mobutu, a Western installed leader in charge, the Soviet threat was minimized from that region. The West did all that it could to preserve Mobutu's regime from any coups until the Cold War between communism and capitalism came to an end with the coming down of the Berlin Wall in 1989. The West had no more use for Mobutu and they allowed him to be overthrown in May 1997 by Laurent

Desire Kabila, a supporter of Lumumba who had helped declare Lumumba a national hero and martyr in 1966.

In summary, there are two issues involved in this chapter:

1. Whether or not Nigeria should apply its diverse "tribal" and religious laws differently and still stay united

Britain, of course, forced Nigeria into a mono-legal system; needless to say, the system was Britain's. It never worked, and it still does not work because of:

a. Nigeria's heterogeneity (language, religion, and cultural differences), and
b. The rule of non-transferability of the law.

To me, the solution is *ex pluribus unum.*

2. Whether or not Nigerian legal reasoning should stem from the natural law theory, according to Burke and African culture, or from legal positivism, according to Britain and John Austin

Nigeria

As effective as legal positivism may have been in England, it violates and ruins the very essence of African jurisprudence due to its separation of law from religion and morality. This system, in the language of Edmund Burke himself, will continue to alienate the Africans. Burke predicted this hundreds of years ago. He was right. It did alienate Africans. It still does. Alienation means estrangement which makes Africans feel like strangers regarding their own laws. It is this lack of internalization and ownership of the law by Africans that impels them to disobey it through bribery and corruption; after all, the separation of law from nature, religion and moral can only make it abstract and impersonal.

The civilian democratically elected administration of Shehu Shagari came into power under the platform of the National Party of Nigeria, NPN, which was one of the five political parties registered by FEDECO for the 1979 elections. Though the country operated a presidential system of democracy this time around (as different from the Westminster parliamentary system of the First Republic —— Sir Abubakar Tafawa

Belewa) the Shagari administration saw the need to carry along without the official support and cooperation of some of the other political parties. It therefore signed a record of cooperation with the Nigerian Peoples Party, NPP, under the leadership of Dr. Nnamdi Azikiwe. The accord was, however, short-lived and soon was when the two parties disagreed on some political issues.

When Shagari came into office in October 1979, Nigeria's economy was relatively buoyant and the general level of prices in the economy was relatively all right. The Shagari administration inherited some handsome external reserves from its predecessor. Some two years after its coming to power, the strains of the high cost of running a democratic government coupled with apparent failure of the ruling party to diversify the nation's economic base which all along had been over dependent on oil revenue, began to show markedly. The situation was now helped by the evident lavish lifestyles and alleged anti-economic activities of some of the NPN top party officials and some top government functionaries which the President failed to put a check on. Meanwhile, the national monthly import bills continued to increase month after month, while both the federal and state governments continued with their plans to obtain various domestic as well as foreign loans to enable them to implement their electoral promises to the people—a need which was made even more expedient by the fast approaching general elections of 1983.

By 1982, it became obvious that for the administration to survive through its tenure economically, something must be done to check the nation's fast dwindling foreign reserves. Shagari's answer to this challenge was his sponsoring of an Economic Stabilization Act in 1982 which empowered his administration to introduce various austerity measures to check the sliding trend of the national economy. As a result of the act, import licensing came under strict rationing and the importation of certain foreign goods into the country was out rightly banned. Efforts were also directed by the government at reviving agriculture and agro-based industries as a means of supplementing the nation's food importations. But each of these measures was either too late or faced sabotage from unpatriotic Nigerians and their foreign collaborators. To make matters worse, the nation's earnings from oil were no longer stable enough to guarantee the servicing and repayment of the numerous foreign loans secured by the federal as well as the state governments, some of which had already begun to mature for repayment.

Furthermore, the political situation in the country during the first term of the Shagari government was far from peaceful. Since after the severing of the NPN-NPP accord of the early life of the Shagari administration, the other political parties in the country began to experiment on possible inter-party alliances aimed at forging a common "progressive" front against the ruling party who they all blamed for the bad shape of the economy.

If the deteriorating economic situation in the country prepared the ground for Shagari's eventual overthrow by the army, the turbulent general elections of 1983 could be said to have provided the last and loudest excuse for the military's intervention on the New Year eve of 1984. The NPN, the party of the government in power, was heavily criticized by all other parties of collusion with the FEDECO (under retired Justice Victor Ovie Whiskey) to return the Shagari administration to power in the August 1983 election, for a second term through electoral malpractice. Also, the governorship elections in some states, particularly Ondo, Oyo, Bendel and Anambra, were very turbulent, and their election results when declared by FEDECO in favor of the NPN met with widespread protests and violent demonstrations leading to the loss of many lives. Chief Akin Omoboroiowo of the NPN, who was declared winner in the gubernatorial election of the pro-UPN Ondo state, had to go into hiding after the FEDECO declaration, apparently to avoid the wrath of the demonstrators. Chief Obafemi Awolowo, the leader of the Unity Party of Nigeria, UPN, described the results of the presidential and governorship elections in the same states as "blatant and brazen daylight robbery."[8] Some of the election results were ultimately challenged in the courts and several of them were nullified on the grounds of electoral malpractices.[9] The depressed economy of the nation saw no improvement during Shagari's second term, which began in October 1, 1983. Widespread commodity shortages, continuously rising level of prices and increasing external debts still characterized the national economy. Therefore, on New Year's Eve of 1984, barely three months into Shagari's second tenure, Major General Muhammadu Buhari toppled the Shagari government through a military coup. Buhari blamed his predecessor for presiding over a corrupt, inept, and insensitive" regime, which increasingly had become "the source of immorality and impropriety"[10] in the country. This brought to a sad end the nation's first experiment with presidential democracy.

Nigerians generally welcomed General Buhari's military regime with great enthusiasm. The expectations of the people from the new government was also very clear as outlined in an editorial by the *New Nigerian* newspaper:

> But by far the most important challenge facing the military administration (of Buhari) is how to revive the economy . . . huge debts have to be paid, essential commodities have to be provided, drought has to be managed, prices have to come down, factories have to reopen and employment raised.[11]

The administration soon set up military tribunals to try the ex-politicians and government functionaries of the ousted civilian administration. Several of the ex-politicians were convicted of embezzlement and abuse of office and as a result they were clamped into jail and their property impounded. Some of these convicts received as much as three, 20-year jail terms to run concurrently. Hoarding of "essential" commodities such as milk, sugar and rice was declared an act of sabotage against the economy and attracted instant forfeiture of the hoarded items as well as instant detention. Soldiers wandered markets and warehouses to search for hoarded goods, as a measure to ease the unabated shortage of essential goods in the markets and shops.

Buhari's second in command and Chief of Staff, Supreme Headquarters, Brigadier Tunde Idiagbon wore a very tough posture both in his appearance and actions in office. On March 20, 1984, he launched a government sponsored nationwide campaign against all manners of indiscipline, as evidence in the public and private lives of Nigerians. This campaign, fondly called "War Against Indiscipline," (WAI) was by design and execution intended to register on Nigeria from the onset the tough, strict posture of the Buhari/Idiagbon administration in charting the nation's march towards economic recovery. The WAI campaign was launched in five phases with each phase focusing on one or another of the Nigerian national life—queuing culture at public places, work ethics, patriotism and nationalism, corruption and economic sabotage and finally environmental sanitation. Though the campaign against indiscipline has been generally criticized for its lack of adequate planning,[12] it nevertheless did something good on our national psyche by creating the awareness in many Nigerians of the need to make collective and relentless efforts towards nation-building.

To help it implement the WAI campaign, the government promulgated several decrees with some of them proving in the end to be very unpopular. One such dreadful decree was the Miscellaneous Offences

Decree, which specified capital punishment for certain crimes such as pushing of hard drugs like cocaine. As if to prove its seriousness with this decree, the government went ahead, unyielding to widespread public and press protests and pleas, to execute Bartholomew Owo and two other convicted cocaine-pushers under the decree. It did not matter to the government that Owo and his companions committed their crimes before the decree came into effect. This retroactive implementation of the Miscellaneous Offences Decree, which led to the execution of this trio, marked the beginning of overt public disenchantment and loss of confidence in the Buhari/Idiagbon administration.

Decree No. 2 and Decree No. 4, of 1984 were two other decrees of the Buhari regime that met with vehement public denunciation. While Decree No. 2 empowered the Chief of Staff Supreme Headquarters to arrest and detain persons indefinitely without trial, Decree No. 4 which was styled the "press gag" decree, sought to protect public office holders as well as the government from unfavorable press reports. Thus, it became virtually impossible for any true, but unfavorable, press reports on the government or its functionaries to run without offending against Decree No. 4. Thompson and Tunde Irabor, both journalists of the *Guardian* newspaper, became its earliest victims.

Decree No. 2 also had its own region of victims, including the irrepressive, aged social critic, Dr. Tai Solarin who was detained for 16 months for no specified reasons. Apparently, his arrest and detention was as a result of his advice to the government to conclude its corrective assignment within six months and return to the barracks. Damica Rafindadi, a former Nigerian Ambassador, headed the oppressive Nigerian Security Organization, NSO, which was responsible for all arrests and detentions of citizens and of aliens alike under the obnoxious decrees. Meanwhile, public outcry for the repeal of these nefarious decrees continued inspite of the government intransigence. Nigeria's Nobel Laureate Wole Soyinka's brave remarks in an interview with *Punch* newspaper depicted the public's disenchantment with the Buhari government. According to Soyinka, "Criticizing the present (Buhari) military government is like talking to the deaf. This government has made up its mind to be deaf to the anguished cries of our people under the severe repression they are undergoing."[13]

Massive lay-offs of workers in the public sector were yet another unpleasant policy of the Buhari era that unleashed untold hardships on many Nigerians. Decrying the effects of these lay-offs on its numerous victims, especially without their retirement entitlements being paid, Professor Samuel Ahiko, a renowned Nigerian economist, was quoted to have remarked, "Retrenching them, retiring them and harassing them are not the answers to our economic situation as they are not a civilized way of doing things. Retiring a quarter of a civil service means retiring a quarter of Pay as you Earn (PAYE)."[14]

By the time Buhari concluded his first year in office, it became obvious to most Nigerians that he was not the kind of leader Nigeria needed at the time to bring about truly feasible solutions to her economic problems. Many, therefore, saw it as a big relief when the Buhari/Idiagbon regime was ousted in a bloodless coup on the 27th of August 1985, barely 20 months after the Buhari coup dismissed Shagari and his team from office.

Major General Ibrahim Babangida, former chief of army staff in Buhari regime, became the new helmsman to pilot the affairs of the nation. He disclosed his reason for overthrowing Buhari when in his address to the members of the Diplomatic Corps three days after his ascent to power, he indicted Buhari's administration for lack of "cohesiveness and unity of purpose that were indispensable in the fulfillment of the objectives which the Armed Forces had set out as their objectives."[15]

The new President Babangida (for that is the title he assumed) further accused his predecessor of allowing some government functionaries and organizations "to trample on the aspirations and basic liberties of our freedom-loving people."[16] The President then justified his coup as a necessary measure taken and "aimed at the restoration and protection of the fundamental rights and civil liberties of our people, assurance of their security and the improvement of their standard of living."[17]

Babangida wasted no time in implementing the plan, which he said his administration had come to execute. He immediately repealed the obnoxious Decree No. 4 and the other offensive decrees and ordered the release of all persons held in jail or detained under any of the abrogated decrees. The Nazi-like atrocities of the NSO were exposed as journalists were invited to the detention cells and allowed to interview their inmates.[18] All of the ex-politicians jailed or detained since January 1984 by the Buhari administration had their cases reviewed and as a result, some of them like Sam Mbakwe, former governor of Imo state, were set free, while others like Barkin Zuwo, former governor of Kano state, had their long jail terms drastically reduced. Former President Shagari and his Vice President, Dr. Alex Ekweme, who had been under detention without trial since their overthrow in December 1983, were cleared from allegations of abuse of office and were set free. This, however, drew criticisms from some sections of the public and press who faulted the logic of the judgment of acquittal and discharge for Shagari and Ekwueme as something of an absurdity. Some argued that it was difficult to conceive of a situation where an executive president of a democratic government would preside over a corrupt government without himself sharing at least in part in the responsibility for the inglorious actions of some of his lieutenants, for whom he failed to check their excesses while in power. Be that as it may, Babangida endeared himself and his administration to the people by his humane posture on human rights. This, in turn, prepared the ground for the eventual formation of several human rights organizations in the country. The Civil Liberties Organization, CLO, formed in October 1987, by Olisa Agbakoba, a lawyer, opened the floodgate. By June 1992, as many as five other human rights organizations had appeared in the Nigerian scene, including the Gani Fawehimni's Solidarity Association, GFSA.[19] Its leader, Gani Fawehimni, a prominent lawyer, has instituted as many as eight law suits against the Babangida administration, over what he termed its "bad policies and programs." In 1990, Fawehimni was arrested and detained for several months by the government for venturing to organize a public lecture on what he termed an "alternative" to the Structural Adjustment Program, SAP, the cornerstone of Babangida's economic policy.

In September 1986, Babangida introduced his pet economic agenda, the Structural Adjustment Program, SAP, as an answer to the economic problems inherited by his administration. Nigerians, however, received the SAP with mixed feelings right from its inception. The SAP had been sold to the nation by the government, as the only feasible alternative to the much-debated proposed negotiations, for loan from the International Monetary Fund, IMF, by the government. Public opposition to the IMF loan was rife, which stemmed mainly from the stringent conditionality of the IMF, which many regarded as "counter productive." In concrete terms, however, SAP meant a deregulation of the economy, a policy whose immediate cardinal effect on the economy was the unprecedented speedy devaluation of the national currency, Naira, against other currencies of the world. The Naira, which hitherto exchange one for one with the US dollar prior to SAP, was exchanging at ₦18 to one US dollar by August 1992. Inflation followed suit at galloping proportions, as prices of both food items and industrial goods shot up. The hardest hit by this economic scenario was the salaried worker, whose pay received no meaningful upward review in line with the SAP-engendered inflation. Minimum wage in many states of the Federation stayed as low as ₦ 250 by May 1992, an amount barely enough to purchase a 2500 gram tin of anchor powdered milk.[20] The extent of the runaway inflation in the economy is typified in the price of a tin of Peak milk, which barely 8 years ago, when Shagari was overthrown, sold for ₦ 0.7 had by July 1992 risen to ₦ 8 per tin.

From his earliest time in office, Babangida clarified his political agenda, which proposed a complete return to civil rule by 1990. He later changed the date to 1992. His transition to a civil rule program provided for a step-by-step return to democracy, beginning from below upwards with the local government elections in 1987. Two political agencies, the National Electoral Commission, NEC, and the Mass Mobilization for Social and Economic Reconstruction, MAMSER, were established to oversee the elaborate transition to civil rule program. The Babangida administration achieved certain political landmarks such as the creation of more Local Government Areas (LGA) and states in November 1991. This brought the number of the local governments in the country up to 554, and his eleven additional new states brought the number of States of the Federation to 30. Two political parties, the National Republican Convention, NRC, and the Social Democratic Party, SDP, were decreed into existence and nurtured initially by the Federal Government as the only two political parties for the country. The NEC, under the chairmanship of Professor Eme Awa, and later under Professor Humphrey Nwosu, had since conducted elections for the local governments, the states, and the National Assembly. The presidential election, scheduled to take place in December 1992, had over 12 candidates in both parties standing for election in the primaries.

The Babangida administration has survived two coups against it since 1986. The latter of these failed coups, led by Major Gideon Okar in April 1990, proved to be the bloodiest coup in the nation's history, with over 70 persons executed amid public pleas for clemency, following the trials of the coup plotters.

Two major factors remain to determine the judgment of Nigerians and history over the Babangida administration when it finally bowed out in 1993. When he annulled the results of a fairly conclusive presidential election that denied Moshood Abiola, the apparent winner, assumption of office, Babangida's decision plunged the nation into political chaos, forcing him to form an interim military-cum-civilian administration headed by General Sani Abacha and Ernest Shoenekan. This uneasy coalition lasted barely two months before Abacha usurped power and imprisoned protesting Abiola to ensure his position. Both Abacha and Abiola died under mysterious circumstances in 1997 and 1998 respectively.

Notes

1. Brian Nelson. *Western Political Thought,* (New Jersey, Prentice Hall, 1982), 113.
2. Chinua Achebe. *Things Fall Apart,* (Connecticut, Fawcett Crest, 1974), 166.
3. T. Okere. *"African Culture,"* A Class Note at Bigard Memorial Seminary, May 1979.
4. Ibid.
5. Niccolo Machiavelli. *The Discourses,* (New York: Random House, Inc., 1950), 148.
6. Ali Mazrui. *The Africans,* (Boston: Little, Brown and Company, 1986).
7. F.P. LeBuffe, *Outline Of Pure Jurisprudence*, (New York: Fordham University Press, 1924), 36.
8. Ibid., 216.
9. Obafemi, Awolowo, "Results Were Day-light Robbery" *National Concord*, (August 19, 1983), 4.
10. Buharis Maiden Broadcast in Radio Nigeria on 1/1/84. Also, *National Concord*, (January 2, 1984), 1.
11. New Nigerian (Editorial), January 5, 1984.
12. Arthur Nwankwor, "Indiscipline Is Systematic Here," *National Concord* (April 9, 1984), 5.
13. Wole Soyinka, (quoted from) Bayo Onanuga (Comp.), "Memorable Quotes," *National Concord*, (August, 28, 1985), 8.
14. Samuel Aluko, (quoted from) Bayo Onanuga, ibid.
15. Ibrahim Babangida, "Address to members of the Diplomatic Corps," *New Nigerian*, September 4, 1985), 2.
16. Ibid., 2.
17. Ibid., 2.
18. See *Vauguard*. (August 31, 1985), 1.
19. See Tony Iyaro, "Like the Mushroom . . ." *Newsweek*, (June 29, 1992), 15.
20. See Wole Oladepo, "The Hard Times," *Newswatch*, (May 4, 1992), 12.

Chapter 10

Igbo Names and Their Meanings

In Africa, the naming of a child is a matter of great importance. Naming is significant because it helps to identify who the child is and where the child will be going in life. The birth of a child in Africa is an occasion of great rejoicing. It is a landmark in the life of the family and a fortunate incident in the collective existence of the community. Numerous considerations influence which name a child is given. The entire continent of Africa considers naming very important though Africans do not share this importance for all of the same reasons.

The Yoruba people of Nigeria have a saying: "We consider the state of our affairs before we name a child." Many African names indicate an event or situation that took place around the time of the child's birth. Africans are very religious people. Thus, a family may, through the name given to the child, be saying that they consider the child's coming as a mark of divine blessing. An Igbo example of this would be the name Chukwueneka, "God has dealt kindly with us."

Some African children are given several names. The choice of names may be based on judgments and observations concerning the child. Examples of these are health, birthmarks, circumstances related to the labor, or those circumstances related to the life or the family of the community. Some children have part of their names from the market day on which they were born, such as the name Okonkwo that shows that he was born on the Nkwo market day.

In Ghana, a child is taught that the name he bears was not lightly given to him and that he must bring honor to the name. A proverb that conveys this message is "A great name is the title only of men of noble deeds." To be named after a distinguished person gives the child the responsibility to fashion his character after the individual whose name he bears.

Other African ethnic groups believe that their child is the reincarnated embodied spirit of an ancestor. The child, who is to be considered reincarnated, is given the name of that relative. The family elder or a priest or priestess may recognize a trait, behavior, or the aura of the ancestor in the newborn infant. The family acknowledges the family member seeking rebirth in the body provided.

A few days after I was born my parents consulted a *dibia* (native doctor) to find out which of their ancestors has come to life again for the first time in the for of their child. My parents were meant to understand that their little baby boy was no one other than the late Nnamani Oke Aneke, my material grandfather. My mother became congested with excitement as she knew that I would be named accordingly, that is, after her very own father. My name was determined as of that day. The fact that I was a reincarnation of my late grandfather was never a secret. Such is considered to be public or communal information. What is never disclosed to anybody, not even to parents, is the number of times one has come to life out of the seven times that one is allowed to return to life (reincarnation) in the Igbo ethnic group.

The Hausa are predominately a Muslim people in West Africa. Their children are given Muslim names and nicknames that may refer to an object, a physical trait, the sequence in which they were born, an event coinciding with the time of birth, or wishes for good health and fortune.

Among the Swahili-speaking people of East Africa, a child is named immediately after birth by an elderly relative or the midwife assisting the delivery. This "childhood name" is somewhat like a nickname that may describe circumstances at the time of birth (Chuke meaning "hatred"), their physical appearance (Panya meaning "mouse" or "tiny"), or their health (Mwatabu meaning "child of sorrow," which refers to trouble in the family or in the birth itself). Seven days after birth, the child is given his adult name usually of Islamic or Biblical origin, and it is always given by the child's parents or paternal grandparents. The oldest boy usually bears the name of his paternal grandfather, and the oldest girl is given the name of her paternal grandmother.

Ceremonies associated with the naming of a child differ from place to place in Africa. The formal bestowing of a name is a very significant event in the child's life. It acknowledges and welcomes the infant as a member of the ethnic group, congratulates the parents, and may make predictions for the child's future. A substantial aspect of the naming ceremony is the role of the aged. The very young and the very old are seen as being very closely connected to each other since the infant has just come from where the aged are preparing to go. Due to this connection, the elder people perform many rituals during the naming ceremony. Some of the rituals preformed may include sprinkling water over the newborn, giving the infant its name, treating the placenta and umbilical cord, or saying prayers.

The naming ceremony of the Yoruba tribe of Nigeria takes place in the parents' house. The ceremony itself is very elaborate, detailed, and precise. Family members and community members attend and always bring gifts. Female relatives and friends present their gifts to the mother, and the males give their offerings to the father. The room is prepared with festive decorations. In the center of the room are containers with water, red pepper, salt, oil, honey, liquor, and kola nuts. The mother gives the child to the elder who will perform the naming ceremony. Water is sprinkled toward the ceiling and on the child. If the child cries when the water is sprinkled on him, it is an indication that the child has come to stay, since only living things can produce noise of their own accord. At this point, the elder whispers the child's name into its ear and then, dipping the tip of his finger into the water and touching it to the child's forehead, announces the name to the rest of the group. Next, the elder puts a little bit of pepper in the baby's mouth to symbolize that the baby will be resolute and have command over the forces of nature. Water is poured in the baby's mouth, symbolizing a wish for his purity of body and spirit and thus his freedom from disease. Then, a little salt is put into the baby's mouth, symbolizing the flavor of wisdom to his lips with the wish that he enjoy power and health like royalty. Honey, then liquor, is touched to his lips, signifying happiness and prosperity. Finally, the infant is given a taste of kola nut, symbolic of the wish for his good fortune. Each of the items is passed around for the people present to partake in as well. The naming ceremony ends, but the festivities of celebrating have just begun. Feasting and dancing may last for hours or days. This is one example of the extensive and honored naming ritual of one African ethnic group.

To conclude, African names carry great weight and importance. It is not merely done on whim or preference. The choice of names may be based on judgments and observations concerning the child, such as reincarnation, health, birthmarks, the circumstances related to the labor itself or the circumstances related to the life of the family or of the community. By just knowing a fellow African's name, another African will already be able to know his tribe as well as some basic information about him. Africans also consider their names to their soul identities. Thus, indeed, it is not until a child has been appropriately named that he is considered a person. In other words, every African name has a meaning and it is quite polite or even endearing to ask an African the meaning of his name.

Some Igbo Names and Their Meanings

A

Adachi	First daughter of God (f)
Adaeze	First daughter of king/queen (f)
Adajie	Her husband's sister (f)
Adaku	Daughter of wealth (f)
Adamma	Queen of beauty (same as Ezeugo) (f)
Adanna	First daughter of the father (f)
Adaobi	First daughter of the home (f)
Adaora	Daughter of the community (f)
Adaugo	Daughter of eagle (of beauty) (f)
Afamefuna	Let my lineage never be lost (f)
Agbakoba	Group is strength (m)
Aghuli	Joy (f)
Aguanuna	Let the lion not fight (m)
Ahanna	In the name of the father (m)
Ajaelo	One who is beyond evil (m)
Ajaero	One who is beyond evil (m)
Ajandu	Sacrifice of life (m)
Akabuogu	The hand is the fight (m)
Akanna	The hand of God (m)
Akuakonam	May I not want (f)
Akubueze	Wealth makes the king/queen (m/f)
Akubuilo	Wealth creates enmity (m)
Akudiuto	Wealth is sweet (m)
Akukalia	Wealth in abundance (m)
Akunesiobike	Wealth strengthens the heart. (m)
Akpunonu	One who never offends (m)

Amachi	Who knows God (m)
Amadi	General rejoicing (m)
Amaka	The beautiful one (f)
Amarachi	Once God is known (f)
Anayo	We pray (m/f)
Anene	Looking up to God (m)
Aniagolu	May the land defend (m)
Anijielo	The land of deliberation (m)
Anike	The land creates (m)
Anochili	The innocent (m)
Anulika	Joy (f)
Anyamele	The eyes see (observe) (m)
Arinzechukwu	The glory of God (m)
Atamuna	Don't bear grudges. (m)
Ayawu (Anyawu)	The sun (m)
Ayilu	Majority (comrade) (f)
Azikiwe	The absence generates anger (m)
Azuka	The absence is great (f)

B

Belonwu	Death surpasses (m)

C

Chekube	Hope in God (*Spera in Deo*) (m/f)
Chiamaka	God is beautiful (f)
Chibuzo	God leads the path (m)
Chibueze	God is king (m)
Chibuogwu	God is the fighter. God leads the fight. (f)
Chi-Chi	God (Goddess) (f)
Chidera	Once God has written (f)
Chidiebele	God is merciful (m/f)
Chidimma	God is good (f)
Chidiuto	God is sweet (f)
Chidubem	May God lead me (m/f)
Chidube	May God lead the way (m/f)
Chiebonam	May God not accuse me (f)
Chiebuka	God is great (m/f)
Chiemeka	God has done good deeds (Thanks be to God) (f)

Chigbo	May God defend (m)
Chigboo	May God prevent evil (m/f)
Chigoo	May God defend (f)
Chigozie	God bless (m/f)
Chijioke	God gives equitably with justice, God gives talent (God is Just) (m)
Chika	God is superior (m/f)
Chikaodili	It's all up to God (m/f)
Chike	Power of God (m)
Chikeluba	God creates wealth (m)
Chilota	May God remember (m)
Chima	God knows (m/f)
Chimauchem	God knows my heart (m/f)
Chimere	God disposes (m/f)
Chimeze	God knows king/queen (m/f)
Chinagolu	God professes my innocence (m/f)
Chinasa	God responds (f)
Chinawaeze	Only God appoints king/queen (God is king maker) (m)
Chinazo	God protects (f)
Chinelo	God plans/ disposes to make it happens/ thought of God (f)
Chinenye	God gives (m/f)
Chinenyendu	God gives life (f)
Chinenyenwa	God gives children (f)
Chineze	God protects from evil/ God defends (m)
Chinoye	God be with us (f)
Chinua	Gods own blessing may God defend (m)
Chinwe	God owns (m/f)
Chinwendu	God owns life (m/f)
Chinweike	God is power (m)
Chinweuba	God is wealth (m)
Chinyere	God gives (grace) (f)
Chioke	Gift of God (m)
Chioma	God is good (f)
Chinyelu	God gives (grace) (f)
Chisomaga	Only God knows (m/f)
Chizimuzo	May God show the way (m/f)
Chizoba	May God guard (protect) (f)

Chuba	God of wealth (m)
Chukusukadibia	God is greater than the priest/prophet (m/f)
Chukwuanugonum	God has heard my voice (m/f)
Chukwuchebe	May God protect (m)
Chukwuchebe	Let God guard (m)
Chukwudi	There is God (God exists) (m/f)
Chukwuebuka	God is great/mighty (m)
Chukwujekwu	God will deliver final judgment (m)
Chukwuma	God knows all (m)
Chuzua	Let God train (m/f)
Chwukwunonso	God is near (m)

D

Daberechi	Lean on God (m/f)
Dike	The powerful one (m)
Dilibe	One for all (m)
Dinobi	One who is in the heart (m)
Dubem	Lead me (God) (m)
Dumebi	God is in charge of my living (m/f)

E

Ebere	Sympathy (m/f)
Eberegbulam	My kindness shall not destroy me (m/f)
Ebubechukwu	Glory of God (m)
Echeumunna	Home of the lineage (m)
Egbeigwe	Thunder (m)
Egonwanne	Brother/sister (sibling) of money (m/f)
Ejike	Not by human power (m)
Ejimnkonye	I owe no one (professes righteousness) (m)
Ejim Ofor	I have justice (m)
Ekele/ Ekene	Thanks (to God) (m)
Ekemma	Beautiful one (f)
Ekene (Dilichukwu)	Let praises be to God (m)
Ekwonaka	Don’t act because you are able (m/f)
Ekwueme	One who does what he says/ one who delivers (m)
Elo	Public place/ gathering place (m/f)
Emeka	Praise be to God (m)
Emenike	Not by force (m)

Enebechi	Looking up to God (m/f)
Eneh	The antelope (m)
Enuwa	The world (m)
Enyi	Elephant (m)
Enyioma	Good friend (m)
Eze	King/queen (m)
Ezedimma	The good king/queen (m/f)
Ezenwa	The king/queen from childhood (m)
Eziechina	Let the lineage not end (m)
Ezenwayi	Queen (f)
Ezimma	The right path (f)
Ezinna	The good father (m)
Ezinne	The good mother (f)
Ezudu	King of *Udu* (oracle) (m)
Ezeugo	King of eagle (same as Adamma) (f)

F

Fuchinanya	Love God (f)

G

Ganiru	Progress (m/f)
Ginikanwa (Nwa)	What is superior to a child? (f)
Golibe	Joy/rejoice (f)

I

Ibeabuchi	No one is God (m)
Ifeakonam	May I not lack (want) (m/f)
Ifeoma	Everything is fine (f)
Ifeama	Right one (also known as Ifeoma) (f)
Ifeanyi	Omnipotent (m/f)
Ifeanyichukwu	God is omnipotent (m)
Ifesinachi	Everything is from God (m/f)
Ifeyinwa	Nothing is like a child (f)
Ifunanya	Love (f)
Igwekamma	Group is better (i.e. two heads are better than one) (m)
Iheoma	The right one (f)
Ijeoma	The right venture (f)
Ikechukwu (Ik)	Power of God (m)

Ikenna/Ikechukwu	Power of God (m)
Ikunna	Paternal home (m)
Ikunne	Maternal home (f)
Ilokansi	Feud is worse than poison (m)
Irobuchi	You don't define me (m)
Iruka	Hope (f)
Iruoma	Good Luck (f)
Isi	Head (m)
Iwe	Anger (m)
Iwuala	Law of the land (m)

J

Jaja	Honored (m)
Jasochukwu	Praise only God (m)
Jideobi	Keep the faith (m)

K

Kambili	Let me live (m)
Kamsi/Kamsiyochukwu	As requested . . . Like I asked God (m)
Kasindu	Full of life (m)
Kelechi/Kenechi	Praise God (m)
Kodioke	What affects one, affects his personal God (m)
Kosisochukwu	As God wishes (m)

L

Lebechi	Look up to God (f)
Lotachukwu	Remember God (m/f)
Lotanna	Remember the father (m)

M

Machebe	Let the spirit (God) protect (m)
Madu	People (m)
Madueke	Humans cannot create (m)
Maduka	Humans are superior (m)
Makuochukwu	Embrace God (f)
Mazi	Sir (m)
Mbadiwe	No is annoying/ refusing is annoying (m)
Mbanugo	The community has heard (m)
Mgborie	Born on Orie market day (f)

Mgbankwor	Born on Nkwor market day (f)
Mgbeke	Born on Eke market day (f)
Mgbafor	Born on Afor market day (f)
Mbanaso	Law of the land (m)
Mbu	The first (m/f)
Mgbechi	God's time (f)
Mukosolu	As I wish (f)

N

Nebechi	Look up to God (f)
Ndidi/Ndidiamaka	Patience is a virtue (f)
Nduka	Life is precious (m)
Ndubisi	Life is primary (m)
Nebolisa	Look up to God (m)
Ngozi	Blessing (f)
Ngozichukwuka	God's blessing is greatest (f)
Ngwu	Holy/sacred tree (m)
Nkechinyelu	The gift from God (f)
Nkechinyere	Gift from God (f)
Nkeiruka	Hope (f)
Nkemakonam	May I not lack (f)
Nkem	Mine (f)
Nkemefula	Let mine not be lost (m)
Nkemdirim	Let mine not be lost/ let mine not be taken from me (f)
Nkemjika	A bird at hand is greater than many in the bush (f)
Nkeonye	To each his own (f)
Nkeoma	The right one (f)
Nkuzi	Teacher (m)
Nmeregini	What have I done? (m)
Nnaemeka	Praise be to God (m)
Nnadi	Father is present (m)
Nnadiuto	Father is sweet (m)
Nnaji	Children of the same father (m)
Nnajiofor	God is just/fair (m)
Nnam	My father (m)
Nnamdi	My father is present, father's name lives on (m)

Nnamani	My earthly father (m)
Nnamigwe	My heavenly father (m)
Nnanna	Grandfather (m)
Nnediuto	Mother is sweet (f)
Nneji	Children of the same mother (m)
Nneka	Mother is superior (f)
Nenna	Her grandmothers look alike (f)
Nkechi	Will of God (f)
Nnengene	Child of spring water (f)
Nenna	Mother of his father (f)
Nneoma	Beloved mother (f)
Nonso	God is near (m/f)
Nonyelum	God be with us (f)
Nwabudike	Son is the father's power (m)
Nwachinemelu	The lucky one / one with God (m)
Nwachukwu	Child of supreme God (m)
Nwadiuko/ Nwaduko	Children are scarce
Nwadinobi	Children are the heart (f)
Nwadiuto	Children are sweet (f)
Nwafor	Child of the third market day (m/f)
Nwagbara	Child of the spirit (m)
Nwakaego	Child is superior to money, more important than money (f)
Nwakibu	You are child (human) (m)
Nwakonam	Let me not lack children (f)
Nwando	Child of the star (f)
Nwandu	Child of life (m)
Nwanagu	A child is a need / everyone wants a child (f)
Nwankwo	Child of the fourth market day (m/f)
Nwangwu	Child of the sacred tree (m)
Nwanne (di namba)	Everyone is related (m/f)
Nwanneka	The relative is superior (f)
Nwanriria	Child of sickness (m)
Nwaokike	Child of the creator (m/f)
Nwaoye/Nwoye	Child of the second market day (m/f)
Nweke	Child of the first market day (m/f)
Nwobodo	Child of the land/community (m)
Nwolisa	Child of God (same as Nwachukwu) (m)
Nwuka	Child of the Sunday (f)

Nzeogwu	One who is beyond evil/devil (m)

O

Obiageli	Child who has come to enjoy (f)
Obiajulu	Mind (heart) has been calmed (f)
Obianuju	One who had come in times of surplus (f)
Obichukwu	The house/heart of God (m)
Obidiago	Sacred heart (m)
Obidimma	The good home (heart) (m/f)
Obidiuto	Sweet home (heart) (m)
Obierika	The home (heart) is great (m)
Obinna	The mind of the father (m)
Obioma	The (generous) good mind/heart (m/f)
Obiora	The heart of the community (m)
Obisike	May the heart be strong (m)
Obodozie	Let the people/ community teach or direct (m)
Obumneme	Am I the cause? (m)
Ochiabuto	Laughter is not happiness (m)
Ochiagha	The leader of war (m)
Ochomma	One who is beauty-conscious (m)
Odenigbo	One who is popular in the land/ one who is in control of the land (m)
Odenigwe	One who is in control of heaven (m)
Odera	Once written (m/f)
Odinkemmelu	What have I done (m/f)
Odinakachuku	It is in the hand of God (m)
Oduu	Tiger (m)
Ofo	Justice (m/f)
Ofobuike	Justice is strength (m)
Ofuruchi	Who has seen God (m/f)
Ogbo	Namesake (m/f)
Ogbodie	One who is like the husband (f)
Ogbonna	One who is like the father, image of his father (m)
Ogechi	God's time (f)
Ogo	Mercy (m/f)
Ogockukwu	God's mercy (m)
Ogoegbunam	Let people not take advantage of my kindness/ Let my mercy not hurt me (m)

Ogonna	Grandfather, father in law (or father's kindness) (m)
Ojijieme	One who is generous with yams / the chief of all crops (m)
Ojiofor	The bearer of justice (m)
Okabonye	Who has it all? (m)
Okafor	Son of the third market day, born on Afor market day (m)
Okechi	The share from God (m)
Okechukwu	The share from God, God's gift (m)
Okenwa	The great child (m)
Okeke	Son of the first day of the week (m)
Okike	Creation (m)
Okochi	The dry season (m)
Okonga	Traditional music (m)
Okongwu	The elderly one (m)
Okonkwo	Son of the fourth market day, Nkwo market day (m)
Okorie	Born on Orie market day (m)
Okoro	A young man (m)
Okoye	Son of the second day of the week (m)
Okpara	First son (m)
Okwudili	It is up to God/ let it be left to God (m)
Okwuejinelo	Discussing a matter peacefully / working out solutions peacefully (m)
Omamma	The beautiful one (f)
Ome	Actor (m)
Omenuko	One who provides when it is scarce (m)
Onyeawuna	Let no one die (m)
Onyedi	One who is like God (m)
Onyedikachi	One who is like God (m)
Onyejietonu	One with (about) whom I brag (boast) (m)
Onyelu	The giver/a giver (m/f)
Onuoha	The voice of the people (m)
Onuora	The voice of the people (m)
Onuwachi	God's world (m/f)
Onodugo	The place of the eagle (m)
Onubuogwu	You don't have to fight with the hand, you can fight with the Tongue. (m)

Onwughalu	Let death/sickness leave me alone (m)
Onuegbu	The mouth never kills (m)
Onwubiko	Death, please don't . . . (m)
Onwudiwe	Death is annoying (m)
Onwukwulueche	Death awaits everyone (m)
Onye Anwuna	Let no one die (m)
Onyema	Who knows it all (m)
Onyebuchi	Who is God (m)
Onyemauche	Who know's God's will? (m)
Onyema (echi)	Who can predict the future? (m)
Onyiye/Onyiyechukwu	Gift (from God) (f)
Onyedikachi	Who is like God? (m)
Okpara	First child (m)
Okparaku	Child of wealth (m)
Orji	*Iroco* (a type of tree) (*Iroko*) (m)
Osisioma	The good/beloved tree (m/f)
Osondu	The fight to save life; one is never exhausted (m/f)
Osufia	The path finder (m)
Oto Narudie	One who grows through her husband (f)
Onyidie	The friend of her husband (f)
Oyiridiya	One who is like her husband (f)
Oyirinwuyeya	One who is like his wife (m)
Oyiludie	One who is like her husband (f)
Ozoemena	Let it not happen again (death) (m/f)

R

Raluchukwu	Leave it to the supreme God (m)

S

Shani	Marvelous (m/f)
Somtochi	Praise God with me (f)
Sopulu Chi	Honor God (m)
Sopuruchi	Honor God (m)

T

Taagbo	It's never too late / today is early (m)
Tabansi	Be patient (m)
Tobe	Praise Him (God) (m)

Tobechi	Praise God (m/f)
Tobechukwu	Praise the supreme God (m)
Tobenna	Praise the father (m)
Tochi	Praise God (f)

U

Uche	The mind (m/f)
Uchechukwu	The Will of God (m/f)
Uchejuna	I have my wits about me (m/f)
Uchenna	The mind of the father (m/f)
Uchechi	The mind of God (m/f)
Uchenwa	The mind of the child (f)
Uchezuike	The mind never rests (m/f)
Udo	Peace (m)
Udodili	Peace be with you (m)
Udodirim	May peace be with me (m)
Ugo	Eagle (m/f)
Ugonna	The eagle from the father (m/f)
Ugochi/Ugochukwu	The eagle for supreme God (created beautifully from God) (m/f)
Udoka	Peace is greatest (m)
Ugonwa	The child of the eagle (The beautiful one) (f)
Uka (Amaka)	Communication (discussion) is good (f)
Ukachi	Discussion from God (m/f)
Ukaegbu	Discussion never hurts (m)
Ukamaka	Communication (discussion) is good (f)
Ujo	Fear (f)
Uloma	The beautiful home (f)
Uwaezuoke	The world is never enough/ the world never satisfies (m)
Unoka	The great home (m)
Unoma	The beautiful home (m/f)
Uwabuaja	The world is dust (m)
Uwakwe	If the world allows (m)
Uzoka	The highway (road) (m/f)
Uzoma	The right way (f)

Y

Yobachi	Pray to God (ask God) (m/f)
Yoolum Chi	Pray to God for me (m/f)

Z

Zahara	Flower (f)
Zelu Njo	Avoid evil/sin (m)
Zikora	Show all (the handy work of God) (f)
Zimuzo	Show me the way (m)
Zobam	Protect me (m/f)

Chapter 11

Proverbs

My interest in African proverbs stems from the fact that it is the most important source of African epistemology. Proverbs are an important literary genre to the Africans. Some have described it as a succinct assertion and others have called it an epigrammatic remark, which could be prognostic in its import.

To the Igbos of South Eastern Nigeria, there is a saying that proverbs are the palm oil with which words are eaten. To speak figuratively and using proverbs is a proof of great eloquence and wisdom. For an adult to speak literally, on the other hand, is like an African without a foofoo, a Chicago winter without wind, a Pope without Latin. It is very didactic and always full of meaning. Proverbs are thought provoking, subject to a variety of interpretations and most suitable for a critical thinker. Finally, it enables the wise to become wiser and helps the naïve and the uninformed to become more confused; hence, most people would describe it as esoteric. And regardless of how it is explained, something that will not change is that Africans love to use proverbs. They admire those who use them skillfully and speeches without them are often considered vapid, tasteless and childish.

Other terms for proverbs include "adages" and "wise sayings." They are like words of wisdom in little capsules with thought-provoking interpretations that lead to critical thinking. This is exactly the reason why proverbs are considered the most important source of African epistemology—a branch of African philosophy.

Igbo Proverbs in English

The following proverbs express the ponderousness of African philosophy and epistemology:

1. He who sees a dead man's mouth sees the folly of not eating what one had in one's lifetime.
2. A man who pays respect to the great paves his way to his own greatness.
3. When a man says yes so does his god.
4. When the moon is shining the cripple becomes hungry for a walk.
5. Looking at a king's mouth one would think he did not suck his mother's breast with it.
6. He who brings kola-nuts brings life.
7. If a child washes his hand he can eat with kings.
8. Let the kite perch and let the eagle perch too. If one says no to the other let his wings break.
9. A toad does not run in the daytime for nothing.
10. The sun will shine on those who stand before it shines on those who sit under it.
11. An old woman is always uneasy when dry bones are mentioned in a proverb.
12. A lizard that jumped from the high iroko tree to the ground said he would praise himself if no one else did.
13. An old woman said, "if the steep hill learns to hurt at the waist and knees, she would learn to walk and rest."
14. If the yam learns to be too hot in the mouth, then the consumer would learn to open his mouth during consumption.
15. Those whose palm-kernels were cracked for them by a benevolent spirit should not forget to be humble.
16. A chick that will grow into a cock can be spotted the very day it hatches.
17. A child's finger is not scalded by a piece of hot yam which its mother puts into its palm.
18. When mother-cow is chewing grass its young ones watch its mouth.
19. If I fall down for you and you fall down for me, it is play according to the dog.

20. A baby on its mother's back does not know that the way is far.
21. If one finger brings oil, it soils the others.
22. Never kill a man who says nothing.
23. Living fire begets cold, impotent ash. Explanation; A child does not always look like any of the parents.
24. An animal rubs its itching back against a tree; a man asks his kinsman to scratch him.
25. A child cannot pay for its mother's milk.
26. The clan is like a lizard; if it looses, its tail it soon grows another.
27. Whenever you see a toad jumping in broad daylight, then something is after its life.
28. Impression without expression is depression.
29. Sin has pancosmic effect.
30. No matter how long the fly keeps flying, eventually, it falls down for the frog to eat.
31. The mother-bed-bug said to the baby-bed-bug, "be patient, whatever is hot will eventually get cool."
32. A child is not disciplined when he ruins the valuable seeds, it's when he ruins the chaff.
33. When the king feeds to his satisfaction, he feels as though his entire community is satisfied.
34. He who is closer to a person is in a better position to perceive his breath.
35. When ukwa fruit is ripe, it falls.
36. Nothing happens before its time.
37. A bad day is not known in the morning.
38. One can only go round a pepper-plant; no one can climb a pepper-tree.
39. A fruit does not fall from the tree.
40. Udala fruit said she is not the only one with a baby whose mouth could be bruised.
41. Whatever distance a runner covers, a walker covers too.
42. If the egg breaks the palm-nut, the stone is disgraced.
43. Whatever that the kite has hatched will never fail to steal chickens. (Like father like son)
44. If a child enquires into what happened to his father too soon, it happens to him too.

45. When an elder falls twice, the content of his bag is exposed to all.
46. The old lady said, "If the hill learns to break the hip, I will learn to rest in between my walk to the top."
47. A perfect "dog-play" entails falling down deliberately for each other.
48. An Igbo man said that since the yam learned to be too hot he has learned to chew it with his mouth open at the same time.
49. The cat will run after he who makes himself like the mouse.
50. I haven't even finished paying the debt I am sure of, let alone the ones that I am not certain of.
51. He who knows that a priest was burned should know that his beard did not survive.
52. When you see a man, you see his manly face.
53. Looking at a man's face you know whether to slap him or not. Explanation; As a man presents himself, so he is treated.
54. One can tell a ripened corn by looking at it.
55. It's a man's countenance that determines whether he should be slapped.
56. He who uses effort does not fall asleep.
57. He who sold his dog and bought a monkey does still have something that squats.
58. The rat said, "he who kills me is not as disdainfully contemptuous as he who asks to see my face after I am killed."
59. A man once said that his anger was not caused by the fact that his wife was seduced, but by what must have been said to his wife about him that made her give in to the seduction.
60. It is by kneeling that a child is breast-fed.
61. Even he who was spoon-fed had to draw his mouth closer.
62. Even the piper has to wipe his mouth once in a while.
63. The dog said she knew right from the beginning that she lacks much stamina and that's why she faced her kneecaps backwards.
64. The chicken said that when she goes to a foreign land she stands with one leg and if others stand with both legs then she does the same.
65. The dog eats feces and the goat's teeth become rotten.
66. He who infers with the bee is stung by it.

67. The chicken said that whatever she chases under the rain must be absolutely important to her.
68. It is only a good path that is followed more than once.
69. If a child throws an elder up in the air, his loincloth covers his face.
70. A short fellow hangs his clothes where he can reach them.
71. A woman can only place the size of her own arm on the husband.
72. You cannot cover a pregnancy with the palm.
73. When a sword cuts a child, he learns to put it in his sheath.
74. When a child roasts a knife on fire, if the knife doesn't cut him, the fire burns him.
75. Would he who has the bee and the mot say he doesn't have what stings?
76. You cannot shave a man's head in his absence.
77. When one takes a child's toy and raises his hand up, the child takes back his belonging whenever the aggressor puts his hand down.
78. When an old lady is asked to be given a baby and she complains that she has no teeth, is she being asked to bite the baby?
79. A child whose hand is filled with meat chases dogs away with a stick.
80. A hen with chicks cannot run from fights.
81. You can't lie down standing up.
82. An elder who eats standing up does he expect the kids to fight as they eat?
83. The knife with a handle is often not sharp and the sharp knife is often without a handle.
84. A child who is given what is beyond him asks, "to whom have I been asked to give this to?"
85. When evil persists, it becomes the custom.
86. A healthy fellow does not know what a leper suffers.
87. A child on the mother's back does not know the distance.
88. He whose life has been blessed by a benevolent spirit feels as though the struggling ones are all crazy.
89. If the land begets a strong cow the land begets a strong man who will arrest it. (when a window is closed, a door is opened somewhere)

90. He who creates a cow will provide it with a tail with which to chase flies away.
91. It is better to win over a case than to win over a fight.
92. If God creates a wild animal it creates a brave man who will tame it.
93. It is wiser to find the dark goat in the daytime before darkness.
94. The stubborn chicken is quiet in a pot of soup.
95. A child who develops elephantiasis as he is being cured of leprosy will soon find what he kept in the evil forest. (cemetery)
96. The deaf do not have to be told when there is pandemonium.
97. A fly without an advisor goes into the grave with the corpse.
98. No one plucks all his fruits the way they are ripened.
99. The tortoise said that in a pandemonium he would kill two people because if anyone else does it would be blamed on him anyway.
100. He who is to eat a toad should eat a fat one so that if he is called a toadeater he might look at it as a badge of honor.
101. He who goes to the toilet at night knows the sleepy flies.
102. The dog that brings a bone carries a bone.
103. Tell me with whom you go and I will tell you who you are.
104. It is by what you say behind others that I know what you say behind my back.
105. When a dog brings a bone, it takes it to the owner.
106. A sleeping goat is lying on its skin.
107. The water in the broken pot awaits the dog. (ones responsibility awaits one no matter the length of delay or procrastination)
108. A day cannot be declared awful until it ends (it is never to late) .
109. He who mistreats a pregnant woman mistreats more than one person.
110. A crab is drowned by (the little amount of water in) the soup after swimming in the oceans and in the seas.
111. People are each other's gods.
112. He who sells his dog and buys a monkey is still keeping a seater animal.
113. A forest that abhors baskets should not grow the mushrooms.
114. He who doesn't eat yams should not have oily lips.

115. He who doesn't steal palm wine should not go around shaking calabashes on palm trees. (He who looks like a duck, walks like a duck, and quacks like a duck is certainly a duck)
116. The goat does not deliver while on a leash.
117. The water kept in the broken pot will continue to wait for the dog. (peoples responsibilities will continue to wait for them no matter the procrastination)
118. He who runs after the chicken should expect a fall.
119. He whose home is on fire does not run after the mice.
120. The trap might hurt the chimpanzee but the chimpanzee will always get home.
121. The monkey with the baby on the back did not know when it plucked and ate the forbidden fruit. (everyone is responsible for his own actions)
122. "See me off" is only a joke, for, who is he who does not know the way to his own home?
123. The honor given to the door is to (bend) bow at the doorway.
124. A pre announced war does not kill the lame. (to be fore warned is to be fore armed)
125. The old lady who sales ogiri spice knows the fly with broken eyes.
126. An elder is never too old at a dance for which he is an expert.
127. A snake that bites a tortoise bites a shell.
128. A grasshopper that is crushed by the train must be deaf. (this proverb is said to he who falls into a danger after repeated warnings)
129. The group is better. (two heads are better than one)
130. As we run away from fire with gunpowder is exactly as we run away from gunpowder with fire.
131. Spontaneity is the weakness of the warrior.
132. Spontaneity if the litmus test with which warriors are determined.
133. A poor man's goat is his cows.
134. Separateness/solitude is the weakness of the snake.
135. The family that bought a sickly goat claimed it died of fats.
136. The blood has its odor. (blood is thicker than water)
137. Every child is beautiful to its mother.
138. Dry meat fills the mouth.

139. When the dry wood is expected to fall, it out-lasts the fresh one.
140. The snake and the snake hunter are both watchful of their lives.
141. Salt and pepper cannot be enemies.
142. Mother and child do not have to eat with lamp.
143. A good Sunday is known by Saturday.
144. He who cleans his teeth with $10.00 should say what he earns through laughter.
145. Nothing happens before its time (God's time is the best).
146. When pride comes first, failure follows.
147. He who doesn't know where the rain started to beat him does not know where it stopped beating him.
148. When a proverb is given about an old basket, an emaciated person begins to examine himself.
149. The vulture said that evil has no duplicate. (two wrongs cannot make a right)
150. The doctor, who cures otoro disease, does he live in the sky?
151. If the rat follows the lizard to swim, the rat remains wet after the lizard is dry.
152. He who asks for his friend's type of haircut will it fit him like his friend?
153. After the rain is over (elsewhere) it continues in the forest.
154. No one prepares palm kernels for ukwa spice that is still on the tree.
155. An antelope that was being pursued by a lion was asked by the mother after it slowed down due to a cut on the leg, "which is worse between a head cut and a leg cut?"
156. Everyone yearns for where he is not (the grass is always greener on the other side).
157. The scent of a woman is best known to he who is closest to her.
158. When the mortar is carrying food it turns its back to the ground.
159. He who dines with the devil should use a long spoon.
160. He who cooks bad food sees it in his stool. (action and reaction are equal and opposite)
161. It takes something which is faster than an animal to kill an animal.

162. A hunter who fails to run as fast as an animal does not kill an animal.
163. If an animal escapes the hunter today, hunting is the next day (tomorrow is another day)
164. Everybody for the thief, one day for the owner.
165. He who takes his bath fully dressed should examine himself.
166. A body that is used to clothing becomes ugly while naked.
167. The fly follows the constipated man because he is always either passing out stool. (or throwing up from the mouth)
168. He who eats food prepared with red palm oil does not pass out dark stool.
169. A fly is not killed in the face of the wound.
170. If an animal runs (fiercely), the hunter pursues it (fiercely) badly.
171. A diarrhea patient does use the coconut leaf for a diaper.
172. He who is a hurry runs into mishap (haste breeds danger hence better be late than the late.
173. What's that between the vulture and the barber?
174. The early beast gets to pass stool on the road. (early bird gets the worm)
175. Whatever is delivered by the snake cannot but be long.
176. A stranger's corpse feels like the wood.
177. He who desires glamour should gather some wealth.
178. A sheep that gives birth to a ram might as well be childless.
179. When the poor is told what it takes to be rich he wants to remain poor.
180. While standing up the youth does not see what the elder perceives sitting down.
181. He who has money should pay for his father's funeral; it is not the oldest child who killed the father. (the tradition is that the oldest child who inherits most of the parents' wealth should be and is responsible for the funeral too)
182. A traveler that passes stool on his way up will meet flies on his way down. (be nice to the people you meet on your way up because you will meet them again on your way down)
183. It's not by opening the eyes very wide that one sees better.
184. Mileage is counted after the race.
185. The lizard wants to sit but the tail doesn't allow it.

186. A baby that keeps the mother from sleeping does not sleep either.
187. The silence of a king/queen is more effective than the voice of a commoner.
188. When a child gets that for which he is a wake, he falls asleep.
189. No one throws a "Hail Mary" pass with his only ball. (Translated with an American expression)
190. No parent fights for his baby because he/she has strength.
191. When one finger gets oil it soils the rest.
192. It is by diplomacy that a leper is taken to his place of quarantine.
193. Whatever a man gives to his fellow man is only to be kept for him as a loan.
194. If a child uses the proverbs which his father uses, let him pay his father's debts.
195. It is not by its strength that a woodpecker cuts though the wood.
196. The earth warm said that it is by justice that he digs into the earth.
197. It does not hurt when the chicken steps on the young one.
198. A word is enough for the prudent.
199. A lonely palm nut is never lost in the fire.
200. When folk deliberate, before hand, they understand each other's signs.
201. He who cultivates under the sun eats under the shed.
202. He who is counting on the mortar for a chair lacks a seat. (backing the wrong horse)
203. The palm wine taper does not ever reveal everything he perceived from the treetop.
204. The relative of the bad dancer is always the one scratching his eyebrow.
205. He who knows the bad appreciates the good the most. (the polar concept in philosophy)
206. A goat that is fed by all dies of hunger. (everybody's business is nobody's business)
207. A goat that is well fed at home does not stray from home.
208. An animal that is being shot by a good hunter does not continue to graze.
209. A dog does not eat a bone that is worn or pinned to its neck.

210. The fire that burns a wealthy man's home only enables him to build a better and new one.
211. When a child cries and points to a location, either of his parents is usually there.
212. Whoever is always being mentioned has something which he has always done.
213. When one is praised for what he does he is encouraged to accomplish more.
214. The dwarf did not create himself. (never judge a man by that for which he is not responsible)
215. Proverbs make the wise wiser and the fool more foolish.
216. Proverbs, according to Chinua, are the oil with which words are eaten.
217. The mind is like a back pack and everyone clings to his own.
218. A child whose favorite meal is being prepared does not fall asleep.
219. When a discussion becomes financial the poor withholds his ideas.
220. Laughter is not pleasure.
221. When an important person is excluded from an important deliberation, it is (voided) repeated.
222. It is by serving a king that one becomes a king.
223. He who cannot follow cannot lead either.
224. The hand that crafted (weave) a basket can always craft another.
225. When the king of the birds is captured he says who made him the king.
226. The king of the birds shall reveal who crowned him, after he is captured.
227. A child at the back does not understand the distance of the pathway.
228. The blind shall catch the grasshopper whenever it rest or perches on his chest. (pertience and perseverance)
229. Where a man's fortune is made is where a man's body is found.
230. The child does not know that "ibi" is a sickness to his father. (a sexually transmitted disease)
231. The only palm nut cannot get lost in the fire. (during roasting)
232. Whenever one wakes up it is his morning.

233. An agreement reached by two is understood by a wink of an eye.
234. He who remembers his death will finish his wealth.
235. Two people running round the house do not know who is doing the chasing.
236. Whoever is forgotten does not forget himself.
237. He whose father is in heaven does not go to hell.
238. It's only with one eye open that a man marries a woman.
239. He who is rejected does not reject himself.
240. One burnt by fire fears even the ashes.
241. As the door opens (in the morning) the mouth (the appetite) opens too.
242. Loudness does not equate strength.
243. Empty barrels make louder noise than those full of oil.
244. The market story is told after the market session.
245. Justice gets one free.
246. The aggressor often dies by aggression.
247. The early beast drinks from the freshest spring.
248. No one leaks his fingers in a rush.
249. One who is afraid of the goat does not (run after) catch the dog.
250. No one gets his first child before his parents.
251. He whose pear is ripped should eat it.
252. The pear has made the king to eat ashes.
253. No one jumps over or across the land (earth).
254. Height does not maturity make.
255. Height does not create maturity.
256. He who cannot show gratitude physically should be able to show it verbally.
257. The forest is a god to the beast .
258. He who plans to say this and that to someone does not know what is going to be said to him in return.
259. Chinua Achebe warned that those whose palm kernel has been cracked by a benevolent spirit should not forget to be humble.
260. The land should not break all hoes even if it is fertile to the yams.
261. The harvester that breaks the yam tuber in a hurry kneels down to dig it out.

262. When a child's fight is broken he feels as though fights are pleasant.
263. Everything bad does not happen to some one alive.
264. A snake seen by an individual is always as long as a python. (people will always exaggerate)
265. When azi itches or yearns for gossip it begins to tattoo his lips.
266. Ask the polygynous woman what she is doing in the other woman's kitchen.
267. When other animals imitate the monkey they break their limbs (jumping).
268. The dog asked for the food to be left for him out there and let him worry about who will take it from him.
269. When the right fingers wash the left, the left wash the right at the same time.
270. Even the flies can stop the work.
271. Looking at a corpse's mouth one sees the folly of not enjoying one's wealth while still alive.
272. A miser should look at a dead person in the mouth.
273. The palm tree is a bed to the vulture.
274. When a home stands it looks as though it is full of wealth.
275. Whatever is used to coil the millipede is disposed with the millipede.
276. When "agbusi" stings the buttock it learns its lessons.
277. When the egg breaks the palm nut, it puts the stone to shame.
278. A child that consumes "akala" consumes his money.
279. When a child cries and points towards a direction, one of his parents is there.
280. When a child hammers his fingers, he throws away the hammer.
281. "Agamegwu" is not god for the pad.
282. Agamegwu does not a good pad make.
283. A traveler is often wiser than the elder.
284. A traveler is often more experienced than the elder.
285. A traveler does not make foes.
286. A friend that becomes an enemy is the worst of enmities.
287. Everyone has a relative abroad (in a foreign land).
288. Brotherly enmity is never skin deep.

289. When a king dies another succeeds him (no one is indispensable) .
290. Every "abada" cloth fits or suits someone out there.
291. A patient man feeds on dried fish.
292. A patient man eats the best-treated fish.
293. He who is given a message for the king is not necessarily asked to capture the king.
294. The messenger does not generate the message.
295. The messenger is only a messenger.
296. When the unfortunate man goes hunting is when the antelopes climb trees.
297. When people urinate together it foams.
298. Today is early. (it is never too late)
299. Winning the judgment is better than winning the fight.
300. When a cunning man dies, a cunning man buries him.
301. A heap of woods is not more than what can be lost in the bush.
302. Something makes something to happen.
303. Whatever happens is made to happen by something.
304. The cocoa yam does not cry "nwee!" for nothing.
305. Okra does not grow taller than he who planted it.
306. Life is coded with destiny.
307. Everyone lives by his destiny (fate).
308. The lizard said that his head is already deep into the red calm wood.
309. It is at the assembly that people know who is who.
310. When one is praised for what he has done he does more. (always be thankful)
311. Every lizard lies on his stomach; it is impossible to spot one with stomach ulcer.
312. A child whose father is the chief judge is seldom convicted.
313. Spend! Spend! is sweeter from another's wallet.
314. The wood (fetcher) gatherer does not gather "agbara" for wood (Agbara itches all over the body).

Igbo Proverbs in Igbo and English

1. Igbo: *Izu ka mma na nneji*. English: Secret deliberations are best among relatives.
2. Igbo: *Aka ka eji egosi nwanne ma adighi, egosi enyi*. English: Everyone knows his own friends but everyone does not know his relatives.
3. Igbo: *nkem bu nkem, nke anyi bu nke anyi*. English: Ours belong to us, mine belongs to me.
4. Igbo: *Ezichaa ofu ofu, ezibe ibuo ibuo*. English: After relating in singles, then we begin to relate in doubles. Explanation: There are different levels, categories and hierarchies of relationship.
5. Igbo: *Nwa adigh nne ya njo*. English: No baby is ugly to its mother.
6. Igbo: *Nsi ebu nafo adigh esi isi*. English: The stool does not smell from the stomach.
7. Igbo: *Bia rie aburo bia yoo*. English: Come and eat is not like come and work.
8. Igbo: *Ozi ezilezi adigh agho*. English: Blame the message not the messenger.
9. Igbo: *Eji anya ama oka chalacha*. English: A ripened corn can be spotted by sight i.e. you can tell a ripe corn by its looks.
10. Igbo: *Okuku gabu oke na ebido na eju*. English: A chicken that is going to be female starts in the egg.
11. Igbo: *Okuku kwachuo akwa ejilu ya mechuo ife*. English: if a cock (rooster) crows too soon, it is used too soon for emulation (sacrifice).
12. Igbo: *Onye chi ya gbalu krisimasi si na ndi ozo na apu ala*. English: he for whom God has celebrated Christmas thinks that others are fooling around.
13. Igbo: *Etigbuo atulu analu ebe osi*. English: when a lamb is unjustifiably killed the owner shows up.
14. Igbo: *Mbosi moto gbulu onye ala amalu na onwelu Nwanne*. English: That a crazy man has relatives is known after he is killed by a car

15. Igbo: *Akata njo Nwata na akataghi mma ya*. English: When a child's misbehavior is mentioned his good behavior is forgotten
16. Igbo: *Onwu nokwulu ajo mmadu, ajo mmadu, anokwulu Nwanne ya*. English: When misfortune is hard on the evil person, he is hard on his brother
17. Igbo: *Dibia onwu na egbu ona agwo mmadu?* English: Does a sick healer heal someone else?
18. Igbo: *Onu bu oka*. English: The speech is an art. Explanation: Think before you speak.
19. Igbo: *Aka na eme azu ogbaa nkiliko*. English: The hand makes the dry fish coil round and round.
20. Igbo: *Nku be ndi na eghelu ndi nni*. English: A people's firewood cooks food for them
21. Igbo: *Ka aka ha nwayi bu ka ona atukwasi di ya*. English: As a woman's hand is so she places it on her husband.
22. Igbo: *Ka Nwayi nwe bu ka onyelu nwa ya*. English: As a woman has is as she gives her kid.
23. Igbo: *Ife nwoke na eme di ya nobi*. English: What a man does is in his heart (mind).
24. Igbo: *Chi na awa eze*. English: God selects the Queen (king).
25. Igbo: *Ijiji na enwero onye ndumodu na eso ozu ana nini*. English: a fly without an advisor goes into the grave with the corpse.
26. Igbo: *Nkita agholu okpukpu sili ka odiba*. English: A dog that was denied a bone said, "let it be"
27. Igbo: *Ikwe bulu nni ochelu ani azu*. English: The motor faces the earth except when it has food.
28. Igbo: *Okuku rapulu onye gbuluya aturo balu ite ofe onu*. English: The hen that bends the neck to the soup in the pot rather than to he who killed it.
29. Igbo: *Okuku adi echefu onye kwolu ya nku na udu mmili*. English: The chicken does not forget he who plucked its feathers during the rainy season.
30. Igbo: *Okuku rapu kwom ojili gini zua umu ya*. English: If the chicken abandons "kwom", the sound it makes, what will it use to train the young ones?
31. Igbo: *Okuku chi umu amaro oso ogu agba*. English: A hen with young ones cannot run from fights.

32. Igbo: *Nwayoo bu ije*. English: Slow and steady wins the race.
33. Igbo: *Gbanu, Gbanu, na agbasi mmanu.* English: He who rushes hurries into trouble.
34. Igbo: *Oji oso agbaku ogwu amaro na ogwu bu onwu*. English: He who rushes into war does not know that war is death.
35. Igbo: *Ife uwa si na akala aka*. English: Life is by destiny.
36. Igbo: *Emeta igede, igede asaba*. English: When "Igede" dance group is treated well and accordingly it begins to sound or play.
37. Igbo: *Onye nwe ozu napa ya nisi*. English: He who owns the corpse carries it by the head. Explanation: He who has a responsibility tackles the lions share of the task.
38. Igbo: *Nwata ana edenye nni nwe nsedebe onu*. English: One who is being fed has the task of bringing close his mouth. Equivalence: Heaven helps those who help themselves.
39. Igbo: *Nne na nwa adi amu oku eri nni*. English: Mother and child do not have to eat with light lit.
40. Igbo: *Mmanu nne nalu na achicha nne*. English: The mother's yeast (oil) has been applied to the mother's bread.
41. Igbo: *Ozugbu nwata nahia sili ya egosina mmadu*. English: He who cheats a child in a sale cautions him not to show it to someone else.
42. Igbo: *Eziokwu bu ndu*. English: Truth is life. Equivalence: The truth shall set you free. English Ezuivalence: Honesty is the best policy.
43. Igbo: *Atuolu omalu omalu, atuolu ofeke ofeba nofia*. English: A wise saying makes the smart smarter and the silly more confused.
44. Igbo: *Ejiro ife eji agba nti agba anya*. English: It is not with what you scratch the ear that you scratch the eye.
45. Igbo: *Ano na ukpotu kpo ete uwotuwo?* English: Does one in ukpotukpo dance to uwotuwo? Equivalence: Jumping from frying pan into the fire.
46. Igbo: *Abia nwaputa imi awapia ya*. English: Sometimes one trims down the nose in an attempt to trim or pull it up. Explanation: Making something worse in an attempt to make it better.

47. Igbo: *Onye ndi ilo gbulu gbulu gbulu na eche ndu ya nche mgbe nine.* English: Whoever is surrounded by enemies guards his life always.
48. Igbo: *Oko koo anu ojekulu osisi mana okoo mmadu ojekulu ibe ya.* English: When an animal feels itchy it goes to a tree stem but when a human feels an itch in the back he goes to a fellow human. Equivalence: No one is an island. Explanation: We need each other
49. Igbo: *Onye anyana nwanne ya.* English: Let no one leave his brother behind.
50. Igbo: *Onye onyeocha cha chulu na agbalu ayali oso.* English: He who has been chased by a white person runs away from milato.
51. Igbo: *Onu kwulu njo ga ekwu mma.* English: The mouth that proclaimed evil shall proclaim peace or righteousness.
52. Igbo: *Onye oku hulu natu ebube egwu.* English: He who has been seriously scalded by fire fears even the ashes.
53. Igbo: *Onyema onye nakulu nnunu egwu?* English: Who knows he who beats the drum for the birds?
54. Igbo: *Onye ala na uche ya yi.* English: The mad man knows what he is doing.
55. Igbo: *Ehina enwero odudu chi ya nachulu ya ljiji.* English: God drives away the flies for a cow without a tail.
56. Igbo: *Ejiro akpata atufue aba ogalanya.* English: No one becomes wealthy by loosing and not conserving his treasures.
57. Igbo: *Ichefuru chechaa akwu onye nwe ya egbulu.* English: After the soldier ant guards the palm fruit, the owner takes it away.
58. Igbo: *Achosia ebe aga abiado aka afuro ya abiado ya na ikpele.* English: If no where else, one can always place one's hands by his knees.
59. Igbo: *Ife onye cho kofu.* English: He who searches finds.
60. Igbo: *Ekwo naka.* English: No one does things just because he can. Explanation: Might is not right.
61. Igbo: *Ekwolu nkita akpiri egosiro ya obu ka obu ife ozo.* English: When one plucks fleas from a dog and fails to show it to him, the dog feels as though it were something else.

62. Igbo: *Agwo na echigha nebe otalu mmadu*. English: The snake always goes back to the scene of the crime or to the scene where it bit the person.
63. Igbo: *Osi ya amaghi ga ama*. English: He who claims not to know will know.
64. Igbo: *Elili ma ngwugwu, ngwugwu ma onye kelu ya*. English: The string (rope) knows the package and the package knows he who tied it.
65. Igbo: *Egoghi na eleghi ona ese okwu?* English: Not buying and not selling, is that a problem?
66. Igbo: *Okwa mmaou nakwa onwe ya*. English: It is at others' funeral that one celebrates his own. Explanation: No one attends his own funeral.
67. Igbo: *Ofu anya ka eji anu nwanyi*. English: Every successful marriage is with one eye closed. Explanation: Couples have to overlook each other's shortcomings.
68. Igbo: *Okuku kpatalu nku eji huo ya*. English: The chicken that fetched the firewood with which it is roasted.
69. Igbo: *Ebuolu ndu ebuolu onwu*. English: We make provisions for death as we make provisions for life.
70. Igbo: *Agadi adi akpo anu ntanta*. English: An elder does not refer to meat as "ntanta" (an alluring term kids use for meat)
71. Igbo: *Afughi ka emelu emee ka afulu*. English: He who does not have much to give gives much of what he has.
72. Igbo: *Okpaka nwata aru, nwata ga agbanari ya na oso*. English: He who abuses a kid will one day be out-ran by the kid.
73. Igbo: *Ana ekwu okwu nsusu ya ana ede*. English: As one talks the nuance and the meanings echo.
74. Igbo: *Otu osisi adigh agho mmadu ngho anya nabo*. English: A stick does not pick one's eye twice.
75. Igbo: *Ndidi ka mma*. English: Patience is the best.
76. Igbo: *Nkpoghali nkpoghali ka eji ele nwankpi*. English: It is by constant movement that a he-goat is sold.
77. Igbo: *Anoro ofu ebe ekiri mmawu*. English: A masquerade is not observed from one spot.
78. Igbo: *Nkita kputa osisi okpunalu onye ono be ya*. English: When a dog picks a bone he takes it to the owner. Explanation: When kids get in trouble parents become responsible.

79. Igbo: *Ebe ifunanya di ebe afu ka udo gadi*. English: It is only where there is love that there is peace.
80. Igbo: *Onwu bu ugwo, onye obuna jiya eji*. English: Death is a loan, which everyone owes which must be paid.
81. Igbo: *Ebe "fune" "fune" di otua, onye ma etu "funa" "funa" ga adi?* English: If "fune" is like this, who knows how "funa" "funa" will be?
82. Igbo: *Ebita akwuo, nekwe ka ebita ozo*. English: Borrowing and paying makes it possible for one to borrow again.
83. Igbo: *Aka adighi nwa ogbenye odi ka omaro ife*. English: When one is poor it seems as though he is foolish (since he is not able to do what he is supposed to do)
84. Igbo: *Nsi gafee orimiri oruo*. English: When poison crosses an ocean it becomes impotent, powerless or ineffective.
85. Igbo: *Onye malu onye ka odi, osolu ya ka odi*. English: He who knows someone as he learns to accept or deal with him as he is.
86. Igbo: *Ji adi esi na odu epu ome*. English: The yam does not germinate from the bottom.
87. Dimaragana, according to Achebe, wouldn't use his knife to cut dog meat because it is a taboo but he offered to use his teeth.
88. Igbo: *Ife enwumelu ite, ite mechaa omee ya enwu*. English: What the goat did to the cooking pot will eventually be done to the goat by the same pot.
89. Igbo: *Oburu onu eji abita ugwo ka eji akwu ya*. English: It is no the tone or tongue with a loan is obtained that it is paid.
90. Igbo: *Agha alalaka adghi eli ngwuro*. English: To be fore-warned is to be fore-armed.

Chapter 12

Conclusion

Nigerian politics, or should I say Western politics in Nigeria, can be seen in the form of conflicts, coups, and corruption. Before I delve into this conclusion, I need to make it clear that there are three major periods that people need to know before discussing politics in Africa. Those periods are pre-colonial, colonial and post-colonial. "Pre-colonial" explains the African situation before the Europeans had a scramble for Africa. "Colonial" is what happened when the Europeans scrambled for Africa. And Post-colonial explains the effects of the colonization of Africa and its people. "Post-colonial" is the contemporary African political situation.

Pre-Colonial

The pre-colonial Africans governed themselves. Kings and Queens ruled over small tribes as well as large empires. Unlike many other places in the world, parts of Africa had a strong matriarchal system. One example is Ghana. Even in places such as Dahomey, where there was a patriarchal system, women still had female leaders. The Lialode of Yoruba had male leaders, however, only women were allowed to administer to women.

Many people know about great African Kings such as Sunni Ali, Sundiata, mai Adris Alooma, and Shaka of Zululand; however, many people don't know that African Queens like Nzinga, the Queen of Sheba, Nefertiti, Cleopatra, Beatrice of Angola, Amina of Hausaland and Ngui Nanaramama, were controllers of the economy and the land, and they fought fierce battles.

The most important aspect of pre-colonial Africa and its politics is that there was no separation between church and state. Religion and politics were pari passu; religious figures were also political leaders. Because African politics were rooted in the fear of God, the people tended to be upright. Pre-colonial Africans perceived corruption, mismanagement, nepotism, and bribery with jaundiced eyes.

The Nature of African Traditional Religion

Most Africans tended to believe in God, the Supreme God, who is the creator, omnipotent, omniscient, ubiquitous, and summon bonum. Right under Him were the minor gods and goddesses, which also included oracles, ancestors, and deities. The minor gods were not worshipped. They were simply reverenced in the same way that the Christian Roman Catholic denomination revere the Virgin Mary and the saints. The ancestors were people who had lived righteous lives and died. Every dead person did not qualify as an ancestor who was worthy of reverence just as not every dead Catholic is worthy of canonization.

Right beneath the minor gods and goddesses were the priests and priestesses, elders, and titled men and women. The priests made the laws of the land; the elders interpreted them using their experience, and the titled people enforced the law. As one can see, special revelations from God made the priests create new laws. The three branches of government could not afford to be corrupt because African traditional belief was such that mischievous behavior had a direct repercussion from the ancestors. In other words, one was punished, one's children were punished, and one's children's children were punished. Hence, there is the famous African saying that sin has a pan-cosmic effect.

Law & Order

There were no prisons in Africa. Hence, criminals never went to jail. Instead, they had a unique way of punishing people who offended the community. The severest punishment was banishment or exile. This was given to people who committed the most egregious abominations. Simply put, people were actually asked to leave their society forever.

The second in severity is capital punishment. In African society, it was an abomination to kill another human being. Therefore, in the case of capital punishment, criminals were asked to hang themselves. This was because no one could shed another's blood except at war. Every person's goal was to rest in peace. The three ways to achieve this were to live righteous life, to receive a righteous burial and then to have a righteous funeral. After an African received a verdict of capital punishment, he or she went through a sacrifice of expiation, which was an act of forgiveness. Then, he hanged himself. The family then gave him a befitting burial. Within a number of weeks, months, or even years in some cases, he or she received a righteous funeral from both the family and the community. This was enough to enable him to rest in peace. When one was sent into exile, on the other hand, he or she never got a chance to rest in peace. Because he died, he would neither be able to get a righteous burial nor a righteous funeral. In other words, whereas capital punishment was a condemnation of the body, exile was a condemnation of the body and the soul.

Needles to say, Africans strongly believed in reincarnation, which means that people come back to life many times. In Igboland, one comes back to life seven times, although it varies from tribe to tribe. Therefore, one had seven chances to live a righteous life and ascend to the spirit world. If one failed to make it in any of the seven lives, he or she remained on earth as a ghost, for Africans did not believe in either heaven or hell.

The third in severity was excommunication. This was when an offender was barred from interacting with any member of the community. The community was equally forbidden from dealing with him or his family until the excommunication was lifted. When one was excommunicated, the family was equally affected. This meant neither he nor anyone of the family could speak to anyone of the community, buy or sell anything, be rescued if the home was on fire, and so on and so forth. This was extremely difficult according to the families that underwent this punishment, because Africans tended to live communal lives.

The next in severity was "akaja." This was when people who stole had the products or items tied on to them as they were paraded around in society. Usually, a song was composed using their names. They were then forced to dance and were disgraced.

The fifth punishment was fines. This was the most common punishment within African Traditional society. Every Africans belonged to a particular age grade. When one committed an offense, he or she was usually referred to his age group for a verdict of whether or not he was guilty. If he was found guilty, the same group determined the amount of fines to be imposed on him by consulting the similar punishments of the past.

Another type of severity involved having the culprit go to the family of the victim and serve them for the rest of his life, especially in the case of murder. That was one-way Africans enslaved people. These are just a few out of many types of punishment in Africa. The community understood this system and there were usually little or no debates when anyone of them was imposed. Of course, there were abominations, which were handled severely and delicately. Some of those taboos included incest, unmasking a spirit of the ancestors, killing a sacred animal, deliberately shedding another's blood, rape, hitting or pushing down an elder, and committing adultery in the marital home.

Colonial Africa

The Europeans met, decided to go into Africa, and then divided the continent up, country-by-country. Britain obtained many parts, such as Nigeria and Ghana; France got the Ivory Coast, and Germany received Cameroon. This proved that Africa was arbitrarily divided. When dividing Africa, the Europeans would not pay any attention to the boundaries of tribes, causing one tribe to be in two different countries that might have been controlled by two different European nations. Lumping different tribes in the same country that had nothing in common led to conflicts. For example, both the Igbo and Hausa tribes were combined to create Nigeria, but both of these tribes had separate governments and religions. The Igbo tribe's religion is described above, whereas the Hausa's became Islamic by Usman Danfodio. However, the European's created a country that combined these two tribes, subjecting both of them to one European government. The Europeans attempted to convert the Hausa tribe to Christianity, rather than Islam, but they failed. As of today, as a matter of fact, Nigeria is half Muslim, a quarter Christian, and a quarter traditional African Religion.

Religion was very important to Europeans, and that was the main reason why they began to colonize Africa. Because the Europeans preached God, love, and peace, those who were unhappy in African societies were the first converts. However, as the Europeans got more converts, they also began to take more control by implementing government, police, prisons, and taxes that went back to Europe. The old governments were gradually disposed of starting with the female rulers, who were replaced with a type of government called indirect rule. Britain was the fist to implement this. What happened was that Britain handpicked loyal Africans who governed according to the dictates from the Crown. This was done because there were not enough Europeans in Africa.

As they did this, no African traditions and ways were accepted because they were thought to be barbaric and primitive. Therefore, modernization had to be imposed and taught, starting with parliamentary system. African religion was also considered to be pagan and the Europeans needed to convert them to prevent them from being idol worshippers. All throughout Europe, books and papers depicted Africa as "the white man's burden" that needed to be rescued and redeemed.

At the same time, African treasurers were finding their ways to Europe. This included mineral resources, diamonds, gold, coal, farm products, lumber, hides and trinkets. But despite this, the Europeans were not making any significant developments except for building railroads. This improvement, though, made looting the natural resource and artifacts even easier.

During this time, the Europeans also refused to recognize any significant historical African events. For example, in 1929, the Nigerian women took up arms and performed a staged conflict because the men were letting the Europeans' take over everything. This event, according to the Nigerians, was the Aba Women's War. But for the British, this was the Aba Riot, because they wished to imply disorganization and unruliness among the Nigerians. Hence, by calling it a riot, the Europeans were subconsciously denigrating the Nigerians.

It must be noted, however, that the Africans did not, do not, and will not understand and identify with the European system. After all, the Europeans divided Africa in such a way because the Africans would always be at war with each other, thereby making it easier to conquer Africa.

Africans did not identify with this government that was imposed on them; they had to find a way to fight the system. One of these ways was to sabotage the European government in Africa by any means necessary. People who succeeded were considered to be heroes among Africans. Therefore, it was common to embezzle money, to hire unqualified people, etc. This explains the corruption in African politics today. It wasn't there before colonization. It started during colonization, and it was only a means to bring the colonial government to its knees.

The question to ask, then, is why the European system of government is still in use today in Africa. One reason they don't know the way of traditional governments anymore is because the people who had experienced them are now dead. *Nemo dat quod non-habet*. (No one gives what he doesn't have.) Also, the Africans see the Western government working in other places, so they expect it to work in Africa, as well and the Europeans taught them that everything European was good, and everything African was backward.

Coups

Coups are foreign to Africans. Africans had heard of coups in other parts of the world where other governments were dethroned and replaced by force. The most interesting aspect of coups in Africa is that foreigners or foreign governments caused them. This was easy to achieve because the colonial masters, always tried to control African governments by putting those Africans loyal to them on the throne. Because the government was already corrupt, foreign governments gave a lot of money to some handpicked individuals who promised to overtake the government in return. Most of the time, though, it was not as smooth as this, and often, it ended in bloodshed.

Post-Colonial Africa

Religion

How does religion in Africa today demonstrate, show or portray colonial mentality? The term mentality stems from the word mental, which refers to the mind or the mindset. In other words, though the Africans have been liberated bodily speaking, their minds have not. Consequently, "mental" slavery and mental colonization is still going on in Africa today. There was a famous Nigerian jazz musician known as Fela Anikulapo, and he was also considered a philosopher. One of his songs is called "Colonial Mentality." In this song he made similar points.

African traditional religion, as explained above, worked very favorably with the old ways. Today, in Africa, due to the colonial mentality, African traditional religion is practiced by fewer than 30% of the population. Why is that? Today, the traditional religion is perceived as paganism, devil-worship, barbaric, and backwards. Pupils study Christianity in schools, whereas the traditional religion was not taught because western missionaries controlled the schools and curricula. When the traditional religion is mentioned, it is in contrast to Christianity. It is compared to black magic and voodoo. The terms modernization, civilization, and progress are synonymous with Christianity, whereas all things purely African are synonymous with backwardness and retrogression. As a result, Africa is known as the continent with the highest number of Christians today. In 1980, when Pope John Paul II visited Bigard Memorial Seminary in Nigeria, he announced that more Catholic priests were ordained there than in any other seminary in the world. As a matter of fact, Africans are now sending their missionaries to the Western world for Christianization and servitude.

African Christianity

The term African Christianity refers to the way Africans attempt to worship Christ as though they were practicing their traditional religion. Africans tend to be more fanatical when they practice Christianity than the Europeans. Women are not allowed to walk into the church without head ties or wearing long pants. People have to fast for several hours before receiving the Holy Communion. People are not allowed to receive the Holy Communion if they owe the AMC or the Peter's Pence. Penitents are punished in public by kneeling in front of the altar during the mass. Communions are not received by hand, only by the tongue. There are no altar girls, only altar boys. Half of the masses are said in Latin. Priests wear sutans all day long. No churches have African names. There are few or no African saints. Masses last between 2-4 hours. Priests and pastors are clairvoyant; they heal the sick and their holy waters are considered miraculous. Every thing African is sinful, such as listening or dancing to African music. Sainthood is acceptable; whereas, ancestor "worship" is diabolical.

Culture

African culture has equally been jettisoned in an attempt to hold tooth and nail to Western ways of life. Take, for example, the African masquerade, which used to serve as a law enforcement agent in Africa but is now considered devilish by the Christians. Previously, Africans celebrated numerous festivals, which are forgotten and avoided today. Instead, they celebrate Christmas, Easter, Independence and Valentine's Day.

At the crux of African culture is music. Today, African traditional music has taken a backseat to Western music. It is a sign of backwardness to be seen dancing to an African tune. An African musician by the name of Bright Chimezie composed a song recently telling a story about what happened to him in a disco hall at Enugu. According to him, people were requesting songs, and he approached the DJ and made his own request. Unfortunately, it was an African song and the DJ responded that the music he had requested did not go well with the people there and also called him "okoro."

In my own experience, I went to Nigeria on a vacation a couple of summers ago, and the next day, my younger brother found me playing one of the songs I purchased in Lagos. It was music from Congo. My brother quickly asked me to keep the door shut so neighbors would not hear me playing that music because it was a disappointment coming from someone from the U.S. He asked me if I did not come home with some rap songs from Eminem, R Kelly, and LL Cool J.

African traditional attire is becoming obsolete in Nigeria today. One is considered primitive if he or she is seen wearing African attire in Nigeria very frequently. Today, women prefer to shop from Western boutiques, and men prefer to wear Western suits in the tropical heat. Every one of them has a handkerchief, and, often they are seen wiping sweat from their faces and armpits. For those with air conditioned cars, homes, and offices, it's more tolerable, but it's an eye sore to find African men walking several miles along the streets of Lagos, Nigeria wearing black polyester and wool suits and ties. African traditional garments, which are usually made of cotton, are seldom in existence.

It is very common for African men in those suits to have grease from Gerry curls dripping from their heads under the tropical sun. Women consider it primitive to be found wearing an African hairstyle. Instead, they choose to perm their hair and put on artificial hair in the form of wigs, all in an attempt to appear like the Western women.

This story could best be summarized by a contingent of African-American delegates from Holy Angels Catholic Parish in Chicago, who traveled to Africa a number of years ago to witness the coronation of their parish priest, Fr. George Clements. They were all dressed in African traditional attires from Chicago. Upon arrival at Murtala Mohammad Airport at Ikeja, Lagos, they were astounded, perplexed, and disappointed because they were the only group wearing traditional garments in the whole airport. Others, especially those who came to receive them, were all found wearing American jeans and European suits.

Masquerades

The masquerade was not used for law enforcement alone. It was used for entertainment as well. During feasts and festivals, masks convened entertainment, especially among the youths. Some of them danced, and others simply ran around with the youths. Today, though, they are no longer in existence because Christians have banned them. Christians claim they are diabolic.

Festivals

In pre-colonial Africa, people had several festivals and feasts to celebrate different occasions. Some were for the harvests, some were for the new year celebration, some were for the end of the year celebration, and others were for family get-togethers, including marriage ceremonies, naming ceremonies, birth ceremonies and fattening ceremonies. Today, all of them have been replaced with Christian celebrations, such as Christmas, Easter, and the independent ceremonies.

Language

Every African tribe has its own particular and unique language. Each language is different from the next because the difference is not simply dialects. In Nigeria, for example, there are as many languages as there are tribes. Therefore, one might conclude that there are over 200 different languages in Nigeria alone. After colonization, the English language became the Nigerian Lingua Franca. None of the two hundred languages were considered good enough to be the official language. Today, schools are taught in English from Kindergarten to the college level. All official transactions are conducted in English. Well-educated Nigerians can seldom speak their own language fluently, let alone write it. Today, it's not unusual for an average Nigerian to be unable to recite the alphabets in his own language, yet most of them speak English and French fluently. Most Nigerians, as a matter of fact, are very proud to point out that their children do not speak or understand our vernacular.

A couple of years ago, I visited a relative in Lagos on my way through Nigeria. I attempted to hold a conversation with one of his children in

Ibo, but the mother was very quick to point out that none of the children spoke our language. She encouraged me to speak in English to him. It was then that I found out that all he knew was pigeon English. In other words, they would rather speak pigeon than our vernacular.

As I spent time in Nigeria, I was reminded that people look down on someone and consider him or her to be uneducated unless he speaks a foreign language in his own homeland. When Africans gather, it is very shameful to consider the fact that none of them can communicate in a language that is not foreign. In America, I have found Indians, Pakistanis, and others speaking in their own languages. When Nigerians gather, chances are that they will either speak English or they will not be able to communicate with each other.

"Engligbo"

This is a term that is commonly used in Nigeria today to describe an average African who cannot complete two sentences in his language without using an English word. It is very common among both educated and so-called "uneducated" Ibo's today. Fortunately, this problem is not found among the Yoruba, Tiv, Hausa, Ibibio, and Fulanis. It is only prevalent among the Igbo's.

Another aspect of African language that has disappeared with Western colonization is the proverb and figurative expressions. Needless to say, short stories and allegories are uncommon parlance thanks to the colonial mentality in Africa today. African languages used to be rich with beautiful proverbs, wise sayings, and idiomatic expressions. It was considered vapid for people to speak in simple sentences. Individuals were eulogized for their oratory skills. Today, all of those linguistic expressions have been jettisoned or discarded for pigeon English.

Names

Before colonization, Africans went by their traditional African names. Once Africa began to be colonized, however, baptism was introduced, during which people were given baptismal names after Western saints. Therefore, as more and more Africans were converted, Western names such as Mary, Peter, and Joseph became more common. These Western names constituted their first names as they retained their African surnames.

After colonization, this practice remained. Today, most Africans continue to identify their children with western names. The irony is that there are no Westerners who give African names to their own children.

This reversal of culture tends to apply to all aspects of African culture. Take the case of marriage. An average African undergoes three different marriages at a time. One is the court wedding, the second is the traditional African wedding, and the third is the Western style wedding. This last wedding usually takes place in a Christian church and a minister presides over it. It is also the most elaborate and expensive of all three weddings.

Food

The same mentality even applies to the food that the Africans eat. In the past, Africans grew their traditional and tropical (where applicable) food crops in abundance. They usually had to export a large portion of the crops, such as groundnuts, millets, soybeans, coffee, tea, maize, and many other items.

Today, Africans cannot even manage to feed themselves. They import food products from all over the world. One of the reasons for this is that a majority of young African men and women migrate to the big cities in search of white-collar jobs. The search for "white" men's jobs (Olu oyibo) is in vogue. No one wants to settle in the villages any more. Farming is considered dirty, primitive, backward, shameful, and African. Therefore, people migrate to the urban areas, looking for clean, Western style jobs. The result is that those cities are overpopulated. Inflation is also rampant because there is too much currency and not enough goods to be purchased.

I must not forget to mention that the African people prefer Western foods to the traditional cuisine. In the past, they had African cakes from oil bean trees, abacha (African pudding), yams, cassava, and uncountable tropical fruits. Today, most Africans don't eat any of them, even though they are both nutritious and delicious. They would rather be found indulging themselves with Western bread, Western biscuits, Uncle Ben's rice and other typical western dishes. Africa has been known for its beers, as well, as palm wine and brukutu. Palm wine is served fresh from the tree and with no preservatives. Doctors recommend it for the eyes due to the yeast content. They are intoxicating and extremely palatable. Today, though, many Africans don't even know what it is because they have stopped growing palm trees and tapping them. Instead, Africans prefer Budweiser from the U.S., Heineken from Germany, and Guinness from Ireland. In the past, they had kaikai spirits (liquor) delicately brewed out of palm wine and from ngwa wine. Today, they are rarely found anywhere in the continent. Instead, they are importing vodka from Russia, scotch from Scotland, whiskey from England, bourbon from the U.S. champagne from France, and wine from Italy.

Matriarchy and Matrilineal Genealogy

Matriarchy is said to have started in Africa and ancient Mesopotamia. That means that in ancient Africa, women dominated the males. Males were not weak. Women were just dominant.

The concept of matrilineal genealogy, or tracing one's genealogy through the mother line, was natural for the Africans. It was not very uncommon, then, for individuals' last names to come from the mothers. Leaders were chiefly queens, even though there were a few kings as well. With colonization, things began to fall apart. The first thing that the Europeans did was to depose women leaders and impose male leaders on the Africans. Even the religion, which had priestesses, was replaced with Christianity, where women could not be ordained as priests by church law. Now, as a result, Africa is completely patriarchal.

Government

As I have stated earlier, African traditional government was pari pasu with religion. Today, there is a separation of church and state. This is one of the reasons why there is corruption in contemporary African government. People no longer have a fear of God in their governmental transactions or dealings. Of course, another reason for corruption was rebelling against the foreign government during colonization. Today, after independence, the governments are still considered to be foreign to the Africans. This is why working for the government, when translated from the Ibo "□ l□ Oyibo" is, literally, "working for the white man."

Mentality

Colonial mentality, for the Africans, can be interpreted as performing actions to keep them from looking black. A good example is what is done to the skin. Many Africans use all sorts of bleach, soap, and creams to make their skin colors look lighter. At first, this habit was only popular among women, but it is now becoming more prevalent among men as well. Another example is the nose. Some people undergo expensive nose surgery to make their noses thinner, like European noses. This is also done with the lips as well. The newest form of plastic surgery, though, is that of the cheekbones. The Africans no longer take pride in the facial characteristics that distinguish the Negroid race from all others.

Colonial mentality is not only shown with the increasing demand for physical alterations, though. It is also predominant in the way the Africans think. Simply put, colonial mentality stresses the belief that black is ugly and inferior, while white is good, beautiful, and superior. This is manifested in every action. They accept Western teachings without questioning them. The best example of this is white dresses that are worn to weddings, while black is worn to funerals. Of course, the angels are painted white, while the devils are painted black in Africa today by Africans.

Medical Technology

In the beginning, Africans were extremely talented in the field of medicine. They used herbs, tree roots, grass roots and tree bark to heal all kinds of diseases, such as epilepsy, blindness, and nervous breakdowns. Unfortunately, they have given them all up for the Western medicine.

During the Nigerian and Biafran War, for example, the Nigerian Government imposed an importation blockade against Biafra. Biafrans became unable to import any war equipment or ammunition. As a result, for three years, "necessity" compelled them to invent their own weapons. Among their creations were rifles, bullets, gunpowder, ogbunigwe (a land mine that killed people in masses), and everything else.

Biafrans were also unable to import medicine, so they had to resort to the traditional healing devices. For example, I once saw them make blood clot by the simple application of the juice from ugbufe leaves or the bobochi. Another time, I had ringworm on my head. My grandmother mixed a concoction with soot in her cooking pot and applied it to my head twice a day. Within a week, I was cured.

Once, I was sick. When I was ten, I was going blind in one eye. My parents took me to the best Western hospitals in the country. Yet, it continued to get worse. In the end, I was taken to the most glamorous and expensive eye clinic in the city of Nkalagu. Nkalagu is where much of the cement is manufactured in Nigeria; therefore, many Westerners work there. This, of course, meant that there were also many Western doctors who practiced there.

What the Western doctors concluded was that I would go blind in one of my eyes. My parents would not accept this diagnosis. That is when my parents decided to take me to a native doctor who lived in my village, less than a mile from my home. When I got there, I was astounded to find that he was a young man in his 30's. He looked in my eyes and knew what the disease was immediately. He sat me down, went outside, and came back with some tree roots. He laid me down flat on the ground, blew at one end of the root, and the juice came out from the other end of the root into my eyes. I lay there for 30 minutes. He then gave me some of the roots and told my mother to repeat the process 4 times a day. In 3 weeks, I was healed.

Even madness was curable with traditional medicine. When I was a kid, one of my friends suddenly became crazy. Rather than taking him to the hospital, his parents took him to a native healer. The healer mixed together some herbs for him to drink every few hours. After a while, he was cured. Since then, he has only had one relapse, which was quickly reversed by the same healer. Now, he leads a perfectly normal life.

One of the most common diseases in Africa, malaria, was often curable with the traditional ways. The most common remedy was the Dogo Yaro, which killed the malaria parasite that is typically transported via mosquitoes. Every part of the tree was used. Some would soak or boil the bark in water and drink it, while others simply ate the leaves, which would heal you more rapidly, but had a distinctive bitter taste. Even though, the Dogo Yaro remedy is free and effective, the expensive malaria pills are typically the preferred prescription because it is Western; that is all!

African medicinal skills were best applied to setting and healing broken bones. First, an expert would set the broken bone, and then would place an herb salve on the skin. After that, they would create a cast out of clay soil and wrap it with another cast fashioned out of wood and string. The herbs would heal the bones, soother the skin, and simulate air movement all of which would make the injured area heal quicker. This method was perfected during the war, but once the war was over, all traditional techniques took a backseat to the preferred Western style of healing.

Summary

What I have been trying to say is that the Western influence in Africa, to this day, has not helped to liberate the Africans. Instead, it has led to what Ali Mazrui has termed in his book, *The Africans* "Modernization without Industrialization," and also "Western taste without Western skills."

Glossary

Affirmative Action	A system that was set up by the government to compensate women and minorities, who were victims of past discrimination.
Afronanism	An ideology that emanates from African philosophy with an "oba" (An altruistic and prudent leader) to uphold the values which they cherish most.
Agalo	Temporary African tattoo
Akaja	Public humiliation
Alu	An abomination
Amamife	Wisdom
Animism	European term for the African Traditional Religion
Biafra	An Igbo nation that lost a civil war to Nigeria in 1970 and was forced to remain part of Nigeria
Chad Republic	A neighboring country to Nigeria
Chukwu	The Supreme God
Confucianism	One of the major world religions
Coup de tat	Taking over the government by force
Dis-Africanization	Doing anything unbecoming an African
Ezinuno	The family
Ex Pluribus Unum	Unity in diversity
Ichie	Council of elders
Igbo	The most populous ethnic group in southern Nigeria
Imani	One of the seven African principles
Kujichagulia	One of the seven African principles
Kuumba	One of the seven African principles
Kwashioko	Malnutrition
Legal Positivism	A philosophical theory that claims that kings or leaders make the law

Lolade	Women leaders in the Yoruba ethnic group
Lolo	A titled Igbo woman
Matrilineal	Tracing genealogy through the mother
Mazi	Mister
Mmehie	Offense
Nia	One of the seven African principles
Nsoani	A taboo
Nze	Priest or Priestess
Oba	An altruistic and prudent leader
Obi	One of the greatest Igbo leaders
Odo	A masquerade
Ogbanje	A changeling
Ofaka	Justice is highest
Ofobike	Justice is strength
Ofodi	There is justice
Ofodile	Justice works
Ofoegbu	Justice never kills
Ofor	Justice
Omenani	African tradition
Omu	Palm leaf
Otu umuada	Association of family daughters
Ozor	Titled people
Polyandry	A marriage between a woman and several husbands at the same time
Polygamy	A combination or the practice of both polygyny and polyandry
Polygyny	A marriage between a man and several wives at the same time
Proverb	Wise saying aphorism or adage
Summum bonum	All goodness
Ufie	Red mud that women rub on their bodies to make their skin smooth
Ujamaa	One of the seven African principles
Ujima	One of the seven African principles
Uli	A dark liquid that women use in their beauty regime
Umoja	One of the seven African principles
Umuada	An important group of females or family daughters that is considered powerful and sacred.
Ujamaa	One of the seven African principles

Uzii — Europeans refer to it as the fattening period, but it is actually a period of three to six months, before the wedding, when future brides are groomed, nurtured, and educated on family matters.

Bibliography

Abraham, Willie E. *The Mind of Africa*. Chicago: University of Chicago Press.

Abrahams, Peter. *Tell Freedom*. New York: Alfred A. Knopf.

Achebe, C. *A Man of People*. London: Heinemann Educational, 1966.

Achebe, C. *Arrow of God*. London: Heinemann Educational, 1964.

Achebe, C. *No Longer at Ease*. London: Heinemann Educational, 1960.

Achebe, Chinua. *Things Fall Apart*. New York: Anchor Books, 1994.

Adams, J. *The Unnatural Alliance: Israel and South Africa*. London: Quartet Books, 1984.

Ajayi, J. F. A. *Christain Misstions in Nigeria 1941-1891: The Making of a New Elite*. Evanston, IL: Northwestern University Press, 1965.

Ake, C. *A Political Economy of Africa*. Chicago: Longman, 1981.

Akintoye, S.A. *Emergent African States: Topics in Twentieth-Century African History*. Chicago: Longman, 1977.

Allen, Francis. *The Borderland of Criminal Justice: Essays in Law and Criminology*. Chicago: University of Chicago Press, 1964.

Aniadi, I.C.K. *Our History and Cultural Heritage*. Onitsha, 1967.

Arikpo, Okoi. *Development of Modern Nigeria*. New York: Penguin.

Armah, A.K. *The Beautyful Ones are Not Yet Born*. Boston: Houghton Mifflin, 1968.

Aubert, Vilhelm, ed. *Sociology of Law*. Baltimore: Penguin Books, 1969.

Ayisi, E.O. *An Introduction to the Study of African Culture*. London: Heinemann, 1972.

Baeta, C.J., ed. *Christianity in Tropical Africa*. London: Oxford University Press for International African Institute, 1968.

Bane, Martin J. *Catholic Pioneers in West Africa*. Dublin: Clonmore & Reynolds, 1956.

Basden, G.T. *Among the Igbos of Southern Nigeria*. London: Frank Cass and Company Ltd. 1968.

Beier, Ulli, ed. *Introduction to African Literature*. Evanston: Northwestern University Press.

Berman, Harold and William Greiner. *The Nature and Functions of Law*. New York: The Foundation Press, 1966.

Biko, S. *I Write What I Like: A Selection of his Writings*. London: Heinemann Educational, 1979.

Black, Donald. *The Behavior of Law*. New York: Academic Press, 1976.

Blackstone, Sir William. *Commentaries of the Laws of England*. Oxford, 1970.

Blyden, E.W. *Christianity, Islam and the Negro Race*. London: Whittingham Press, 1887.

Boahen, A.A. *Topics in West African History*. London: Longman, 1965.

Bond, G. *African Christianity: Patterns of Religious Continuity*. New York: Academic Press, 1979.

Borne, Etienne and Francoise Henry. *A Philosophy of Work*. London: Sheed and Ward, 1938.

Brand, Myles and Douglas Walton. *Action Theory*. Boston: D. Reidel Publishing Co., 1980.

Brandt, Anthony. *Reality Police: The Experience of Insanity In America*. New York: William Morrow and Company, Inc., 1975.

Brett, Peter. *An Inquiry into Criminal Guilt*. Sidney: The Law Book Co. Australia, Ltd., 1963.

Bromber, Walter. *Crime and the Minds*. New York: Macmillan Company, 1965.

Brooks, Alexander, ed. *Law, Psychiatry and the Medical Health System*. Boston: Little, Brown and Co., 1974.

Brown, Phillip. *Radical Psychology*. New York: Harper & Row, 1973.

Buckland, W.W. *A Text-Book of Roman Law*. Cambridge: Cambridge University Press, 1946.

Cairns, H. *Law and the Social Sciences*. New York: Harcourt, Brace and Company, 1935.

Cambell, Colin, and Paul Wiles, eds. *Law and Society*. Oxford: Martin Robertson, 1979.

Carver, T.N. *Essays in Social Justice*. Cambridge, Mass., 1915.

Chambliss, William, ed. *Crime and the Legal Process*. New York: McGraw-Hill Book Company, 1969.

Chambliss, William and Robert Seidman. *Sociology of the Law: A Research Bibliography*. Berkeley, California: The Glendessary Press, 1970.

Chambliss, William. *Functional and Conflict Theories of Crime*. New York: MSS Modular Publications, 1973.

Chambliss, William, ed. *Criminal Law in Action*. Santa Barbara, California: Hamilton Publishing Company, 1975.

Chambliss, William and Milton Mankoff, eds. *Whose Law: What Order?* New York: John Wiley and Sons, 1976.

Coulter, Jeff. *Approaches to Insanity*. New York: John Wiley & Sons, 1973.

Curtin, Philip D. *African History 1964*. Boston: Little, Brown, 1978.

Curtin, Philip D., ed. *Africa Remembered*. Madison: The University of Wisconsin Press, 1967.

Chraibi, D. *Heirs to the Past*. London: Heinemann Educational, 1971.

Clark, J.P. *America, Their America: Autobiography*. London: Heinemann Educational, 1964.

Cleckly, Hervey. *The Mask of Sanity*. 5th ed. St. Louis: C.V. Mosby Company, 1976.

Crowder, M., ed. *West African Resistance: The Military Response to Colonial Occupation*. New York: Africana Publishing Corporation, 1971.

Cusie O' Brien, D.B. *The Mourides of Senegal: The Political and Economic Organization of an Islamic Brotherhood*. Oxford: The Clarendon Press, 1971.

D'Arcy, Erick. *Human Acts: An Essay in their Moral Evaluation*. Oxford: Clarendon Press, 1963.

Danquah, J.B. *The Akan Doctrine of God: A Fragment of Gold Coast Ethics and Religion 1944*. London: Frank Cass, 1968.

David, Rene and John Brierley. *Major Legal Systems in the World Today*. London: Stevens and Sons, 1968.

Davidson, B. *Africa in Modern History: The Search for a New Society*. London: Allen Lane and Penguin Books, 1978.

Davidson, B. *The African Genius*. Boston: Little, Brown, 1969.

Davidson, B. *Discovering Africa's Past*. London: Longman, 1978.

Davidson, B. *Modern Africa*. London: Longman, 1983.

Davidson, B. *The People's Cause: A History of Guerillas in Africa*. Harlow: Longman, 1981.

Davis, F. James. *Society and the Law*. New York: Free Press, 1962.

Davis, Lawrence. *Theory of Action*. Englewood Cliffs: Prentice-Hall, Inc., 1979.

Davis, Philip E., ed. *Moral Duty and Legal Responsibility*. New York: Appleton-Century Crofts, 1966.

Decalo, S. *Coups and Army Rule in Africa: Studies in Military Style.* London: Yale University Press, 1976.

De Graft, J.C. *Muntu*. London and: Heinemann Educational, 1977.

Deng, F.M. *African of Two Worlds: The Dinka in Afro-Arab Sudan.* New Haven and London: Yale University Press, 1976.

Denoon, D. and B. Nyeko. *Southern Africa since 1800.* London: Longman, 1972.

Dettwyler, Katherine A. *Dancing Skeletons.* Prospect Heights, IL: Waveland Press, Inc., 1994.

Diamond, Arthur. *Primitive Law*. London: Watts and Company, 1935.

Du Bois, W.E.B. *The World and Africa: An inquiry into the Part which Africa has Played in World History.* New York: Vikings Press, 1947.

Durkheim, Emile. *Division of Labor in Society*. New York: Free Press, 1967.

Eacker, Jay. *Problems of Philosophy and Psychology*. Chicago: Nelson-Hall, 1975.

Eckhoff, Torstein. *Justice: Its Determinants in Social Interaction.* Rotterdam: Rotterdam University Press, 1974.

Ehrlrich, Eugen. *Fundamental Principles of the Sociology of Law*. New York: Russell & Russell, 1962.

Ekechi, F.K. *Missionary Enterprise and Rivalry in Igboland 1857-1914.* London: Frank Cass and Company Limited, 1971.

Ekwensi, Cyprian. *Jagua Nana*. London: Granada Publishing, 1961.

Elias, T.O. *The Nigerian Magistrate and the Offender*. Benin City: Ethiope Publishing Co., 1972.

El Zein, A.H.M. *The Sacred Meadows*. Evanston, IL: Northwestern University Press, 1974.

Engelhardt, H. and S. Spiker. *Mental Health: Philosophical Perspectives*. Boston: D Reidel Publishing Co., 1976.

Equiano, O. *Equiano's Travels: His Autobiography 1789*. Abridged edition edited by P.E. Edwards. London: Heinemann Educational, 1967.

Eterovich, Francis, *Aristotle's Nichomachean Ethics: Commentary and Analysis*, Washington: University Press of America, 1980.

Evan, William, ed. *Law and Sociology*. New York: Free Press, 1962.

Ewig, A.C. *The Morality of Punishment*. London: Kegan, Paul, Trench, Trubner & Co., Ltd., 1929.

Ezorsky, Gertrude, ed. *Philosophical Perspectives on Punishment*. Albany: State University of New York Press, 1972.

Farah, N. *From a Crooked Rib*. London: Heinemann Educational, 1970.

Farrer, Austin. *The Freedom of the Will*. New York: Charles Scribner's Sons, 1960.

Feiberg, Joel and Hyman Gross, eds. *Punishment: Selected Readings*. Belmont: Dickenson Publishing Co., 1975.

Feiberg, Joel and Hyman Gross, eds. *Responsibility: Selected Readings*. Belmont: Dickenson Publishing Co., 1975.

Fifoot, C.H.S. *History and Sources of the Common Law*. London: Tort and Contract, 1949.

Frazer, Sir James G. *The Golden Bough: A Study in Comparative Religion*. London, 1890.

Freund, Julien. *The Sociology of Max Weber*. New York: Random House, 1968.

Friedmann, Wolfgang. *Legal Theory*. 5th ed. London: Stevens & Sons, 1967.

Fuller, L. L. *The Morality of Law*. New Haven, Connecticut: Yale University Press, 1964.

Fuller, L. L. *The Law in Quest of Itself*. Boston: Beacon Press, 1940.

Geertz, C. *The Interpretation of Cultures*. New York: Basic Books, 1973.

Gilsenan, M. *Saint and Sufi in Modern Egypt: An Essay in the Sociology of Religion*. Oxford: The Clarendon Press, 1973.

Gluckman, Max. *The Judicial Process among the Baratse of Northern Rhodesia*. Manchester: Manchester University Press, 1955.

Golding, Martin P. *Philosophy of Law*. 1974.

Gower, L.C.B. *Independent Africa*. Cambridge: Harvard University Press, 1967.

Green, M.M. *Ibo Village Affairs*. London: Sidgwick & Jackson, ltd. 1947.

Green, Thomas F. *Work, Leisure, and the American Schools*. New York: Random House, 1968.

Gunther, John. *Inside Africa*. New York: Harper & Brothers, 1953.

Gurvetch, Georges. *Sociology of Law*. London: Routledge and Kegan Paul., 1947.

Gutteridge, W. *Military Regimes in Africa*. London: Methuen, 1975.

Haley, A. *Roots*. Garden City, NY: Doubleday, 1976.

Hall, Jerome. *General Principles of Criminal Law*. (2nd ed.) Indianapolis: Bobbs-Merrill Co., 1947.

Halleck, Seymour. *Psychiatry & the Dilemmas of Crime*. Berkeley: University of California Press, 1967.

Hampshire, Stuart. *Thought and Action*. London: Chatto and Windus, 1959.

Harrison, D. *The White Tribe of Africa in Perspective*. London: BBC Publications, 1981.

Harrison, Ross, ed. *Rational Action*. Cambridge: Cambridge University Press, 1979.

Hart, Bernard. *The Psychology of Insanity*. Cambridge: Cambridge University Press, 1968.

Hart, H. L. A. *Punishment and Responsibility*. Oxford: Oxford University Press, 1968.

Hart, H. L. A. *The Concept of Law*. London: Oxford University Press, 1961.

Hart, H. L. A. *Law, Liberty, and Morality*. Stanford, CA: Stanford University Press, 1963.

Hastings, A. *A History of African Christianity, 1950-75*. Cambridge: Cambridge University Press, 1979.

Hay, M.J. and S. Stichter. *African Women South of the Sahara*. Harlow: Longman, 1982.

Hegel, G. W. F. *Philosophy of Right*. New York: Oxford University Press, 1952.

Herpin, N. *Les Sociologues Americians et Le Siecle*. Paris: P. U. F., 1973.

Hillman, James. *The Myth of Analysis*. New York: Harper & Row Publishers, 1972.

Hills, Stuart. *Crime, Power, and Morality: The Criminal Law Process in the United States*. Scranton, PA: Chandler Publishing Company, 1971.

Hinsie, Lelana and Robert Campbell. *Psychiatric Dictionary*. 4th ed., New York: Oxford University Press, 1970.

Hiskett, M. *The Development of Islam in West Africa.* Harlow: Longman, 1984.

Hoch, Paul and Joseph Zubin. *Psychiatry and the Law*. New York: Grune & Stratton, 1955.

Hoebel, E. Adamson. *The Law of Primitive Man*. Cambridge, Massachusetts: Harvard University Press, 1967.

Hoebel, E. Adamson. *The Law of Primitive Man*. Cambridge: Harvard University Press, 1954.

Hoggart, Richard. *The Uses of Literacy*. London: Penguin Books, 1957.

Honderich, Ted. *Punishment: The Supposed Justification*. London: Penguin Books, 1969.

Hook, Sydney, ed. *Determinism and Freedom*. New York: Macmillan Co., 1912.

Horne, Herman. *Freewill and Human Responsibility*. New York: Macmillan Co., 1912.

Horwitz, George. *The Spirit of Jewish Law*. New York: Central Book Co., 1953.

Ingleby, David, ed. *Critical Psychiatry: The Politics of Mental Health*. New York: Pantheon Books, 1980.

Isichei, Elizabeth. *Igbo Worlds*. London: Macmillan Education Limited, 1977.

Jahn, Jahnheinz. *A Bibliography of Neo-African Literature*. New York: Frederick A. Praeger.

Joachim, H. H. *Aristotle: The Nichomachean Ethics*. ed., D. A. Ross, Oxford: Clarendon Press, 1955.

Jones, David. *Crime and Criminal Responsibility*. Chicago: Nelson-Hall, 1978.

Jones, J. W. *The Law and Legal Theory of the Greeks*. Oxford: Oxford University Press.

July, R.W. *A History of the African People*. London: Faber, 1970.

Keim, Curtis A. *Mistaking Africa*. Boulder: Westview Press, 1999.

Kenyatta, J. *Facing Mount Kenya: The Tribal Life of the Kikuyu 1938*. London: Henemann Educational, 1971.

Kitchen, H. *United States Interest in Africa in the 80's*. New York: Praeger, 1983.

Kunene, M. *Anthem of the Decades*. London: Heinemann Educational, 1981.

Kwamena-poh, M.A. *African History in Maps*. Chicago: Longman, 1982.

Lanning, G. and M. Mueller. *Africa Undermined, Mining Companies and the Under-development of Africa*. Harmondsworth: Penguin Books, 1979.

Laye, C. *A Dream of Africa*. London: Collins, 1966.

Le Vine, V.T. and T.W. Luke, eds. *The Arab- African Connection*. Boulder:

Westview Press, 1979.

Leape, J. *Business in the Shadow of Aparthied: U.S. Firms in South Africa*. Lexington, MA: Lexington Books, 1984.

Leith-Ross S. *African Consolation Piece: A Picture of Igbo Life*. London: Hutchinson, 1944.

Leith-Ross S. *African Women: A Study of the Igbo of Nigeria*. London: Faver, 1934.

Lowie, Robert. *Primitive Society*. New York: Harper Torchbook, 1961.

MacGaffey, W. *Modern Kongo Prophets: Religion in a Plural Society*. Bloomington: Indiana University Press, 1983.

MacPherson, J.M. *Blacks in America: Bibliographical Essays*. Garden City, NY: Doubleday, 1971.

Mahfouz, N. *Children of Gebelawi*. London: Heinemann Educational, 1981.

Maine, Henry S. *Ancient Law*. Boston: Beacon Press, 1956.

Malinowski, Bronislaw. *Crime and Custom in Savage Society*. New York: Harcourt Brace and Company, 1926.

Mandela, N. *No Easy Walk to Freedom: Articles, Speeches and Trail Addresses*. London: Heinemann Educational, 1965.

Martin, M.L. *Kimbangu: An African Prophet and his Church*. Oxford: Basil Blackwell, 1975.

Mazrui, A.A. *The African Condition: the Reith Lectures 1979*. London: Heinemann Educational, 1980.

Mazrui, A.A. *Africa's International Relations: the Diplomacy of Dependency and Change*. London: Heinemann Educational, 1977.

Mazrui, A.A. *Political Values and the Educated Class in Africa*. London: Heinemann Educational, 1978.

Mazrui, A.A. and M. Tidy. *Nationalism and New States in Africa from about 1935 to the Present*. London: Heinemann Educational, 1984.

Mazrui, A.A. and M. Tidy. *The Trial of Christopher Okigbo*. London: Heinemann Educational, 1973.

Mbiti, J.S. *African Religions and Philosophy*. London: Heinemann Educational, 1969.

Mbiti, J.S. *An Introduction to African Religion*. London: Heinemann Educational, 1975.

McDonald, Lynn. *The Sociology of Law and Order*. Montreal: Book Center Inc., 1976.

McEvedy, C. *The Penguin Atlas of African History*. Harmondsworth: Penguin Books, 1980.

Mertz, P. M. and R.A. Arab. *Aid to Sub-Saharan Africa*. Boulder: Westview Press, 1983.

Miers, Suzanne and Igor Kopytoff, ed. *Slavery in Africa*. Madison: The University of Wisconsin Press, 1977.

Morris, Herbert, ed. *On Guilt and Innocence*. Berkeley: University of California Press, 1976.

Murphy, Jeffrie. *Kant: The Philosophy of Right*. London: Macmillan, 1970.

Murphy, Jeffrie, ed. *Punishment and Rehabilitation*. Belmont: Wadsworth Publishing Company, 1973.

Murphy, Jeffrie. *Retribution, Justice, and Therapy*. Boston: D. Reidel Pub., Co., 1979.

Mwangi, M. *Going Down River Road*. London: Heinemann Educational, 1973.

Mwangi, M. *Kill Me Quick*. London: Heinemann Educational 1973.

Mwase, G. S. *Strike a Blow and Die: A Narrative of Race Relations in Colonial Africa*. London: Heinemann Educational, 1969.

Myers, III, D. *U.S. Business in South Africa: The Economic, Political and Moral Issues*. Bloomington: Indiana University Press, 1980.

Nadar, Laura, ed. *Law in Culture and Society*. Chicago: Aldine Publishing Company, 1969.

Nation, R.C. and M. V. Kauppi, eds. *The Soviet Impact in Africa*. Boston: D.C. Heath, 1984.

Neamen, Judith. *Suggestion of the Devil: The Origins of Madness*. Garden City: Doubleday, 1975.

Nelson, Brian R. *Western Political Thought*. Englewood Cliffs: Prentice-Hall, Inc., 1982.

Ngugi wa Thiong'o. *Detained: a Writer's Prison Diary*. London: Heinemann Educational, 1981.

Ngugi wa Thiong'o. *Devil on the Cross*. London: Heinemann Educational, 1982.

Ngugi wa Thiong'o. *Petals of Blood*. London: Heinemann Educational, 1977.

Nkosi, L. *Tasks and Masks: Themes and Styles of African Literature*. Harlow: Longman, 1981.

Nkrumah, K. *Consciencism: Philosophy and the Ideology for Decolonization*. London: Panaf Books, 1970.

Nkrumah, K. *Neo-Colonialism: The Last Stage of Imperialism*. London: Panaf Books, 1965.

Nsugbe, Philip O. *Ohafia: A Matrilineal Igbo People*. Oxford: Clarendon Press, 1974.

Nwabara, S. N. *Igboland: A Century of Contact with Britain 1860-1960*. London: Hodder and Stoughton, 1977.

Nzimiro, Ikenna. *Studies in Ibo Political Systems*. London: Frank Cass and Company Limited, 1972.

Ogot, B.A. and J.A. Kieran. *Zamani: A Survey of East African History*. Nairobi: East African Publishing House, 1968.

Okonkwo, M. N. *A Complete Course in Igbo Grammar*. Nigeria: Macmillan, 1979.

Olaniyan, R., ed. *African History and Culture*. Harlow: Longman, 1982.

Olaniyan, R. *Nigerian History and Culture*. Harlow: Longman, 1984.

Oppenheimer, Heinrich. *The Rationale of Punishment*. London: University of London Press, 1913.

Osia, K. *Israel, South Africa and Black Africa: A Study of the Primacy of the Politics of Expediency*. New York: University Press of America, 1983.

O'Sullivan, P.N. *Intention, Motives, and Human Action: An Argument for Free Will*. Queensland: University of Queensland Press, 1977.

Ousmane, S. *The Money Order with White Genesis*. London: Heinemann Educational, 1972.

Ousmane, S. *Xala*. London: Heinemann Educational, 1976.

Oyono, F. *Houseboy*. London: Heinemann Educational, 1966.

Oyono, F. *The Old Man and the Medal*. London: Heinemann Educational, 1970.

Packer, H. *The Limits of the Criminal Sanction*. Stanford: Stanford University Press, 1968.

Parfitt, T. *Operation Moses: The Story of the Exodus of Falasha Jews from Ethiopia*. London: Weidenfeld and Nicolson, 1985.

Parkin, David J. *Palms, Wine, and Witnesses*. Prospect Heights, IL: Waveland Press, Inc., 1972.

Parrinder, G. *African Traditional Religion*. London: Scheldon Press, 1976.

Paulme, Denise, ed. *Women of Tropical Africa*. Berkeley: University of California Press, 1963.

P'Bitek, Okot. *African Religions in Western Scholarship*. Nairobi: East African Literature Bureau, 1971.

Pepinsky, Harold. *Crime and Conflict: A Study of Law and Society*. New York: Academic Press, 1976.

Perham, Magery. *Native Administration in Nigeria*. New York: Oxford University Press, 1988.

Podgorecki, Adam. *Law and Society*. London: Routledge and Kegan Paul, 1974.

Quigg, Philip W., ed. *Africa*. New York: Frederick A. Praeger, 1964.

Quinney, Richard. *Crime and Justice in Society*. Boston: Little, Brown, and Company, 1969.

Quinney, Richard. *Criminal Justice in America*. Boston: Little, Brown and Company, 1974.

Ra Cliffe, B. *Structure and Function in Primitive Society*. London: Cohan & West Ltd., 1959.

Rander, T.O. *Peasant Consciousness and Guerilla War in Zimbabwe*. London: James Currey, 1985.

Ranges, T.O. and I. Kimambo, eds. *The Historical Study of African Religious*. Berkeley: University of California Press, 1972.

Rogers, B. *White Wealth And Black Poverty: American Investments in Southern Africa*. Westport, CT. And London: Greenwood Press, 1976.

Savage, Katharine. *The Story of Africa: South of the Sahara*. New York: Henry Z. Walck, Inc., 1961.

Sawer, Geoffrey, ed. *Law in Society*. London: Oxford University Press, 1965.

Schubert, Glendon, ed. *Judicial Decision-Making*. Glencoe, IL: Free Press, 1963.

Schur, Edwin. *Law and Society: A Sociological View*. New York: Random House, 1968.

Segal, Ronald, ed. *Modern Poetry from Africa*. Baltimore: Penguin Books, 1963.

Shaw, T. M. and K.A. Heard. *The Politics of Africa: Dependence and Development*. New York: Holmes and Meier, 1979.

Shelton, J.A. *The Igbo-Igala Borderland*. Albany: State University of New York Press, 1971.

Skinner, B.F. *Beyond Freedom and Dignity*. New York: Knopf, 1971.

Sohn-Rethel, Alfred. *Intellectual and Manual Labor*. New Jersey: Humanities Press, 1978.

Shorter, Edward, ed. *Work and Community in the West*. New York: Harper & Row Publishers, 1973.

Sorabji, Richard. *Necessity, Cause and Blame: Perspectives on Aristotle's Theory*. Ithaca: Cornell University Press, 1980.

Soyinka, W. *Myth, Literature and the African World*. Cambridge: Cambridge University Press, 1976.

Soyinka, W. *The Man Died: Prison Notes of Wole Soyinka*. London: Rex Collings, 1972.

Stephen, James Fitzjames. *Liberty, Equality, and Fraternity*. Cambridge: Cambridge University Press, 1967.

Stevens, Shane. *By Reason of Insanity*. New York: Dell Publishing Co., Inc., 1979.

Sullivan, W.C. *Crime and Insanity*. Garden City: Doubleday & Co., Inc., 1970.

Sumner, William. *Folkways*. Boston: Ginn and Company, 1986.

Sweetman, D. *Women Leaders in African History*. London: Heinemann Educational, 1984.

Sylvester, A. *Arabs and Africans: Five Years of Arab- Africans Economic Cooperation*. London: The Bodley Head, 1981.

Szasz, Thomas. *The Manufacture of Madness*. New York: Harper & Row, Pub., 1970.

Szasz, Thomas. *The Myth of Mental Illness*. New York: Harper & Row, Pub., 1967.

Talbot, P.A. *The Peoples of Southern Nigeria*. London: Frank Cass & Company Ltd., 1969.

Tangri, R. *Politics in Sub-Saharan Africa*. London: James Currey, 1985.

Timasheff, Nicholus. *An Introduction to the Sociology of Law*. Cambridge, Massachusetts: Harvard University Press, 1939.

Trimingahm, J.S. *The Influence of Islam upon Africa*. Harlow: Longman, 1968.

Turk, Austin. *Criminality and Legal Order*. Chicago: Rand McNally, 1969.

Uchend, Victor. *The Igbo of Southern Nigeria*. New York: Holt, Reinehart & Winston, 1965.

Uchendu, P.K. *The Role of Nigerian Women in Politics*. Enugu, Nigeria: Fourth Dimension Publishing Co., 1993.

Umeasiegbu, R.N. *The Way We Lived*. London: Heinemann Educational Books, 1969.

Unger, Robert. *Law in Modern Society: Toward A Criticism of Social Theory*. New York: The Free Press, 1976.

Valente, William. *Law in the Schools*. Columbus: Charles E. Merrill Publishing CO., 1980.

Versey, Godfrey. *Personal Identity: A Philosophical Analysis*. Ithaca: Cornell University Press, 1974.

Vold, George. *Theoretical Criminology*. New York: Oxford University Press, 1958.

Walker, Nigel. *Punishment, Danger and Stigma*. Totowa: Barnes & Noble Books, 1980.

Webster, J.B. *The Revolutionary Years: West Africa since 1800*. Harlow: Longman, 1967.

Wicker, Brian M. A. *Work and the Christian Community*. London: Darton, Longman and Todd Ltd., 1964.

Worku, D. *The Thirteenth Sun*. London: Heinemann Educational, 1973.

Zahan, D. *The Religion Spirituality and Thought of Traditional Africa*. Chicago: University of Chicago Press, 1979.

Zell, H.M. *A New Reader's Guide to African Literature*. London: Heinemann Educational, 1983.

Index

About the Author

Dr. Nkuzi Michael Nnam hails from Akpugo in Nkanu Local Government Area of Anambra State, Nigeria. He was born to Nnamigwe and Adajie Nwaonuma. He obtained a Bachelor's degree (Summa Cum Laude), a Master's degree, and a Ph.D. in philosophy at DePaul University in Chicago, U.S.A. He is currently an Associate Professor of Philosophy and the Director of African and African-American Studies at Dominican University in River Forest, Illinois.

Dr. Nnam has published numerous articles and is the author of the book *Anglo-American & Nigerian Jurisprudence*.